To Bind Up the Wounds

To Bind Up the Wounds

CATHOLIC SISTER NURSES IN THE U.S. CIVIL WAR

Sister Mary Denis Maher

Contributions in Women's Studies, Number 107

Greenwood Press

NEW YORK • WESTPORT, CONNECTICUT • LONDON

Library of Congress Cataloging-in-Publication Data

Maher, Mary Denis.
  To bind up the wounds : Catholic sister nurses in the U.S. Civil
War / Mary Denis Maher.
    p. cm.—(Contributions in women's studies, ISSN 0147–104X ; no. 107)
  Bibliography: p.
  Includes index.
  ISBN 0–313–26458–9 (lib. bdg. : alk. paper)
  1. United States—History—Civil War, 1861–1865—Medical care.
2. United States—History—Civil War, 1861–1865—War work—Catholic
Church.   3. United States—History—Civil War, 1861–1865—Women.
4. Monasticism and religious orders for women—United States—
History—19th century.   5. Nursing—United States—History—19th
century.   I. Title.   II. Series.
E621.M34   1989
973.7′75—dc20   89–2217

British Library Cataloguing in Publication Data is available.

Library of Congress Catalog Card Number: 89–2217
ISBN: 0–313–26458–9
ISSN: 0147–104X

First published in 1989

Greenwood Press, Inc.
88 Post Road West, Westport, Connecticut   06881

Printed in the United States of America

∞™

The paper used in this book complies with the
Permanent Paper Standard issued by the National
Information Standards Organization (Z39.48–1984).

10 9 8 7 6 5 4 3 2 1

Contents

Acknowledgments

To the Sisters of Charity of St. Augustine for personal and financial support in this as in many other projects in my life, my prayerful gratitude.

To the archivists of all the religious communities for generous and easy access to their archives, my overwhelming appreciation. Special thanks to Sr. Romauld Burns of the St. Louis Sisters of Mercy for arranging her schedule for me to use material in Vicksburg, Mississippi; to Sr. Campion Kuhn of the Holy Cross Sisters, Saint Mary's, Notre Dame, Indiana; to Sr. Aloysia Dugan of the Daughters of Charity, Emmitsburg, Maryland; to Sisters Alberta and Anne Francis of the Sisters of Charity of Our Lady of Mercy, Charleston, South Carolina; and to Sr. Laura Marie Watson of the Sisters of Charity of Cincinnati, Ohio. They all shared both their extensive archives and their community life with me during the process of this work.

To the personnel of the Cleveland Public Library, especially in the History Department, who assisted me in utilizing the vast resources of its holdings; and to the staff of the medical library at St. Vincent Charity Hospital, Cleveland, who quickly secured copies of many difficult-to-find nursing and medical journal articles, my special gratitude.

To Fr. William Burn, archivist of the Diocese of Charleston, South Carolina, for the opportunity to leisurely and comfortably research the papers of Bishop Patrick Lynch, my deep appreciation.

To Roberta Wollons at Case Western Reserve University, Cleveland, Ohio, for her genuine interest and persistent questions on earlier versions of this book, my gratitude. To Case Western Reserve University for a Graduate Alumni Award which funded a research trip to Charleston, South Carolina, my thanks.

To Sr. Michael Francis, OSU, and Ann Trivisonno, friends and colleagues at Ursuline College, Pepper Pike, Ohio, and Terry Peck Maher, my sister-in-law, for their kindly but perceptive comments and judicious editing, especially when my own interest and energy flagged, my continued pledge of mutual support.

To Teddi Denk, who first deciphered my innumerable drafts and put everything on the word processor, to Sr. Allan Kenzig, CSA, who later assisted me in making the revisions, and to Sr. Mary Patricia Barrett, CSA, for the generous use of the facilities of CSA Health and Human Services, Richfield, Ohio, my utmost admiration and personal thanks.

And as always, to my parents, William and Iola Maher, for their love and belief in me, my love and prayers.

To Bind Up the Wounds

Introduction

"It seems strange that [the sisters] can do with honor what is wrong for other Christian women to do," mused Confederate nurse Kate Cumming, struggling to understand why she could not obtain enough women to help nurse the wounded Southern soldiers.[1] Not everyone had the same perceptions about the work of the sisters. A Vermont senator in 1871 sought to disallow funds to rebuild a war-ravaged orphanage for the Sisters of Charity of Our Lady of Mercy. Their cause had been advanced because of their unwavering care of both Union and Confederate soldiers in Charleston, South Carolina, but he dismissed the claim by saying, "They have done no more than their duty"—any patriotic citizen would have done as much, he felt.[2]

Nevertheless, almost fifty years later, in 1921, another Congressman, Rhode Island Representative Ambrose Kennedy, would speak on behalf of establishing a monument in Washington, D.C., for the "Nuns of the Battlefield,"[3] whose "services were not only conspicuously national; they were also singular and unique."[4] These nuns were part of the almost 600 Roman Catholic sisters of twenty-one separate religious communities of twelve different orders who nursed sick and wounded soldiers during the US Civil War, 1861–1865.[5]

Were the sisters pathbreakers for women's activities, as Cumming suggested, and thus deserving of honor and respect? Were they just ordinary citizens with special skills doing their patriotic duty as the senator implied, and thus not worthy of any special consideration? Or were their services singular and unique, as Representative Kennedy testified, qualifying them for a national monument?

Together, these three comments by outside observers—one a nurse who had direct contact with the sisters, one a Northern senator who opposed a Southern state's petition for restitution, and one far removed from the battles or the politics of the Civil War who was impressed by the historical data—identify three major aspects of the sisters' services: commitment to religious duty, skilled service, and their singular and unique example for other women.

The mission of the sisters in nineteenth-century America was to carry out works of Christian charity by teaching, caring for orphans, nursing the sick, and providing spiritual assistance for the dying. Particularly in their mission to serve the sick, the sisters could be considered pathbreakers. Even though nursing one's own family members was an acceptable and expected occupation, nursing as a profession or lifelong commitment was almost unknown, except among Catholic women's religious communities. However, in a sense, they could also be merely doing their duty. For example, some sisters had nursed wounded soldiers in the Revolutionary War and the War of 1812, as well as in the cholera epidemics between 1830 and 1860. In addition, they had established some twenty-eight hospitals by 1860.[6] Yet the sisters were indeed unique and singular among the few thousand women who cared for the sick during the Civil War. They demonstrated not only a strong religious commitment in their work on the battlefield, in the government hospitals, and on military transports, but also very practical skills, which enhanced this service.

Thus, in order to understand the unique role and special function of the sisters in the Civil War, four fundamental questions must be answered:

Who were the religious communities of sisters who served in the war and how did they become involved?

Where did the sisters nurse and what did "nursing" consist of during the Civil War era?

How were the sisters and their work regarded by the doctors, other female nurses, the military, and governmental officials and the soldiers themselves?

Why were the sisters willing to serve and how did they view their services?

Answering these questions is difficult since little has been written about these sisters and their service. In spite of the qualifications the sisters brought to their Civil War work, neither the history of religion in America,[7] (including the history of American Catholicism),[8] nor the history of nineteenth-century American women[9] give more than scant reference to Catholic sisters prior to or during the war.[10] Catholic hospitals or other health-care institutions do not receive even a heading in the index of such works. Neither is there a single volume covering the history of

Catholic health care in the United States,[11] as there is for education or Catholic social service. While the history of nursing[12] and of Civil War medical history[13] offers some brief mention of the sisters' services rendered during the war, the pages generally are as mute as the cannons now in the Civil War parks.[14]

Similarly, literature on other women in the Civil War is also limited. Writing shortly after the war, historian Frank Moore remarked, "The story of the war will never be fully or fairly written if the achievements of women in it are untold. They do not figure in the official reports; they are not gazetted for deeds as gallant as were ever done; the names of thousands are unknown beyond the neighborhood where they live or the hospitals where they loved to labor; yet there is no feature in our war more credible to us as a nation, none from its positive newness so well worthy of record."[15]

Even though more than a hundred articles based on women's experiences were published between 1865–1914, mostly firsthand accounts by female nurses, teachers of freedmen, U.S. Sanitary Commission workers and others,[16] a twentieth-century women's historian could still lament that while "the Civil War has produced tons of literature, there are few studies of the contributions of women."[17]

Unlike their more prolific female nurse counterparts, the sisters left little written material concerning their experiences in the Civil War. Fires, lack of awareness of the historical value of such documents, little desire or incentive for the sisters to record their experiences, and an overriding sense that they were simply extending their works of charity by caring for the sick and providing assistance for the dying left little material from which to study and evaluate the experiences of these women.[18] Sufficient material does exist, however, in primary and selected secondary sources relating to the official records of the Civil War and in the official medical and surgical history of the war. In addition, secondary sources relating to medical history, nursing accounts, and other memoirs do exist. These sources provide sufficient evidence to construct a composite picture of the Roman Catholic sister nurse during the Civil War.

NOTES

1. Kate Cumming, *Kate: The Journal of a Confederate Nurse*, ed. Richard B. Harwell (Baton Rouge: Louisiana State University Press, 1959), p. 178.

2. *Congressional Globe*, Third Session of the Forty-first Congress, Mar. 3, 1871, pp. 2008–2009.

3. The monument was erected at the corner of Rhode Island and Connecticut Avenues in 1924 and depicted, in bas-relief, sisters from the twelve different orders of the twenty-one separate communities who nursed in the war.

The efforts of Mrs. Mary Ryan Jolly, supported by the Ladies Auxiliary of the Ancient Order of Hibernians, had made the research and monument possible.

4. Hon. Ambrose Kennedy, "Speech of Hon. Ambrose Kennedy of Rhode Island in the House of Representatives, Mon., Mar. 18, 1918," *Federal Register*, Mar. 18, 1918, Washington, D.C.: U.S. Government Publications, 1918, p. 4.

5. The term "nun" and "sister" are both encompassed by the term "women religious." Until 1983 the former terms had precise and distinct meaning in canon law: "nuns" were those with solemn vows of poverty, chastity, and obedience with strict rules of enclosure and devoted completely to lives of prayer; "sisters" had simple vows, modified rules of enclosure, and were engaged in charitable works in addition to their focus on prayer. "Order" was the term applied to a group with solemn vows, and "community" was used for sisters in simple vows, as well as for a smaller unit of sisters within an order or a larger community. However, in common speech, the terms, "sister," "nun," and "woman religious" were and are used interchangeably and will be so used here unless their canonical meaning is intended and specifically noted.

6. Ann Doyle, "Nursing by Religious Orders in the United States," *American Journal of Nursing* 29 (July-Dec. 1929): 775–786, 959–969, 1085–1095, 1197–1207, 1331–1343, 1466–1484.

7. See Sydney Ahlstrom, *A Religious History of the American People* (New Haven: Yale University Press, 1972); Edwin Gaustad, ed., *A Documentary History of Religion in America*, 2 vols. (Grand Rapids: William B. Eerdmans, 1982); Robert Handy, *A History of the Churches in the United States and Canada* (New York: Oxford University Press, 1977); Winthrop Hudson, *Religion in America: An Historical Account of the Development of American Religious Life*, 3rd ed. (New York: Charles Scribner's Sons, 1981); Martin E. Marty, *Pilgrims in Their Own Land: 500 Years of Religion in America* (New York: Penguin Books, 1984); Mark Noll et al., eds., *Eerdman's Handbook to Christianity in America* (Grand Rapids: William B. Eerdmans, 1983).

8. See Jay P. Dolan, *The American Catholic Experience: A History from Colonial Times to the Present* (Garden City, NY: Doubleday, 1985); John Tracy Ellis, *American Catholicism*, 2nd ed. (Chicago: University of Chicago Press, 1969), p. 293; James Hennesey, *American Catholics: A History of the Roman Catholic Community in the United States* (New York: Oxford University Press, 1981); John Gilmary Shea, *History of the Catholic Church in the United States*, 4 vols., (New York: John G. Shea) 1886–92.

Dolan and Hennesey do give some attention to women, as do other recent works, such as John Tracy Ellis and Robert Trisco, eds. rev. ed., *A Guide to American Catholic History* (Milwaukee: Bruce Publishing Co., 1982); James Hennesey, *American Catholic Bibliography, 1970–1982* (Notre Dame: Cushwa Center Working Papers, Series 12, No. 1, Fall, 1982) and the *Supplement to American Catholic Bibliography*, Series 14, No. 1, Fall, 1983.

9. In general, little is written on women in religion. For exceptions to this, see Janet Wilson James, ed., *Women in American Religion* (Philadelphia: University of Pennsylvania Press, 1980). Several of the twelve articles in this book originally appeared in *American Quarterly*. See also Rosemary Radford Ruether and Rosemary Skinner, eds., *Women and Religion in America: A Documentary History*, 3 vols. (San Francisco: Harper and Row, 1981, 1983, 1986). Volume I deals with the

nineteenth century, Volume II with the colonial and revolutionary periods, and Volume III with the twentieth century. The volumes have excellent footnotes, an index, and illustrations. There are, of course, some individual volumes on women in various religious organizations in the nineteenth century. See R. Pierce Beaver, *All Loves Excelling* (now published under the title *American Protestant Women in World Missions: History of the First Feminist Movement in North America*) (Grand Rapids: Eerdmans, 1968), rev. ed. 1980. Amanda Porterfield, *Feminine Spirituality in America* (Philadelphia: Temple University Press, 1980).

10. For notable attempts to address the void, see Sr. Mary Ewens, *The Role of the Nun in Nineteenth-Century America* (New York: Arno, 1978); Sr. Barbara Misner, "A Comparative Social Study of the Members and Apostolates of the First Eight Permanent Communities of Women Religious within the Boundaries of the United States, 1790–1850." Ph. D. Diss., Catholic University of America, 1981; Margaret Susan Thompson, in "Discovering Foremothers: Sisters, Society and the American Catholic Experience," *U.S. Catholic Historian* 5 (Summer/Fall 1986): 273–290, indicates that she is working on an integrated history to be published by Oxford University Press, entitled *The Yoke of Grace: American Nuns and Social Change, 1808–1917.*

11. See Ursula Stepsis, CSA, and Dolores Liptak, RSM, eds., *Pioneer Healers: The History of Women Religious in American Health Care* (New York: Continuum-Crossroad, 1989). The most extensive treatment of Catholic hospitals is contained in the dated John O'Grady, *Catholic Charities in the United States* (Washington, D.C. 1930, rpt. Arno, 1971), pp. 183–212.

12. The classic history of nursing is Mary Adelaide Nutting and Livinia Dock, *A History of Nursing*, 2 vols. (New York: G.P. Putnam's Sons, 1907–1912). See also Anne Austin, *History of Nursing Source Book* (New York: G. P. Putnam's Sons, 1957); Vern and Bonnie Bullough, *The Care of the Sick: The Emergence of Modern Nursing* (New York: Prodest, 1978); Josephine A. Dolan, *Nursing in Society: A Historical Perspective* (Philadelphia: W. B. Saunders, 1978); Philip and Beatrice Kalish, *The Advance of American Nursing* (Boston: Little Brown, 1978).

13. George W. Adams, *Doctors in Blue: The Medical History of the Union Army in the Civil War* (New York: Henry Schuman, 1952); Horace H. Cunningham, *Doctors in Grey: The Confederate Medical Service* (Baton Rouge: Louisiana State University Press, 1958).

14. Ellen Ryan Jolly, *Nuns of the Battlefield* (Providence, RI: Providence Visitor, 1929). However, the work, through using archival material and personal interviews, has no footnotes and reflects Jolly's uncritical admiration and praise for those who nursed.

15. Frank Moore, *Women of the War: Their Heroism and Self-Sacrifice* (Hartford, CT: S. S. Scranton, 1867), pp. v-vi.

16. Mary Elizabeth Massey, *Bonnet Brigades* (New York: Alfred A. Knopf, 1966), p. 187.

17. Catherine Clinton, *The Other Civil War: American Women in the Nineteenth Century* (New York: Hill and Wang, 1984), p. 219.

18. See letter to the author, dated Nov. 29, 1985, from archivist Sr. Mary Hyacinth Breaux, O. Carm., for a typical response to a request for archival materials. She wrote, "We know that a great deal of Archival material was destroyed in Thibodaux [Louisiana], because people did not know the value of

such things." See also letter dated Nov. 15, 1985, from archivist Sr. Constance Golden, RSM, stating, "The nightmare of every archivist apparently occurred. Some well-intentioned person typed from the original and then disposed (!!!) of it."

Nuns of the Battlefield Monument, Washington, D.C. Columbia Historical Society, David Blume, photographer; Ms. 367, James M. Goode *Outdoor Sculpture of Washington* Papers.

Daughters of Charity with doctors and soldiers. Satterlee Hospital, Philadelphia. Courtesy, St. Joseph's Provincial House Archives.

Daughters of Charity in the kitchen. Satterlee Hospital, Philadelphia. Courtesy, St. Joseph's Provincial House Archives.

Daughters of Charity outside the kitchen and storeroom. Satterlee Hospital, Philadelphia. Courtesy, St. Joseph's Provincial House Archives.

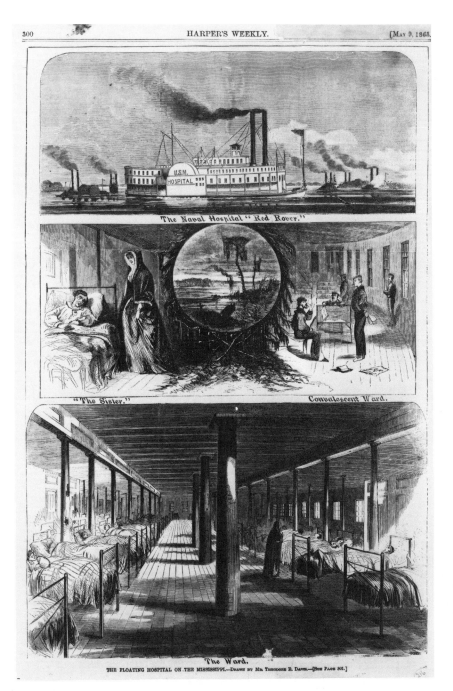

The Naval Hospital "Red Rover."

"The Sister."

Convalescent Ward.

The Ward.

THE FLOATING HOSPITAL ON THE MISSISSIPPI.—Drawn by Mr. Theodore R. Davis.—[See Page 301.]

Holy Cross Sisters on the Red Rover hospital ship. *Harper's Weekly*, May 9, 1863.

Sister Colette O'Connor, RSM, with doctors and soldiers. Douglas Military Hospital, Washington D.C. Courtesy, Archives, Sisters of Mercy, Province of Baltimore.

1

Catholic Sisters in Mid-Nineteenth Century America

"What or *who* are they?" queried a curious group of onlookers surrounding five Daughters of Charity coming to Marietta, Georgia, to nurse Confederate soldiers in 1863. "Are they men or women?" the bystanders continued, wondering what kind of strange uniform the country had adopted. "Surely, the enemy will run from them," another responded. Finally, when one sister spoke, many of the people clapped their hands, shouting, "She spoke! She spoke!"[1]

This Civil War incident reflects the fact that Catholic nuns in the United States at mid-nineteenth century were little known and less understood by most Protestant and even Catholic Americans. However, the truth is that in the 1850s, just prior to the war, Catholic sisters did belong to the worlds of the immigrant Roman Catholic and of nineteenth-century American women, sharing some of the qualities and characteristics of each. They were organizers of educational, health, and social-service institutions in a period when some of their female Protestant counterparts were going to foreign lands as missionaries. In addition, they were women possessed of the qualities of piety, purity, submissiveness, and domesticity in a time when those qualities were set as a feminine ideal by male and female alike. Yet, unlike their Protestant contemporaries, these sisters had lifelong vows of poverty, celibacy, and obedience, were dedicated to a life of service to others, and lived in community with like-minded women. Thus, they were a striking alternative to women in the socially expected and approved married state. However, the sisters were generally abhorred, misunderstood, or criticized as aberrations of foreign devils because of the apparent constrictions of their lifestyle, as symbolized by their strange garb, their structured life, and the convent walls. Thus, the real values of sisterhood, and the sisters' special opportunities for service, which were unavailable to other nineteenth-century women, were unknown or overlooked. Only through the experiences of the Civil War would the sisters' qualities of committed service, experience in caring for the sick and educating others, and the ability to organize and move on quick notice become visible to many Americans.

To understand the change that the Civil War made in the public's experience and understanding of the sisters, the larger context of American Catholicism must be examined. The Roman Catholic Church in America to which these sisters belonged might best be characterized by Alexis de Tocqueville, himself of French Catholic background. Struck by the religious atmosphere of the country, de Tocqueville, in his visit to the United States in 1830, characterized the more than one million American Catholics he found as "very submissive and very sincere... loyal in the practice of their worship and full of zeal and ardor for their beliefs."[2] Catholics were found by the observant Frenchman to "form the most republican and democratic of all classes in the United States." Explaining this phenomenon, de Tocqueville said Protestantism promoted independence, while Catholicism emphasized human equality. "It mingles all classes of society at the foot of the same altar, just as they are mingled in the sight of God," he wrote.[3] Poverty, social inferiority, and minority status all contributed, de Tocqueville concluded, to the development of the democratic spirit among American Catholics, even if the nature of their beliefs may not have given them "any strong impulsion toward democratic and republican opinions."[4]

Between 1785 and the beginning of the Civil War, these Catholics grew from a group of twenty-five thousand to a church of over one million, with nearly a third coming to the United States in the decade before the attack on Fort Sumter.[5] Church historian John Tracy Ellis characterized American Catholicism at mid-century as the religious faith of a minority who suffered from traditional prejudice. Furthermore, their predominantly foreign cast caused increased attacks, which accentuated the differences of Catholics from their fellow citizens. Politically, Catholics were usually Democratic, since that party was friendliest to their interests. Generally, they belonged to the poorer class and lived in the rising industrial towns of the East and Midwest. Nevertheless, they enjoyed America's religious freedom, which enabled Catholicism to expand without interference from government.[6]

To serve this church, priests and nuns from European countries were recruited and supported until enough Americans could join or start their own seminaries and communities.[7] While the clergy largely organized and serviced parishes, the women religious, who numbered over 1,500 by mid-century, had established forty-one communities of twenty-three orders, whose main purpose was to establish and staff institutions of education, health, and social welfare.[8]

The first community in the United States was the French Ursulines, who in 1727 pioneered education for women with a female academy for ages seven to fifteen in New Orleans.[9] They were followed in 1790 by cloistered Carmelites at Port Tobacco, Maryland, but the majority of the early communities were active religious of simple vows devoted to works of education and charity, such as care of orphans and the sick poor. Though many of the early communities were European in origin, primarily French and Irish, and later German, American women soon joined or started their own communities. The commitment of women's religious communities, both those founded by American women and those of mixed immigrant and American women,[10] was strong from the beginning in responding to needs of the evolving American Church. For example, Saint Elizabeth Bayley Seton, a wife, mother, and convert from the Episcopal Church, began the first American community—the Sisters of Charity—in 1809, the first free parochial school in 1810, and the first Catholic orphanage in 1810 in Emmitsburg, Maryland. The community later established the first Catholic hospital in St. Louis in 1828.[11]

By 1812, two other American communities, the Sisters of Loretto and the Sisters of Charity of Nazareth, were established in the Kentucky wilderness. They were followed ten years later by Dominican Sisters at Saint Catharine, Kentucky. Completing the roster of active communities founded by American-born women or women who had been assimilated into American life were the Baltimore-based Oblate Sisters of Providence, a community of Black sisters formed to work among their own people, and the Sisters of Charity of Our Lady of Mercy, located in Charleston, South Carolina, both begun in 1829.[12] Seton's Sisters of Charity (later called Daughters of Charity), the Sisters of Charity of Nazareth, and the Sisters of Charity of Our Lady of Mercy were involved in education, health care, and social service; the Sisters of Loretto and the Dominicans were primarily teachers of young women.[13]

Charitable institutions staffed largely by these active sisters' orders, as well as by their independent branches, and other communities that started before the war preserved the religious faith of the immigrants and assisted them in adapting to their new environment, thus partially insulating them from prejudice.[14] For example, increasing immigration and periodic epidemics demonstrated the need for Catholic hospitals. Thus, St. Vincent's Hospital was established in New York City in 1836 so that poor immigrants could have spiritual comfort and relief from the conditions that Catholics often faced in Protestant hospitals.[15] Medical historian Charles Rosenberg described some of these conditions and underscored the reasons that prompted Catholics to build their own institutions and find sisters dedicated to the corporal works of mercy to staff them. He cited, as an example, a lay Boston trustee at Massachusetts General Hospital in 1851 who, alarmed at the number of Irish-Catholic laborers treated there, suggested that it might be advisable to build a "cheap building" or rent one in the vicinity of the hospital in order to care for these "ignorant immigrants." "They cannot appreciate," he explained, "and do not really want some of those conveniences which would be deemed essential by most of our native citizens."[16]

The famous preacher Reverend Lyman Beecher epitomized many views about Catholics when he said, in 1834: "The Catholic Church holds now in darkness and bondage nearly half the civilized world . . . It is the most skillful, powerful, dreadful system of corruption to those who wield it, and of slavery and debasement to those who live under it."[17]

Anti-Catholic lectures, tracts, newspapers, riots, and burnings were often the result of the antagonism.[18] Among the more popular of anti-Catholic writings were the titillating tales of convent horrors, promoted by the lecture-circuit authors of two of the most famous novels. Rebecca Reed's *Six Months in a Convent* (1835)[19] offered tales of austere practices, and Maria Monk's *Awful Disclosures of the Hotel Dieu Nunnery in Montreal* (1836)[20] graphically described fables of infants, born of priest-nun relationships, murdered and buried in convent basements.

As Mary Ewens has demonstrated in her study of this literature, sisters, especially in the three decades preceding the Civil War, were generally depicted as "mournful prisoners doomed by unhappy love affairs to lives of sinful indolence."[21] The purpose of these publications, from the Protestants' point of view, was well stated in the preface to Reed's novel, which said that if the book has:

this blessed effect in guarding the young women of our land against the dangers of early impressions imbibed at convents in favor of a form of religion which is to be *tolerated* but never to be *encouraged* in a free country, it will do more even than the laws can do in suppressing such outrages as the riot at Charleston; for if Protestant parents will resolve to educate their daughters at Protestant schools and patronize no more Nunneries, then no more Nunneries will be established in this country and there will be none for reckless mobs to destroy.[22]

In spite of the charitable works of Catholic sisters, much of the knowledge about them was derived from this popular literature, largely the work of anti-Catholic writers or self-styled "escaped nuns," rather than from personal experience. While anti-Catholic incidents and literature of the period disclosed a fear of Catholicism far out of proportion to the actual power and motivations of American Catholics, historian Amanda Porterfield has suggested that the fear was often linked to an obsession with Catholic "perversions of womanhood." Because of the convent exposés,

Porterfield concluded, "imaginative Protestants perceived convent chastity as an escape from the Christian responsibilities of marriage and as an excuse for sexual promiscuity between monks and nuns."[23]

The emotionalism engendered by these tales, coupled with public anti-Catholic sentiment, was perhaps epitomized in the burning of the Ursuline Convent in Charlestown, Massachusetts, on August 11, 1834. The incident was apparently inspired by misinformation circulated in the Boston area by Rebecca Reed, who had been dismissed as unsuited for religious life after a six-month period. In addition, it was incorrectly rumored that Elizabeth Harrison, a sister who had left briefly because of a nervous breakdown and then re-entered, was being held by force against her will. A mob of about fifty men, who first looted the building, proceeded to desecrate the chapel and frighten the sisters and pupils who got out; they ultimately burned the four-story academy and convent. Subsequent trials were considered farcical, the legislature refused to compensate the diocese, and the Ursulines were forced to return to Canada.[24]

The austere practices of early rising, hours of prayer, rules of enclosure within the convent, and withdrawal from society, family, and friends that were portrayed in the popular novels did have some basis in the lifestyle of the sisters. Nevertheless, the reality of the lives of the sisters, who largely ran the alternative social institutions for the immigrant church, was far different from the stereotype of the nun as sex-crazed or unwillingly constrained. A young woman in nineteenth-century America joined a community in her twenties or early thirties, went through a period of trial of several months to a year as a postulant, then received the habit of the order with a white veil or bonnet for a one- to two-year term as a novice. Temporary vows of poverty, chastity, and obedience and promises to live according to the constitutions of the community were made for one to three years, and a black veil or bonnet replaced the white as a sign of the professed sister. After the temporary period was over, the sister would make final vows for life.[25]

During these years of probation, a sister, with the guidance of more experienced sisters, learned the spirit of the community and the prayers and practices of the group and was trained in the work that the community undertook. During all these times, assisting with the "common" work of cooking, cleaning, mending, and making habits was generally part of a sister's life. Those communities of European origin with strong enclosure rules and solemn vows might have lay sisters do the manual labor while the "choir" sisters engaged in the teaching. In these periods of gradual assimilation into the religious lifestyle, the sister could leave the community, or be dismissed or encouraged to leave if she did not seem fitted for the life.

The community itself would have a mother superior ruling the group with the aid of a council of senior sisters, varying according to community, but an ecclesiastical superior—the bishop or some priest designated by him—exercised extensive powers over the life of a community. These powers might include confirming the election of a superior, sometimes appointing or removing the superior, and imposing corrections on sisters.[26] Church or canon law governed much of what was part of religious life: types of vows, rules regarding how the superior was to govern, religious practices, and the habit.

However, as Mary Ewens has demonstrated, the Church's formal role definition for nuns was generally based on a twelfth-century view of a woman as immature, inferior, evil, incapable of directing her own life, and requiring constant surveillance lest she fall.[27] Thus, this type of life, "frozen into Canon law regulations," Ewens concluded, was the result of a medieval society with an economic system in which fathers sometimes sent their daughters to convents for financial rather than religious motives.[28]

Communities differed in their own internal rules and practices. For example, those communities with European origins, such as the Sisters of Mercy or the Sisters of Charity (who amalgamated with the French Daughters of Charity in 1850) or the Sisters of St. Joseph of Carondolet (who separated from France) often had years of tradition and written rules and customs. American communities, often formed or encouraged by bishops desperately in need of someone to begin schools and services for the poor, did not have written documents. However, the sisters were often encouraged to utilize sections from the rules of other, more established communities, thus creating similar practices among many groups of women religious.

In spite of the Church's often archaic view of women religious, the needs of the American wilderness and the developing country certainly did not allow for well-built European convents with walls, for adherence to a rigid schedule of the day, or for rules of strict seclusion from the public. Not surprisingly, sometimes there were tensions between the sisters and some bishops, between the bishops with Rome, or between the American sisters and their European motherhouses over understanding or carrying out various regulations.

Nevertheless, the nuns often came from European communities, for whom America was missionary territory. This was in contrast to the sisters' Protestant counterparts in the American women's benevolent and missionary societies, who frequently turned their attention to foreign mission lands.[29] Indeed, the U.S. Church was officially considered "mission country" by the Vatican until June 29, 1908.[30] The struggles to meet the demands of this mission and frontier country are recounted in the early histories of most communities. For example, Sr. Frances Jerome Woods, in chronicling the work of congregations of women in the South, recounted stories of sisters planting and harvesting fields, chopping wood, struggling with snakes and other animals, being flooded out, and doing other manual work to fix up buildings for their early convents, schools, and hospitals. Those sisters that came from European countries to start American branches often saw themselves as coming to convert the savage Indians.[31] The American women who joined the communities might be aware they were probably not going to be converting Indians, at least not in the East and Midwest of the country. Nevertheless, the frontier experiences, the long distances from other Catholic settlements, and the physical hardships of establishing themselves and their schools caused the sisters to be clearly aware that this was pioneer mission territory as far as Catholics were concerned.

Cognizant of these conditions, the six archbishops and twenty-six bishops gathered together in 1852 for the First Plenary Council of Baltimore declared in their pastoral letter: "The wants of the Church in this vast country, so rapidly advancing in population and prosperity, impose on us, your pastors, and on you, our children in Christ, peculiar and arduous duties." After delineating the need for churches, more clergy, and Catholic education for youth, the letter stated, "Not only have we to erect and maintain the Church, the Seminary, and the School-house, but we have to found Hospitals, establish orphanages and provide for every want of suffering humanity, which Religion forbids us to neglect."[32] The sisters were the major contributors to this plea for health, education, and social-service institutions.

Renouncing marriage, motherhood, and home, the nuns lived an alternative life in a communal, single-sex setting and worked in these educational, health, and social-welfare institutions, where they held responsible, powerful, and influential positions. As Ewens has demonstrated, entrance into convent life, even in a hierarchical, patriarchal church, often gave these women leadership opportunities not available to many other women in mid-nineteenth-century America.[33]

Joseph Mannard, studying the relationship of these pioneer nuns to the antebellum ideology of domesticity, concluded that such divergence from traditional behavior of the "true women" did not reflect or foster changes in the sisters' value system. Little evidence exists, he determined, to suggest that the nuns challenged their continued subordination to males within church and society or criticized the male exclusiveness of the Catholic clergy and hierarchy.[34] Basically, Mannard believed they accepted the gender distinctions and accompanying sex roles as defined by the ideology of domesticity, and that they attempted to pass these ideals on to other women. "If nuns helped pioneer new variations on traditional roles and greater participation for women beyond the immediate family circle," he concluded, "the effect was only to broaden the meaning of the female sphere without questioning the validity of that concept."[35] Mannard's research suggests, rather, that nuns, by practicing "maternity of the spirit," fulfilled the functions of domesticity and conformed to its assumptions about the female nature.[36]

This women's sphere of domesticity, as reflected in letters, in diaries of white Protestant New England women, in the sermons preached in the late eighteenth and early nineteenth centuries, and as popularized in women's magazines, was in that place of salvation: the home. Separated from the arena of the world in which men labored in an arduous but energizing fashion, women were supposed to find satisfaction, happiness, and salvation in domestic occupations, spiritual care, and maternal destiny; their vocation was "to stablize society by generating and regenerating moral character."[37] Middle- and upper-class women especially, between 1820 and 1860, were merely "female appendages" to male activity in labor, business, politics, and the professions.[38]

James Kenneally suggested that to many American Catholics, the broad concept of true womanhood was an acceptable and familiar model. The concept rested in part on a Christian tradition that held that such a pattern was designed by God, exemplified by the Virgin Mary, and revealed by a Pauline interpretation of scripture and natural law. Furthermore, Kenneally noted that the belief was reinforced by biological differences and supported by a historical tradition proclaiming the supremacy of man. Consequently, numerous Catholics believed in distinct spheres of activity for each sex. Woman's sphere, of course, centered around her position as perpetuator of the race and nucleus of the family.[39] However, the extent to which American Catholic women, North or South, were influenced by these concepts of domesticity through sermons in their own churches, general popular magazines, and other forces, such as lectures, newspaper articles, or contact with Protestant women, remains to be examined in extensive detail by studying their letters, diaries, or journals.[40]

Education, religion, and sisterhood, as described by Nancy Cott, were all key concepts in developing the ideology of domesticity, regardless of the apparent lack of written evidence linking Roman Catholic women and nuns to the ideology of true womanhood.[41] It is reasonable to presume that Roman Catholic nuns themselves might have easily identified with many of these concepts. The two studies of Roman Catholic sisters, by Misner and by Ewens, when placed in the context of other studies on women and religion in the early nineteenth century,[42] suggest that the American women religious were not anomalies, even though they appeared suspect because of the different manner in which they expressed their ideals of womanhood.[43]

Education, for example, though seen as a responsibility of the mother in the nineteenth-century American family, was not a lifelong career. However, most religious communities were engaged in teaching, provided in-service training for their members, and saw their role as educators of future wives and of their families. Furthermore, the permanent vows the sisters took committed them for life to these educational activities.

Similarly, religion and piety, the signs of the nineteenth-century woman's virtue and the source of her strength, were prized because they did not take her away from her "proper sphere," her home.[44] Religion as practiced by the sisters, however, was seen by Catholics, at least, as a "higher calling" than marriage and the family. Sisters, therefore, were considered generous and self-sacrificing in giving up the pleasures and comforts of home, not as selfishly denigrating the ideas of true womanhood by their lifestyle. Some communities even used the title "Mother" for each of the sisters, and all communities had an understanding that sisters were the "brides of Christ."

Further, women, viewed by both Church and State as weak and ill-prepared to make important decisions, often looked to sisterhood with other women as a means of companionship and of exercising some influence on society. Most of the benevolent and missionary societies of the period, which were part of the Protestant revival movement, developed out of this model. Even though sisterhood, as practiced in Catholic religious communities, was otherwise unknown in the United States, some of its values often appealed to some Protestant women, like Catharine Beecher, who were intent upon social and educational reform.[45] In this model, they found an alternative to the primary calling of a woman to marriage and a family. Perhaps a major difference between the Protestant social reformers[46] and Roman Catholic sisters, however, was that the Protestant women were just beginning to form or join voluntary, benevolent, missionary, or reform organizations.[47] Developing institutions would come later. The sisters, on the other hand, already lived in an organized and structured form of benevolent and missionary association. Thus, they could devote themselves to building, developing, and administering social reform institutions, establishing places of salvation in the world. Thus, education, religion, and sisterhood reflected values of domesticity the sisters shared, though expressed differently, with Protestant women.

Nevertheless, the nineteenth-century American Catholic Church, like the rest of society, did not expect women to act independently. Thus, major decisions in religious communities usually required at least the approval of the bishop or his representative. The question of the authority of the community versus that of a local bishop was, perhaps, the single most important factor in the difficulties that arose as the sisters within each community moved from pioneer groupings to more structured institutions.[48] Despite this, the women religious did hold most of the responsibility for their own finances, for the day-to-day management of their institutions, which grew from one-room cabins to brick buildings, and for the future expansion of their works of education, health care, and social services. Further, sisters had opportunities for education and on-the-job training, "careers," administration, and a relative independence in their work, all of which were rarely achieved by other nineteenth-century women.[49]

As a result of the interaction of the nuns with their milieu, both European and American attitudes toward nuns were gradually modified. The American view eventually changed from one of hostility to one of acceptance and respect, and the Catholic church slowly became aware that some of its obsolete European role definitions for nuns had to be changed if sisters were to work effectively in a different cultural setting.[50]

Many of the role conflicts that developed were actually the result of cultural clashes between European and American values that were apparent in other aspects of American Catholic life.[51] The European values were codified in the canon law for religious, which governed every aspect of their lives: daily schedule, clothing, work, rules on enclosure. The prevailing European concept of a sister as one who had solemn vows and hence was cloistered was somewhat clarified by the decision in 1864, that, with few exceptions, all sisters in America should take simple vows, thus modifying the regulations regarding the cloister.[52]

Ewens points out that in the decade of the 1860s, sisters generally continued to play the same roles they had earlier. The American foundations of European motherhouses begun during the earlier period gradually became Americanized as adaptions, such as the addition of American members, the pressure of bishops, and other factors worked to lessen their foreign characteristics.[53] The Civil War, of course, hastened this change. With approximately one-fifth of the sisters in the United States involved at some point in nursing,[54] their schedules were disrupted, and they were exposed to a greater cross-section of Americans.[55]

As part of the largely immigrant Catholic Church, Roman Catholic sisters belonged to a minority group, and were misunderstood and even hated because of foreign or strange ways. Though not part of the culture of nineteenth-century Protestant, middle-class, married women, whose life and values set the standards for domesticity, the American sisters did reflect qualities of purity, piety, service, and submissiveness in their lives. The sisters' nineteenth-century feminine, domestic qualities were strikingly enhanced by their life in a female religious community, with values of a common goal of service to all those in need, organization for that purpose, and mutual support. Above all, the sisters' training and experience in nursing and other social services, done out of a missionary purpose rather than a reforming, professional zeal, made them generally admired, though sometimes envied, by Protestant women. However, the essence of the mission and the purpose of all Catholic women religious was the desire to make the Catholic religion better understood and known through continuing charitable works of education, social service, and health, especially for the immigrant Catholic Church and for the poor. Thus, on the eve of the Civil War, the sisters possessed those qualities that would ultimately set a standard for skilled nursing care, modify decades of negative attitudes about their lives, and win understanding and appreciation for themselves and for their Church.

NOTES

1. Archives of the Daughters of Charity, Emmitsburg, MD, (ADC), *Annals of the Civil War*, Vol. I, p. 13.
2. Alexis de Tocqueville, *Democracy in America*, eds. J. P. Mayer and Max Lerner (New York: Harper, 1966), p. 414.
3. de Tocqueville, p. 265.
4. de Tocqueville, p. 266.
5. Edwin Gaustad, *Historical Atlas of American Religion* (New York: Harper and Row, 1975), pp. 36, 42, 111.
6. John Tracy Ellis, *American Catholicism*, rev. ed. (Chicago: University of Chicago Press, 1956), pp. 82–83.
7. Sr. Mary Christine Sullivan notes in her study, "Some Non-Permanent Foundations of Religious Orders and Congregations," *U.S. Catholic Historical Society Records and Studies* 31 (Jan. 1940), 7–118, that in these approximately seven communities, which did not survive due to "fire, floods, lack of subjects, misunderstanding, calumny, and even persecution," the foundresses (except for the Visitandine Nuns at Georgetown, District of Columbia), were of European origin (pp. 8–11). See also Barbara Misner, "A Comparative Social Study of the Members and Apostolates of the First Eight Permanent Communities of Women Religious within the Boundaries of the United States, 1790–1850," Ph.D. Diss., Catholic University of America, 1981. Misner indicates that by 1830, the eight permanent communities, which included two cloistered communities (the Carmelites and the Visitandines), totaled 1,441 members (Misner, p. viii).
8. Elinor Dehey, *Religious Orders of Women in the United States* (Hammond, IN: W. B. Conkey, 1930). My own examination of the official Catholic directories for 1850 indicates the impossibility of getting accurate figures, as each diocese reported statistics in different ways, and total numbers of sisters were not given, though some dioceses did list the number of sisters at given institutions. The best method to ascertain the number might be to request the figures from each individual community still in existence that kept a register, if the record has not been destroyed by fire or other calamity.
9. John Tracy Ellis, *Catholics in Colonial America* (Baltimore: Helicon Press, 1965), p. 249.
10. Though a sociological profile of these sisters in antebellum America would be valuable to have, the data remain fragmentary or nonexistent. Misner, as a part of her dissertation, did a computer analysis on what information was available on the first eight permanent communities of women religious; she acknowl-

edges that while more information can be found about these women than for any other group of women of similar size (1,441) during the early nineteenth century, "Much of the data was not available." Misner, pp. vii-viii.

11. Ellis, *American Catholicism*, pp. 54–56.

12. Misner, pp. vi-vii.

13. Misner, pp. vi-vii. See also Dehey for specific information on each community.

14. See Dehey for dates and names of these communities. These data are also summarized in a table in Sr. Evangeline Thomas, *Women Religious History Sources: A Guide to Repositories in the United States* (New York: R. R. Bowker, 1983).

15. Jay Dolan, *The Immigrant Church*, p. 130.

16. Charles Rosenberg, "And Heal the Sick: The Hospital and the Patient in Nineteenth Century America," *Journal of Social History* 10 (Summer 1977): 438.

17. Lyman Beecher, quoted in Hennesey, p. 119.

18. Hennesey, pp. 116–127.

19. Rebecca Reed, *Six Months in a Convent* (Boston: Russell, Odeorne and Metcalf, 1835).

20. Maria Monk, *Awful Disclosures of the Hotel Dieu Nunnery in Montreal* (New York: Howe and Bates, 1836).

21. Sr. Mary Ewens, *The Role of the Nun in Nineteenth-Century America* (New York: Arno, 1978) p. 250.

22. Reed, p. 13.

23. Amanda Porterfield, *Feminine Spirituality in America* (Philadelphia: Temple University Press, 1980), p. 122.

24. "Destruction of Charleston Convent from Contemporary Newspaper Accounts," *U.S. Catholic Historical Records and Studies* 13 (May 1919): 106–119. For another view see James Kenneally, "The Burning of the Ursuline Convent: A Different View," *Records of the American Catholic Historical Society* 90 (Mar.-Dec. 1979): 15–22.

25. The general information in this and the following paragraphs is drawn largely from Ewens, pp. 105–122.

26. See Sr. Patricia Byrne, "Sisters of St. Joseph: The Americanization of a French Tradition," *U.S. Catholic Historian* 5 (1986): 256.

27. Ewens, p. 326.

28. Ewens, p. 326.

29. See Keith Melder, "Ladies Bountiful: Organized Women's Benevolence in Early Nineteenth Century America," *New York History* 48 (July 1967), 231–254. Mary B. Treudly "The Benevolent Pair: A Study of Charitable Organization Among Women in the First Third of the Nineteenth Century," *Social Service Review* 19 (Dec. 1940): 509–522.

30. Ellis, *American Catholicism*, p. 124.

31. Woods, pp. 104–105.

32. Peter Guilday, ed. *The National Pastoral Letters of the American Hierarchy (1792–1919)* (Maryland: The Newman Press, 1954), p. 187.

33. Ewens, especially conclusion, pp. 326–331.

34. Joseph Mannard, "Maternity of the Spirit: Nuns and Domesticity in Antebellum America," *U.S. Catholic Historian* 5 (Summer/Fall 1986): 322.

35. Mannard, p. 324.

36. For another view, see James Kenneally, "Eve, Mary, and the Historians: American Catholicism and Women," in Janet W. James, ed., *Women in American Religion* (Philadelphia: University of Pennsylvania Press, 1980). He says that ladylike qualities, nurtured and fostered by the institutional Church, made nuns ideal for teaching children, Blacks, and Indians, and for running orphanages and nursing the infirm and aged. On the other hand (p. 197), these activities, wherein sisters performed as administrators and superiors, or natural "male roles," sometimes led to clashes with the hierarchy. Of the twelve nuns listed in *Notable American Women*, six had difficulties with male superiors (pp. 197–198).

37. Nancy Cott, *The Bonds of True Womanhood* (New Haven: Yale University Press, 1977), p. 92.

38. Ronald Hogeland, "The Female Appendage: Feminine Life Styles in America, 1820–1860," *Civil War History* 27 (1971): 104–114.

39. Kenneally, p. 191.

40. Colleen McDannell, *The Christian Home in Victorian America, 1840–1900* (Philadelphia: Temple University Press, 1986). She compares Protestant and Catholic homes and devotes one chapter to Catholic domesticity (pp. 52–76). McDannell noted that it took almost fifty years before Irish Catholic immigrants developed a Victorian domesticity similar to Protestant sensibilities, mainly due to their social and economic situation. Thus, the time lag precludes any definitive comparisons being made between Catholic and Protestant concepts of domesticity in the antebellum period.

41. Cott cites the current uses of the term "domesticity," p. 1. All uses apply only to the Puritan Protestants.

42. See those by Welter, Cott, and Porterfield.

43. Misner, p. 287.

44. Welter, pp. 152–153.

45. Catharine Beecher, *The American Woman's Home* (New York: J. B. Ford, 1870), p. 451. See also Kathryn Sklar, *Catharine Beecher: A Study in American Domesticity* (New Haven: Yale University Press, 1973), pp. 171–172.

46. As Rosemary Reuther and Rosemary Keller in *Women and Religion in America: The Nineteenth Century: A Documentary History* (San Francisco: Harper and Row, 1981) point out, there was no uniformity within the ranks of Protestant reformers. Tension existed between conservative and radical, educational and abolitionist reformers, debating whether woman's sphere was to be exercised within the home and church—the extension of the private, domestic world—or within their own moral judgment and reason in the larger world beyond the home (p. 300).

47. See Carolyn Gifford, "Sisterhoods of Service and Reform: Organized Methodist Women in the Late Nineteenth Century: An Essay on the State of the Research," *Methodist History* 24 (Oct. 1985): 15–30.

48. Misner, p. 253.

49. Mannard, p. 322. For a view of late-nineteenth-century reformers who did develop institutions, see Estelle Freedman, "Separation as Strategy: Female Institution Building and American Feminism, 1870–1930," *Feminist Studies* 5, No. 3 (Fall 1979): 513–529.

50. Ewens, p. 12.

51. Ewens, p. 12.

52. Ewens, pp. 204–217.

53. Ewens, p. 217.

54. The one-fifth figure is derived from the available statistics of the communities that served in the Civil War.

55. Ewens, pp. 250–251. See also Dolan, *The American Catholic Experience*, pp. 121–124.

2

Backgrounds of Catholic Nursing in the United States in the Nineteenth Century

Roman Catholic sisters, in spite of their minority status and misunderstood life, offered the only source of trained nurses for the Civil War, especially in its chaotic beginnings. The significance of their contribution becomes clearer when it is viewed in the context of early efforts to develop almshouses and private hospitals, to provide nursing care, and, (a movement led by Florence Nightingale) to reform nursing. Those on both sides of the Atlantic who decried the conditions of these early health-care institutions turned to the model of the religious sisterhoods, especially the Roman Catholic nursing communities, examples of how single Protestant women might be religiously motivated and organized to carry out this nursing care. An examination of this nursing history and the care that was given by the sisters in Catholic and other early hospitals in the three decades before the war will demonstrate that sisters were uniquely positioned by their traditions, their experience, and their community constitutions to provide nursing care when the Civil War began.

Although the first hospital in the continental United States was established in 1658 by the Dutch West India Company in Massachusetts for sick employees,[1] the sick were ordinarily cared for within the family by mothers, sisters, and wives. Strangers and travelers who fell ill were generally taken in by benevolent families and nursed back to health or buried. However, epidemics of cholera, typhoid, and smallpox, along with immigration and emigration patterns, changed this system of home or even company nursing care. Two types of hospitals gradually developed: the voluntary hospital, supported by private philanthropy, such as general hospitals in Pennsylvania (1751), New York (1775), and Mas-

sachusetts (1821), and the almshouse hospital established by cities, beginning with Philadelphia in 1713, where William Penn provided the
necessary leadership. Some, like Charity Hospital in New Orleans, which
was established in 1737 by a private gift of a sailor, took both poor and
paying patients.[2] By 1840, most of the major American cities had almshouses, which included infirmaries for the sick and poor and pest houses
for the isolation of contagious diseases. Social medical historian Paul
Starr stated that these early hospitals were considered, at best, unhappy
necessities, filthy, overcrowded, and used as combinations of prisons,
poorhouses, pest houses, and homes for the aged. Contagious diseases
spread rapidly in them, and the mortality rates were high.[3]

In the almshouses, most of the care was given by the other inmates.
In the hospitals, nursing, done by women of the lower classes who were
sometimes recruited from the almshouses or penitentiary, was classed
with scrubbing the floors; no special training was expected or desired.[4]
Even at its best, nursing was considered a domestic art and, as such, was
passed from person to person by word of mouth and by demonstration.
Keeping the patients clean and giving them nourishment was the major
responsibility, and there were no nurses at night except in emergencies.
Regular inspection of hospitals or nursing care was not done.[5]

The early hospitals kept very few medical records, usually just ad-
missions and discharges, summaries of age and nationality, and a statement of the disease and condition on discharge.[6] Thus, other than a
general awareness of deplorable conditions surrounding these early institutions, little is actually recorded about the hospitals or the specifics
of the care of patients in them. For example, in trying to reconstruct
the early history of city hospitals, historian Harry Dowling said that
historians know much more about when and where these almshouses
were built than about the care given the patients. Even so, the data consist
of a date and a geographical location.[7] Nursing historians Adelaide Nutting and Lavinia Dock, using an 1854 article describing Bellevue Hospital
in New York as an example of the fragmentary information about early
nursing, noted that "not a word was said about the nursing or the care
of the patients."[8]

In the decade before the Civil War, a few doctors, notably Dr. Joseph
Warrington of Philadelphia and Dr. Marie Zakrzewska of the New England Hospital for Women in Boston, provided some basic lectures and
instruction in cleanliness for female nurses on the maternity cases. In
spite of these efforts, however, there were only fifty women trained by
Dr. Warrington between 1839 and 1850, and Dr. Zakrzewska had only
one applicant in 1859.[9] There were some printed materials, like Warrington's *The Nurses Guide* (1839), on the nursing of women and children,
and a few on general nursing.[10] While they were intended, for the most

part, for home nursing, these materials were used by some of the early hospital nurses, religious as well as secular.[11]

In the United States, where ties with England had always been close, the English example of Florence Nightingale and her nursing reforms was influential even though there was also an independent American reform movement.[12] However, even in 1844, when Nightingale first knew with certainty that her vocation lay among the sick in hospitals, she did not have the actual practice of nursing in her mind. She had spoken to Dr. Samuel Howe, husband of Julia Ward, of "devoting herself to works of charity in hospitals," thinking that the qualities needed to relieve the misery of the sick were tenderness, sympathy, goodness, and patience. But after a brief experience of nursing some family members, she realized that only knowledge and expert skill could bring relief, even though it was universally assumed that being a woman was the only qualification needed for taking care of the sick.[13]

Concurrent with Nightingale's interest in devoting herself to the sick, nursing reform in England was developing out of the high-church religious revival of the 1840s and 1850s. The new Anglican sisterhoods, as women's historian Martha Vicinus has demonstrated, saw nursing the sick poor as one of their prime objectives, reviving the ancient tradition of the religious vocation of nursing. Similar reforms, she pointed out, were also being undertaken by Roman Catholic nuns in France and Lutheran deaconesses in Germany. Although all these religious orders, both in England and on the Continent, put little emphasis upon formal training, Vicinus concluded they set "new standards of cleanliness and conscientiousness."[14]

Thus, when Nightingale went to the Crimean Peninsula in 1853, during the war between Russia and the allied powers, which included England, twenty-four of her thirty-eight nurses were from Anglican and Roman Catholic religious orders. In fact, as Mary McAuley Gilgannon has demonstrated, it was the Sisters of Mercy from Ireland and from England who gave Nightingale's Female Nursing Establishment "whatever semblance it possessed of being a cohesive body."[15] The women's success in the Crimea brought fame to Nightingale's nurses and a heightened public interest in nursing as a vocation. Both Nightingale and her nursing reformers and the religious orders benefited from these achievements.[16]

The specific example of the Roman Catholic sisters in Europe and England was laid before the English people by another advocate of nursing reform: author, art historian, and lecturer Mrs. Anna Jameson. She followed the lead of physician and philanthropist Dr. Robert Gooch in publicly advocating a Protestant nursing order. An 1855 lecture, entitled "Sisters of Charity Abroad and at Home," cited example after example of what Roman Catholic sisters had done throughout Europe as inspiration for her challenge to the British,[17] even though she was "not a friend of nunnaries [sic] . . . [or] even of Protestant nunnaries."[18] The lecture was so well received that it was later published in England and America.

She acknowledged that while some concepts of Catholicism were repugnant, such as images of "forced celibacy and seclusion," and other traditions Protestants regarded "with terror, disgust, and derision," Jameson suggested that just as the British used old cathedrals and colleges for pious ends and social benefits, Protestant women could dispense with some of the ornaments and appendages of Catholicism and retain the basic concept of nursing.[19]

As American reformers such as Catharine Beecher, Jane Woolsey, and Mary Livermore were to do in the United States, Jameson concluded with a resounding plea for Protestant women to follow the example of the "well-trained" Roman Catholic sisters in the Crimea who "held on with unflagging spirit and energy . . . meeting all difficulties with a cheerful spirit and a superiority which they owed to their previous training and experience, not certainly to any want of zeal, benevolence, or intelligence in their Protestant sisters of the better class."[20]

Jameson acknowledged that British doctors in the Crimean War, who felt that any experiment with volunteer nurses "*must* end in total failure" in spite of Nightingale's sometimes controversial efforts to win their confidence and support, were "loud and emphatic" in their admiration of the Catholic sisters.[21] Reasoning, then, that men did not object to women as nurses but only to Protestant women as nurses, she brought her argument to a logically ordered conclusion: "Now, do they mean to say that there is anything in the Roman Catholic religion which produces these efficient women? or that it is impossible to train any other women to perform the same duties with the same calm and quiet efficiency, the same zeal and devotion? Really I do not see that feminine energy and efficiency belong to any one section of the great Christian community."[22]

Vicinus concluded that nursing and religious commitment were closely linked in the minds of the educated British public because no one believed that anyone but a sister would be willing to do the work.[23] Even the advocates of reformed nursing from Evangelical or nonconformist backgrounds, who wished to move leadership out of the hands of High Anglicans and wanted "commitment without incense," unanimously agreed that religious inspiration was essential if gentlewomen were to consent to a lifetime of unpleasant work.[24]

These views were similarly applied in America, though in the United States anti-Catholic sentiment made women of any religious grouping somewhat suspect. Thus, according to the Bulloughs, Protestant reformers in America who, as in England and Europe, greatly admired the work of the Catholic nursing orders, sought to mobilize Protestant women for works of charity without establishing convents.[25]

On a smaller scale than Catholics, Protestant churches also trained nurses, usually called deaconesses.[26] Four Lutheran deaconesses were first brought by Pastor Theodore Fliedner in 1849 to Pittsburgh from Kaiserswerth, Germany, where the movement had begun and flourished. The Pittsburgh Infirmary, founded by Rev. Dr. William A. Passavant, was one of four Lutheran hospitals started by him before the Civil War. When the war broke out, Dr. Passavant offered the deaconesses' services to Miss Dorothea Dix, Superintendent of the Union army female nurses, who received them graciously.[27] The Episcopal Church also began a deaconess movement, organized in 1855 by the Reverend Horace Springfellow in Baltimore. Though short-lived as a group, they did staff St. Andrews's Infirmary there.[28] The first Episcopal sisters, distinguished from deaconesses by vows and enclosure, were loosely organized in 1845 and formally established in 1852 by Rev. William A. Muhlenberg, who started a dispensary in New York City which later became St. Luke's Hospital.[29]

In spite of these efforts by Protestant sisterhoods to provide better nursing care, two factors, according to the Bulloughs, limited their expansion. First, the communities lacked sufficient recruits to adequately staff expanding numbers of hospitals. More seriously, there was antagonism from Protestants who saw such groups as havens for secret Catholics, causing even Muhlenberg to dissolve his sisterhood for a time.[30]

In addition to these religiously organized groups, in 1813 the Ladies' Benevolent Society of Charleston, South Carolina, began nursing the sick at home in the first known example of organized, untrained, lay nursing in America.[31] Furthermore, women who were thwarted in their attempts to be part of the larger medical field in antebellum America—often a difficult task—sometimes were forced to undertake nursing as an alternative, at least during the Civil War.[32] For example, Dr. Mary Walker was the only woman who officially practiced medicine during the Civil War; it is believed that others, like Esther Hill Hawkes, who was denied the opportunity to serve as a doctor, turned to nursing.[33]

Thus, in spite of some reform efforts, neither in nursing nor in medicine was there a strong background, tradition, or experience in caring for patients among women in the United States. On the other hand, although there were no doctors among them, the Roman Catholic sisters who served in the Civil War, regardless of whether they came from European or American communities or whether their community was devoted primarily to nursing care or to other forms of charity, came from a long tradition in which care of the sick was done from religious motivation.

That tradition had its beginning in the Middle Ages, where devotion to the sick for religious reasons caused an important forward step in nursing. To assist in carrying out the religious ideal, medieval men and women developed various Catholic institutions, especially hospitals and nursing orders devoted to relieving pain and suffering.[34] Unfortunately, many of these institutions were closed, the lay groups disbanded, and religious orders dissolved during the Protestant Reformation.[35] Though male nurses, many of whom were part of the monastic orders or lay groups, largely disappeared, Catholic nursing orders organized after 1500 were for women.[36] Whatever may have been the detrimental effects of the Protestant Reformation on Catholics, one result was to put the care of the sick in the hands of female religious communities, who devoted their lives to this work by serving in institutions that were closely connected to, as well as controlled by, the Catholic hierarchy. This single-minded devotion to the sick, which was supported by visible institutional structures as well as regulated by some of the constricting rules of religious life, would eventually be brought to the United States or adapted in some way by the communities that would come or be started two centuries later.[37]

Aware of the value of dedicated people serving others, but also aware of the constrictions of cloistered female religious life, St. Vincent De Paul initiated the most important development in nursing in Catholic countries by founding the Sisters (later called Daughters) of Charity in seventeenth-century France. In his work with convicts and galley slaves in France, he first founded the Congregation of Priests of the Missions. During his work, he became acquainted with two noblewomen, Madame de la Chassaigne and Madame de Brie, who spent most of their time aiding the poor or nursing the sick. In the beginning he simply organized a society of ladies to help in better distributing food and services for the needy. Later, a community was established under the direction of Louise de Marillac. As the community developed, it underwent various modifications in theme and purpose; however, by 1634, de Marillac assumed leadership of what was by then called Sisters of Charity. Vincent De Paul was opposed, though, to either the earlier ladies of charity or the sisters becoming nuns since he felt there was a real need for women who could visit with the sick in their homes. This visiting would have been almost impossible for nuns, who were bound under strict, cloistered rules, which kept them within the confines of their convents.[38] He wrote: "It is true [there were] religious [orders] and hospitals for the assistance of the sick, but before your establishment there was never a community destined to go and serve the sick in their houses. If, in some poor family, anyone fell sick, he was sent to the hospital, and this separated the husband from his wife, and the children from their parents."[39]

Other communities of sisters, focusing on similarly active ministries, rather than the contemplative prayer ministries of nuns, soon followed.

Some were based on ideas of Vincent De Paul and emphasized care of the sick, along with education and other works of charity. For example, by 1816, Mary Aikenhead of Cork founded the Irish Sisters of Charity; she later was in charge of Dublin's St. Vincent's Hospital, the first hospital in Ireland to be served by nuns. The Sisters of Mercy, several branches of which came to the United States, were founded in 1827 by Catharine McAuley in Dublin. Though these communities and others were distinct in name, purpose, regulations, and dress, the differences were often indistinguishable in the view of the ordinary person, and all sisters were often called Sisters of Charity or Sisters of Mercy after these early communities, which focused on charitable works.

Concurrent with the developments in Europe, the medieval legacy of care of the sick done by religious orders, as revitalized by Vincent De Paul and Louise de Marillac and as carried out by the formation of apostolic communities of women religious, was being developed in North America. The first attempt to train nurses on the North American continent was made by the Ursuline nuns of Quebec, who, about 1610, taught the Indian women to care for their sick.[40] In 1639, three Augustinians from Dieppe, France, whose community had been established in 1155 as hospital sisters, also came to Quebec to nurse Indian smallpox victims in a New World Hotel Dieu.[41] The first whites to be nursed by sisters were soldiers of the Revolutionary Army suffering from smallpox and scarlet fever contracted during the siege of Quebec. They were taken to Hotel Dieu and cared for by the Augustinians, as were both Americans and French in the Battle of Three Rivers in 1776.[42]

Although there were these examples of French Canadian sisters nursing in North America, hospital care in the continental United States was started primarily by American-founded communities. Particularly influential in forming American concepts of nursing was the work of Elizabeth Ann Bayley Seton: wife, mother, and widow, and the first native-born American to be canonized a Roman Catholic saint.[43] After her conversion to Catholicism, she organized the St. Joseph's sisterhood at Emmitsburg, Maryland, in 1809. The group soon adopted the rule of the Sisters of Charity of St. Vincent De Paul, and a union with the French society was effected in 1850. From the beginning, care of the sick was a major work of this community. Between 1828 and 1860, these Sisters of Charity (later called Daughters of Charity) opened eighteen hospitals in ten different states and the District of Columbia;[44] these constituted more than half the twenty-eight Catholic hospitals established before the Civil War.[45] Other communities soon followed the Sisters of Charity in establishing hospitals for the sick and diseased.

Similar to the findings of the medical and nursing historians cited earlier, facts on the establishment of these Catholic institutions and the care provided by them are also sparse. Ann Doyle, in her research on

nursing by religious orders in the United States, first points out the
difficulty of compiling any comprehensive or complete history of the
contributions made by various religious groups, Catholic or Protestant.
Even the words "hospital" and "nursing," she found, were not used in
early books. Citing both the "limitations and difficulties of the times"
and the "extreme modesty and self-effacement" of the various sisters,
Doyle further suggests that even when brief accounts of the beginnings
of the religious communities were done, the sister historians were largely
teachers and thus often neglected research into the beginnings of hospitals, focusing rather on educational endeavors and the internal history
of the community.[46]

Nonetheless,.from the data that do exist, it can be determined that
sisters took care of patients in at least seven hospitals, often called infirmaries, asylums, or retreats, in the period before 1840.[47] The Baltimore
Infirmary, Maryland, begun in 1823, had four wards, one of which
handled eye cases, was attended by doctors and students from the University of Maryland, and had seven or eight Sisters of Charity by 1827.[48]
Four Sisters of Charity in St. Louis started the St. Louis Mullanphy
Hospital in 1828 in a three-room log house until a brick building was
constructed in 1831. The Baltimore Infirmary is considered the first
instance of women religious in active hospital work in the United States,[49]
and Mullanphy Hospital, the first permanent Catholic hospital.[50] During
the years 1830 to 1840, when yellow fever and cholera scourged Charleston, South Carolina, the Brotherhood of Saint Marino, an association of
mechanics and laborers, rented a house, furnished it with beds, linens,
and other supplies, and then put it under the direction of the Sisters of
Our Lady of Mercy (now called Sisters of Charity of Our Lady of Mercy),
an American community founded by Bishop John England to serve the
poor in his diocese of Charleston, South Carolina.[51] Similarly, the origins
of the St. Vincent Infirmary of the Sisters of Charity of Nazareth, established about 1836, for the sick of Louisville, Kentucky, were in a few
spare rooms of an orphanage built after the cholera epidemics of the
1830s.

As Charles Rosenberg points out in his history of the United States'
cholera epidemics of 1832 and 1849, hospitals were the most immediate
need in cholera-stricken communities, but the need was not easily filled.[52]
Only in a few cities, such as Philadelphia, Baltimore, Louisville, St. Louis,
and Cincinnati in 1832, and in Buffalo, Boston, and St. Louis in 1849,
where various communities of Sisters of Charity allowed their hospitals
to be used for treating cholera patients, could health authorities turn to
hospitals already staffed and functioning.[53]

During these epidemics, sisters were also asked sometimes to staff
other hospitals. For example, Blockley, the municipal almshouse of Philadelphia, was managed briefly by the Sisters of Charity during the chol-

era epidemic of 1832.[54] Admiration was earned by the sisters, Rosenberg concludes, for their practical benevolence, which demonstrated that their lives were "not idled away in the convent living tomb."[55]

The Daughters of Charity were asked to take charge of Charity Hospital in New Orleans in 1834,[56] served at Maryland Hospital in Baltimore from 1834 to 1840, and opened the Richmond Infirmary in 1838. Some of these early beginnings, like Charity Hospital, Mullanphy Hospital (which became St. Louis Hospital in 1930), and St. Vincent Infirmary (which became St. Joseph Infirmary) lasted into the twentieth century. All of them set the pattern of sisters both initiating their own institutions and being asked to staff other public and private institutions.[57]

Although it is not clear what precise tasks were performed by the sisters in these early hospitals, it is presumed the duties involved dressing wounds, bathing the patients, keeping the bedding and rooms clean and aired, preparing and serving food, and providing spiritual support for the suffering and dying.[58] A letter from a priest in Baltimore to Bishop Benedict Flaget in Kentucky stated that the sisters at the Baltimore Infirmary in 1829 received $42 a year each, and that their duties included dressing "sore legs and blisters" and "all the wounds of the women, unless from an operation," and "administering all the medicine."[59]

The Daughters of Charity, the Sisters of Charity of Nazareth, the Sisters of Charity of Our Lady of Mercy, all American-founded communities, were the three communities with sisters in these early hospitals. Numbers are difficult to determine, but generally three or four sisters began in these places, with their number perhaps doubling as needs demanded.[60]

In the period from 1840 to 1860, the Daughters of Charity started additional hospitals. Other women came from Europe to begin communities for visiting the sick in their homes and to start hospitals, as well as to engage in education and other works of charity. Sisters of Mercy, arriving from Ireland in 1843, came with a tradition of visiting the sick in their homes. In the United States, they established their first hospital in Pittsburgh in 1847, another one in Chicago in 1851, and St. Mary's Hospital in San Francisco in 1857. A hospital in Wheeling, Virginia (now West Virginia) in 1853 and in St. Paul, Minnesota, in 1854, were established by the Sisters of St. Joseph of Carondelet, who had come from France in 1836. Sisters of the Poor of St. Francis, coming from Germany to America in 1850, established St. Mary's Hospital in Cincinnati in 1859 and St. Elizabeth's Hospital in Covington, Kentucky, in 1860. Another Franciscan community, the Sisters of the Third Order of St. Francis, founded St. Mary's Hospital in Philadelphia in 1860. In addition, the Sisters of Charity of St. Augustine, brought to Cleveland by Bishop Amadeus Rappe for the express purpose of establishing a Catholic hospital, started St. Joseph Hospital in 1852, which closed in 1856 but was later reestablished as St. Vincent Charity Hospital in 1865. This work is similar to the activities of other religious communities who staffed hospitals for only a period of time, particularly during the various cholera epidemics in the 1840s and 1860s.[61]

Typical of the beginnings of these hospitals between 1840 and 1860 were the three dilapidated log buildings in Detroit that were the start, in 1844, of St. Mary Hospital. Two stables in Rochester, New York, were the beginnings in 1857 for St. Mary's Hospital there. The old ballroom of the Sisters of Mercy residence in Pittsburgh became Mercy Hospital in 1849 to care for men suffering from ship fever aboard boats on the Ohio River. A temporary building was the origin of Wheeling Hospital, Virginia, begun in 1853 by the Sisters of St. Joseph. In contrast to these usual beginnings was St. Joseph Hospital in St. Paul, Minnesota, built in 1854, which was made of stone and was four stories high. Generally, the approximately twenty hospitals established during this period by the sisters, sometimes with the support of the bishop or doctors, were begun in response to acute needs, such as cholera or smallpox.[62]

In addition to the above communities, all of whom were later involved in the Civil War nursing effort, there were several other communities devoted to nursing established prior to the war, such as the Sisters of the Incarnate Word in Texas and the Sisters of Charity of Providence in Washington state. Probably because of geographic location, these communities were not involved in the war.[63] Also, the Sisters of Providence of St. Mary of the Woods, Indiana, who came from France in 1840, and the Sisters of the Holy Cross of South Bend, Indiana, who came in 1843, later established hospitals as a result of their Civil War experience, although they had not been involved with health care before the war.

These early hospitals, opened primarily to meet acute needs and to help the influx of poor immigrants, [64] were small. Perhaps largest was the forty-bed St. Vincent Hospital in New York City; all were greatly handicapped by lack of resources and personnel. The major reason for this was that the people on whom the sisters had to depend for support were mostly newly arrived immigrants, who were hard pressed in obtaining even the necessities of life.[65] For example, the Daughters of Charity reported that Detroit Bishop Paul Lefevre was anxious to tell the people that the sisters would open a hospital in 1845 and that they should support it by bringing bedding and articles to furnish the wards. Nevertheless, the sisters recounted that they only got "a few bed ticks, somewhat longer than pillow-ticks, with a little straw in them."[66]

While by modern standards the sisters had little special preparation when they opened their first hospitals, they were reported to have "zeal, self-sacrifice and sympathy for the suffering that made them an inspiring challenge to Protestant institutions."[67] Although some doctors and various reformers decried the lack of adequate medical care in most public institutions, most nursing historians state that methodical attendance of the sick was probably undertaken until well into the nineteenth century only by the Catholic religious orders in both the United States and England.[68] For example, Robin O'Connor has found that in contrast to lay nurses, "The Catholic sisterhoods trained their own members well, creating educated and disciplined nurses." He noted that New York City, Baltimore, and Philadelphia often hired the Daughters of Charity for emergency nursing service, and a few cities, such as Mobile, Alabama, in 1830, and Augusta, Georgia, in 1834, established hospitals with the intent of having Catholic sisterhoods manage them.[69]

There are few written records of the nursing practice even during these years just before the war. Judging from the practice of medicine at the time, it is reasonable to suppose, as Doyle believes, that it was very simple and probably confined to procuring cleanliness, nourishment, and safety for the sick, and to the administration of simple medicine. In addition, the work of the sisters was extended to the kitchen, the laundry, supervision of the wards, and care of the spiritual welfare of the patients.[70]

Although written documents concerning the actual training and nursing practice in Catholic hospitals may seem sparse to most nursing and medical historians, an extemely important set of documents has been overlooked by them. The rules and constitutions of communities with European origins, like the Sisters of Mercy, or with European affiliations, like the Daughters of Charity, were used as models by American communities. These contained sections that served as a practical guide to nursing care for the sisters. The constitutions clearly spelled out how the sick were to be regarded and treated, what kind of food should be served, how the linens and rooms should be cleaned, what the schedule of the day should be, how doctors should be regarded, and above all, how the dying should be prepared for death.[71] The reading and studying of these basic documents, which covered all phases of a sister's life, including the specific rules for care of sick sisters as well as directives for sisters visiting the sick or working in hospitals, were a part of the early training and life-long experience of the sisters. In addition, the apprenticeship of these beginning religious with an experienced sister served as formal training in the many aspects of living and working.

These same constitutions and commentaries of both Sisters of Charity and Sisters of Mercy also provided conventional wisdom and nursing training. These regulations exhorted the sisters not to warm the broth for the infirm more than an hour, lest it become too salty,[72] to make sure that those who are very weak "occasionally have something nice to eat and drink,"[73] and to cleanse frequently the mouths of the sick, as well as their bodies, for fear of canker sores. In addition, the sisters were reminded that complete ventilation, without permitting draughts of air to flow on the patient, was essential, and that with doctors, the "sisters' manners should be ever reserved, polite, and self-possessed, attentive to take directions, vigilant and exact in fulfilling them."[74] Further, sister pharmacists should take great care to keep the drugs in a good state.

These simple and practical attempts to regard the patients with dignity and keep them clean and well-fed seem almost insignificant by modern standards. However, in contrast to the general conditions of care in the almshouses and city hospitals, these measures were extremely important for the health and well-being of the patients. The generally small houses, called hospitals, cleaned and fitted up by the sisters to care for the sick, were primitive compared to twentieth-century institutions, yet these beginning hospitals were exactly the type of structures that would be used to house the wounded in the early years of the war.

Furthermore, the overall spiritual context in which the care of the sick was carried out by all communities was clearly and similarly expressed. The Daughters of Charity, for example, gave as the first rule in the section on sisters in hospitals:

The end for which the Daughters of Charity are sent to a Hotel-Dieu or hospital is to honor Our Lord Jesus Christ, the Father of the sick poor, both corporally and spiritually; corporally, by serving them and giving them food and medicine, and spiritually, by instructing the sick in what is necessary for their salvation; advising them to make a good general confession of their past life, that by this means those who die may depart hence in the state of grace, and they who recover may take the resolution never more with the help of God's grace, to offend Him.[75]

The Sisters of Mercy in their constitutions reminded the sisters that in visiting and caring for the sick they were part of a long line of saints, both men and women following Jesus Christ, who performed many miraculous cures, had great tenderness for the sick, and gave His powers of healing to His Apostles and followers.[76] Though this spiritual motivation was the primary cause of the commitment of the sisters before, during, and after the Civil War, nonetheless, it was the practical focus of their training that ultimately earned them the respect of doctors and soldiers alike. As the commentary on the Mercy constitutions stated: "The sisters should not only evidence compassion, but a practical desire to relieve and promote the temporal comfort of the sufferer as much as they can."[77]

On the eve of the Civil War, then, the only source of any kind of trained nurses—male or female—existed primarily in the twenty-eight Catholic hospitals, which were run by several different women's religious communities. Additional communities, though not primarily nursing orders, would join these communities and demonstrate that caring and

compassion, especially when combined with a tradition of trained experience or willingness to learn on the part of those sisters with no
experience, could make a significant difference in the quality of care
given to the wounded and dying Union and Confederate soldiers.

Some twenty years after the war, Sanitary Commission worker and
later women's rights leader, Mary Livermore, set the sisters' work in the
context of the nursing issues of the period:

I am neither a Catholic, nor an advocate of the monastic institutions of that
church. Similar organizations established on the basis of the Protestant religion,
and in harmony with republican principles, might be made very helpful to
modern society, and would furnish occupation and give position to large numbers of unmarried women, whose hearts go out to the world in charitable intent.
But I can never forget my experience during the War of the Rebellion. Never
did I meet these Catholic sisters in hospitals, on transports, or hospital steamers,
without observing their devotion, faithfulness, and unobtrusiveness. They gave
themselves no airs of superiority or holiness, shirked no duty, sought no easy
place, bred no mischiefs. Sick and wounded men watched for their entrance
into the wards at morning, and looked a regretful farewell when they departed
at night. They broke down in exhaustion from overwork, as did the Protestant
nurses: like them, they succumbed to the fatal prison-fever, which our exchanged
prisoners brought from the fearful pens of the South.[78]

Thus, the sisters in the United States, whether of American or European origin, brought to the Civil War four major contributions. First,
they brought a tradition and history of commitment to nursing derived
from centuries of European sisters being involved in care of the sick.
Second, they earned the recognition on both sides of the Atlantic, from
Nightingale and others who desired to initiate reforms for the better-
ment of the sick, that the sisters with their two-fold combination of
nursing skills and religious commitment offered a model for certain
aspects of care of the sick. Third, the communities running the Catholic
hospitals, which had been started to meet emergencies of diseases and
epidemics, showed a willingness to consider service in other hospitals
when the need arose. Fourth and foremost, the written regulations of
their community life served as a training manual for how patients should
be treated, and their religious community life itself provided the daily
living experience and personal example for other women religious in
the practice of these regulations.

While the restrictiveness of many of the regulations surrounding the
sisters' lives perplexed and puzzled many Americans, the practical nature
of their nursing work, learned in a community setting where the written
regulations were demonstrated, passed down to newer members, and
inculcated in the beginnings of their hospitals, made these sisters unique
as a group of women when they served the sick and wounded in the

Civil War. No other group of women had the tradition, organization, commitment, or hospital and nursing experience to bring to the desperate needs of the war. The Civil War would provide the sisters with the opportunity to put these practical skills, so admired by the doctors, and their religious commitment, so appreciated by the soldiers, to work in a larger setting. Thus, in spite of the anti-Catholicism of the antebellum period, there was a recognition that the sisters had a contribution to make in the care of the sick, that they had a history of coming to aid in other crises, and that they could work with medical and governmental authorities in these situations.

NOTES

1. Anne Austin, *History of Nursing Source Book* (New York: G. P. Putnam's Sons, 1957), p. 304.

2. Charles Rosenberg, "The Origins of the American Hospital System," *Bulletin of New York Academy of Medicine* 55 (Jan. 1979): 13. See also Harry Dowling, *City Hospitals: The Undercare of the Underprivileged* (Cambridge: Harvard University Press, 1982), pp. 16–21; Vern L. and Bonnie Bullough, *The Care of the Sick: The Emergence of Modern Nursing* (New York: Prodist, 1978), p. 63.

3. Paul Starr, *The Social Transformation of American Medicine* (New York: Basic Books, 1982), p. 155.

4. Bullough, p. 104.

5. John O'Grady, *Catholic Charities in the United States* (Washington, D.C. National Conference of Catholic Bishops, 1930; rpt. New York: Arno, 1971), p. 193.

6. Ann Doyle, "Nursing by Religious Orders in the United States," *American Journal of Nursing* 29 (Aug. 1929): 966.

7. Dowling, p. 14.

8. Mary Adelaide Nutting and Lavinia Dock, *A History of Nursing*, vol. 2 (New York: G.P. Putnam's Sons, 1907–12), p. 331.

9. Nutting and Dock, p. 342; 347.

10. Austin, pp. 330–331.

11. Doyle, p. 966.

12. Bullough, p. 105.

13. Cecil Woodham-Smith, *Florence Nightingale* (New York: McGraw-Hill, 1951), pp. 34, 38.

14. Martha Vicinus, *Independent Women: Work and Community for Single Women, 1850–1920* (Chicago: University of Chicago Press, 1985), pp. 88–89.

15. Mary McAuley Gilgannon, RSM, "The Sisters of Mercy as Crimean War Nurses," Ph.D. Diss. University of Notre Dame, 1962, p. 2.

16. Vicinus, p. 89.

17. Anna Jameson, *"Sisters of Charity" and "The Communion of Labour": Two Lectures on the Social Employment of Women* (London: Longman, 1859), pp. 20–23.

18. Jameson, p. 34.

19. Jameson, p. 18.

20. Jameson, p. 142.

21. Gilgannon, pp. 94–95.

22. Jameson, p. 132.

23. Vicinus, p. 89.

24. Vicinus, p. 89. See also Richard Shyrock, *The History of Nursing: An Interpretation of the Social and Medical Factors Involved* (Philadelphia: W. B. Saunders, 1959), p. 287.

25. Bullough, p. 105.

26. While there were Methodist, Evangelical, and Mennonite deaconesses at a later period, none was organized at the time of the Civil War.

27. Doyle, "Nursing by Religious Orders in the United States," *American Journal of Nursing* 29 (Oct. 1929): 1200.

28. Doyle, "Nursing by Religious Orders in the United States" *American Journal of Nursing* 29 (Nov. 1929): 1331–1334.

29. Doyle, "Nursing by Religious Orders in the United States," *American Journal of Nursing* 29 (Oct., Nov., Dec. 1929): 1197–1207; 1331–1143; 1466–1484.

30. Bullough, p. 33.

31. Victor Robinson, *White Caps: The Story of Nursing* (Philadelphia: J. B. Lippincott, 1946), p. 373–374.

32. See John B. Blake, "Women and Medicine in Antebellum America," *Bulletin of the History of Medicine* 39 (March-April 1965): 106–111. See also Mary Walsh, *Doctors Wanted: No Women Need Apply* (New Haven: Yale University Press, 1977). Walsh credits Harriot Hunt with being the first woman to practice medicine successfully in America, p. 1. Elizabeth Blackwell is the first woman doctor to receive an M. D. degree.

33. See Gerald Schwartz, ed., *A Woman Doctor's Civil War: Esther Hill Hawks' Diary* (Columbus, SC: University of South Carolina Press, 1984). Esther Hawks actually spent most of her time teaching in a school for freedmen, rather than as doctor or even nurse.

34. See Robinson, p. 372.

35. Bullough, p. 53.

36. Bullough, p. 54.

37. Bullough, p. 54.

38. Bullough, p. 62.

39. St. Vincent De Paul, quoted in Bullough, p. 62.

40. Josephine Dolan, *Nursing in Society: A Historical Perspective* (Philadelphia: W. B. Saunders, 1978), p. 193.

41. Robinson, pp. 372–373.

42. Doyle (July 1929), 775.

43. Bullough, pp. 104–105.

44. William Cavanaugh, "The Hospital Activities of the Sisters During the Civil War and Their Influence on the Catholic Hospital System Movement up to 1875," Masters Thesis, Catholic University of America, 1931, p. 13.

45. It is difficult to establish the exact number. The Cavanaugh thesis gives twenty-eight (pp. 13 and 14), yet one hospital listed simply changed hands from the Mercy Sisters to the Daughters of Charity. O'Grady implies twenty-five (p. 185–188), yet doesn't give the names of all of them. Doyle lists two "infirmaries" not included in Cavanaugh. Lack of records and some hospitals started that did

not continue also contribute to the difficulty in gathering exact numbers. General hospitals, hospitals for the insane, maternity, and infant-care hospitals sometimes were listed and sometimes not. Some institutions were also part hospital and part orphanage. Terms like "infirmary," "asylum," and "retreat" were often used synonymously. The official Catholic almanacs of the time did not have consistent data, as they were dependent on each individual diocese sending in information somewhat in the fashion each chose. *The Metropolitan Catholic Almanac* (Baltimore: John Murphy & Co., 1861) lists twenty-eight, and that may have been the source for Cavanaugh.

46. Doyle (July 1929): 779. See Barbara Misner, "A Comparative Social Study of the Members and Apostolates of the First Eight Permanent Communities of Women Religious within the Boundaries of the United States, 1790–1850," Ph.D. Diss. Catholic University of America, 1981, pp. 211–234, for some recent archival research on the sisters' care of the sick between 1830–1850.

47. Doyle (Aug. 1929): 962

48. O'Grady, p. 183.

49. Doyle (July 1929): 775.

50. O'Grady, p. 183.

51. Doyle (July 1929): 783.

52. Charles Rosenberg, *The Cholera Years: The United States in 1822, 1849, and 1866* (Chicago: The University of Chicago Press, 1962), p. 119.

53. Rosenberg, pp. 95, 119.

54. O'Grady, p. 191.

55. Rosenberg, p. 139.

56. See Stella O'Connor, "Charity Hospital at New Orleans: An Administrative and Financial History, 1736–1941," *Louisiana Historical Quarterly* 31 (Jan. 1948), 6–109.

57. Doyle (July 1929): 783–84.

58. Doyle (July 1929): 782–83.

59. Misner, pp. 278–79.

60. Misner, p. 212.

61. Data on the names and dates of the communities and hospitals are taken from Doyle (July and Aug. 1929): 775–785, 959–969.

62. Doyle (Aug. 1929): 961–62.

63. Doyle (Aug. 1929): 960.

64. O'Grady, p. 192.

65. O'Grady, p. 185.

66. Misner, p. 218.

67. O'Grady, p. 191.

68. Bullough, p. 104.

69. Robin O'Connor, "American Hospitals: The First 200 Years," *Hospitals* 50 (Jan. 1, 1976): 67.

70. Doyle (July 1929): 781.

71. Archives of the Sisters of Mercy of Vicksburg, Mississippi, (ARSMV), Handwritten copy of Mother M. de Sales Browne's *Constitution of the Sisters of Mercy* and *A Guide for the Religious Called Sisters of Mercy, Part I and II.* Although the *Guide,* compiled by Mother Mary Francis Bridgeman, who was with Nightingale in the Crimea, was not published until 1866, it grew out of a series of

discussions designed to establish some conformity among the practices of the Irish Mercy sisters. Presumably, though, the oral tradition of these directions for care of the sick would have been handed down to the Sisters of Mercy in the United States from those who came from these foundations in Ireland. See Gilgannon, pp. 371–372. Further, there was a written commentary on the Rule and Constitution, written by the founder Mother Catharine McAuley (Gilgannon, 378–383). See also Archives of the Daughters of Charity, Emmitsburg, Maryland (ADC), *Constitution of the Daughters of Charity of St. Vincent de Paul* (Paris: Motherhouse, 1954), and Sister Louise Sullivan, trans., *Spiritual Writings of St. Louise de Marillac* (Albany, NY : De Paul Provincial House, 1984).

72. ADC, *Constitutions*, p. 141.

73. ADC, *Constitutions*, pp. 142–43.

74. ARSMV, *A Guide for the Religious Called Sisters of Mercy*, Part I and II, p. 41.

75. ADC, *Constitutions*, p. 136.

76. ARSMV, handwritten copy of *Constitution of the Sisters of Mercy*, n.p.

77. ARSMV, *A Guide*, p. 29.

78. Mary Livermore, *What Shall We Tell Our Daughters: Superfluous Women and Other Lectures* (Boston: Lee and Shepard, 1883), pp. 177–178.

3

Medical Care and Lay Female Nursing During the Civil War

As the Civil War began, armies of soldiers and officers, supplies of weapons and ammunition, military strategies on land and sea, and support of politicians and citizens alike were the major governmental and military issues. Almost overlooked in the early planning on either Union or Confederate side was the need for medical and nursing personnel to care for the thousands of men who would become sick or wounded during the course of the war. Disorganization and chaos characterized the early efforts of medical personnel as the casualties of the war overwhelmed their inadequate staff, makeshift facilities, untrained assistants, and limited medical knowledge. Even when these limitations were addressed during the course of the war, wounded and sick men needed more care than the doctors and hospitals could provide. Nurses were desperately needed to dress wounds, distribute medicine and supplies, keep patients clean and fed, offer support when nothing more could be done, and coordinate all these tasks. Disabled soldiers pressed into service for these duties simply did not suffice.

However, women of the North and South, willing to extend their maternal care, domestic skills, and moral values to the larger home of their country, eagerly stepped forward to offer their services when the governments were pleading for male volunteers to fight. Whether providing general support for the soldiers by sewing, making bandages, sending food packages, raising money, or specifically rushing to temporary hospitals to nurse, the women found a new role outside their homes. While attempts were made in the North by reformer Dorothea Dix and by the US Sanitary Commission to coordinate these efforts, the suddenness of the war, the lack of experience, and the disorganization surrounding the volunteer efforts added to the general consternation of male doctors faced with a mass of women moving into their domain.

The patriotic women, anxious to do what they believed they could do best—care for the sick—did expand the public's awareness of what women could do in improving the care given to the wounded and ill. However, prejudices against females caring for strange men, particularly when good will and not skill was the women's main contribution, were only partly overcome in the four years of the war. Nevertheless, what many doctors were willing to accept, and what some did get, were Roman Catholic sisters who were trained and organized, had experience, and would care for the sick with dedication and quiet good order. To understand why the sisters became the preferred nurses and were able to change attitudes about the place of women in nursing, and to highlight the value of training for those who would care for the sick, three aspects of Civil War medical care must be examined: first, the chaotic state of medical knowledge, practice, and facilities at the beginning of the war; second, the absence of any nursing care, and the women's efforts to express their patriotism and concern by rushing to fill this gap; and third, the resulting attitudes toward what these women did, and how they were regarded by doctors and soldiers. These issues provide the context in which the unique role of the sister nurse can be understood.

The catastrophic nature of the war was grasped by wound dresser and poet Walt Whitman, who observed, "So much of a race depends on what it thinks of death, and how it stands personal anguish and sickness." He found the main interest of the Civil War and its significance to be in the "two or three millions of American young and middle-aged men, North and South,... especially the one-third or one-fourth of their number stricken by wounds or disease" rather than in the "political interests involved."[1] The impact of the war is best revealed in the mortality statistics, which directly reflected the medical aspects of the conflict.

In the 2,196 battles fought, in which 67,000 Union soldiers were killed, 43,000 died of wounds; 250,000 died from disease; and some 130,000 were left with scars, amputations, and other lifetime reminders of the common people's war. Among the Confederates, approximately 94,000 died of wounds, and 164,000 of disease.[2] Though pictorial representations often show Civil War soldiers with bayonets and sabres, only 56 of the 922 Union wounds caused by these weapons were fatal. However, the small leaden Minié ball caused 94 percent of the wounds and the canister (a metal cylinder packed with small shot and fired from a cannon) about 6 percent for both Confederate and Union soldiers.[3]

The diseases, such as typhoid, dysentery, diarrhea, measles, smallpox, and fevers, such as erysipelas, caused the greatest death toll on both sides, with Confederate soldiers having a disproportionate share of respiratory-pulmonary diseases in the first year-and-a-half of the war.[4]

Medical historian Richard Shryock has estimated that the average soldier was ill between two and three times each year, with the annual mortality rate from sickness more than 5 percent. Compared with male civilians of military age, servicemen were five times as likely to become ill, and they experienced a mortality rate that was five times as high as that of those who remained at home.[5]

The inital belief of both sides that the conflict would be short caught everyone, including the Federal Army Medical Department, unprepared for many aspects of a prolonged and decimating war. There was no general military hospital and only one army-post hospital; it had forty-one beds in Fort Leavenworth, Kansas.[6] A medical staff of ninety-eight officers, but little support staff, no ambulances, and no nursing corps composed the rest of the Medical Department.[7] Though some surgeons resigned to aid the Southern states, the Confederacy was even less prepared.

While modern practice would judge Civil War surgeons as "deplorably ignorant and badly trained," they actually were better trained than the generation of physicians preceding them.[8] As Confederate medical historian Horace H. Cunningham and Union historian George W. Adams both pointed out, the rise of American nationalism during the second and third decades of the nineteenth century had contributed to the increasing number of native medical schools. Most of these were in the North, so that the South experienced a "medical dependence on the North as marked as [its] economic dependence,"[9] according to Cunningham. Nevertheless, in spite of schools, students still continued in the traditional mode of obtaining their training in the offices of older practitioners, who served as preceptors.[10]

By the antebellum period, opportunities for medical education had improved somewhat in both the North and South. For example, medical journals and professional societies existed to support the doctor in his practice.[11] Furthermore, Southern medical institutions increased in number, and their faculties compared favorably with those in the North from both a quantitative and a qualitative standpoint. In spite of some doctors with lack of experience, Cunningham credited the South with having some of the most competent medical men in the nation on the faculties of growing medical schools with relatively high standards. In spite of these growing opportunities for medical education, many young doctors in both the North and the South still began their careers without having had the opportunity to observe an operation closely, let alone perform one.[12]

While some Civil War doctors were often accused by coworkers of a lack of training or knowledge, general ineptitude, disregard for the patients, and drunkenness,[13] many were competent and concerned for their patients. For example, Walt Whitman, who worked as a wound dresser in various Washington hospitals and had seen "many hundreds of them [doctors]," said:

I must bear my most emphatic testimony to the zeal, manliness, and professional spirit and capacity, generally prevailing among the surgeons, many of them young men, in the Hospitals and the army. I will not say much about the exceptions, for they are few; (but I have met some of those few, and very incompetent and airish they were) I never ceas'd to find the best young men, and the hardest and most disinterested workers, among these Surgeons, in the Hospitals. They are full of genius, too.[14]

However, the difficulties and strains of practicing medicine under inadequate and crowded conditions, with erratic supplies and often meager food, were overwhelming burdens for many doctors who had to assume leadership of military hospitals. As a consequence, Medical Director Dr. John Brinton, cousin of General George McClellen, was grateful for money sent by Northern men and for food and supply boxes sent by women. He recalled:

During my short stay at Mound City Hospital [Illinois], I first learned what it really was to be in authority. The responsibility which to me was always commensurate with the authority, weighed heavily upon me. I did my best to get for the patients in the hospitals all the comforts I could not only from the government supplies but also with the aid societies which at that time were springing up everywhere in the west and the east.[15]

In addition, Brinton also had to perform rites for the dead when he was left without a chaplain.

Basic medical knowledge taken for granted today was unknown to Brinton and other doctors. While anesthesia was used just prior to the Civil War (1846) and chloroform was administered by some surgeons,[16] whiskey forced down a man's throat by attendants holding him prone for the surgery (often amputation) was common on the battlefields of the North and South. More significantly, Joseph Lister's first paper on antiseptic surgery was not published until 1867, and Louis Pasteur's discoveries on the germ theory of infection were not known in America.

Consequently, while Civil War surgeons knew that carbolic acid would clean out infected wounds, they did not think to use it to sterilize instruments. In spite of their practical wartime experience with wounds, surgeons still believed that infections were caused by "noxious effluvia" arising from filth and carried through the air. Thus, while ordinary cleanliness in hospitals and fresh air was known to be important and later incorporated in the designs of government-built hospitals in the latter half of the war,[17] "laudable pus" in a wound was seen as desirable, and a surgeon's hands seemingly had nothing to do with the spread of disease.[18]

Dr. William Keen, who utilized his wartime experience in writing extensive scientific monographs after the war, graphically described the conditions:

We operated in our old blood-stained and often pus-stained coats.... We used undisinfected instruments from undisinfected plush cases, and still worse, used marine sponges which had been used in prior pus cases and had been only washed in tap water. If a sponge or an instrument fell on the floor it was washed and squeezed in a basin of tap water and used as if it were clean.... The silk with which we sewed up all our wounds was undisinfected. If there was any difficulty in threading the needle we moistened it with (as we now know) bacteria-laden saliva, and rolled it between bacteria-infected fingers.... In opening wounds... maggots as large as chestnut worms abounded in the Summer. While disgusting they did little or no harm....[19] We were wholly ignorant of the fact that the mosquito, and only the mosquito, spreads yellow fever and malaria.... We did not even suspect that the flea and rat conspired to spread the bubonic plague and that the louse was responsible for the deadly typhus.[20]

While innumerable doctors on both sides kept careful diaries and journals, in which they described and often illustrated the illnesses and surgical procedures they were doing,[21] these were not available for circulation during the war. In any case, the exigencies of the battlefields, the demands in the field and general hospitals, and the hazards of the blockades, especially for the Southerners, left little time to study new techniques and methods. Thus, the same general medical knowledge, surgical techniques, and beliefs about disease and sanitation prevailed among both Union and Confederate doctors.

Physical facilities for the sick were also woefully lacking throughout most of the war in the South and in its early stages in the North. At first, schools, churches, warehouses, private residences, and public buildings on both sides were all hurriedly pressed into service as general hospitals, but most were poorly furnished and badly managed. As the war proceeded, private hospitals sometimes had contracts with the government, and soldiers went to them, hoping the government would pay their bills for what they believed would be better care.[22]

The usual procedure on both sides was to transfer a seriously sick soldier from the field or regimental hospital, usually located in a canvas tent, to a "general" hospital, which was not restricted to men of any particular military unit.[23] However, even the facilities for transporting the wounded to these hospitals were inadequate. The war began with no ambulance system for either army. The Union army, after the devastating campaigns of 1862, finally had ambulances taken from the authority of the Quartermaster Corps and placed under Dr. Jonathan

Letterman, medical director of the Army of the Potomac, who gradually developed a system of adequate, better designed ambulances.[24]

On the Confederate side, early battles around the capital of Richmond, Virginia, all filled to overflowing the buildings of Richmond and the surrounding areas held by the Confederates. As a result, in late 1862, Surgeon-General Samuel P. Moore, with the assistance of hospital directors William S. Carrington, Samuel H. Stout, and James McCaw, and with monies from the Confederate Congress, finally organized a Confederate hospital system and began building military hospitals.

Many efforts were made to address the problems. The widespread belief about poisons circulating in the air and the recommendations from the Crimean War doctors in regard to the value of fresh air had three effects: tent hospitals in the field were in use until the end of 1865; general hospitals of canvas were erected in 1862; and the design of the pavilion hospitals, initially built under Union Surgeon William A. Hammond's direction in 1862, provided excellent ventilation. By the end of the war, the Union claimed 204 hospitals and 136,894 beds, ranging in size from Satterlee Hospital in Philadelphia, with 3,500 beds, to Hospital #20 in Tullahoma, Tennessee, with 100.[25] Ultimately, the Confederates had about 150 general hospitals, with about 50 located around or in Richmond. The 8,000-bed Chimborazo Hospital, near Richmond, was believed at the time to be the largest ever built in the world.[26]

As a result of these building efforts, Joseph J. Woodward, Assistant Surgeon General, could claim that "never before in the history of the world, was so vast a system of hospitals brought into existence in so short a time." He further cited the Union's practice of putting these hospitals under medical directors rather than ordinary officers, which had been the practice in the Crimean War. A consequence of this action, he felt, was a very low mortality rate and little spread of disease in these hospitals.[27]

Walt Whitman's comment, though, may have been closer to the truth experienced by those who worked day in and day out with the "system," especially in the first two years of the war:

There are, however, serious deficiencies, wastes, sad want of system, etc., in the Commissions, contributions, and in all the Voluntary, and a great part of the Governmental, nursing, edibles, medicines, stores, etc.... Whatever puffing accounts there may be in the papers of the North, this is the actual fact. No thorough previous preparation, no system, no foresight, no genius. Always plenty of stores, no doubt, but always miles away; never where they are needed, and never the proper application. Of all the harrowing experiences, none is greater than that of the days following a heavy battle. Scores, hundreds of the noblest young men on earth, uncomplaining, lie, helpless, mangled, faint, alone, and so bleed to death, or die from exhaustion, either actually untouch'd at all, or merely the laying of them down and leaving them, when there ought to be means provided to save them.[28]

Although from a later perspective the disease mortality rate was appalling, army leaders thought their record was quite satisfactory compared with that of previous wars.[29] Yet much unnecessary illness was caused by the utter lack of preparation and subsequent inefficiency of the medical services. Shryock notes, though, that this inefficiency was not the fault of any one group. Sharing in responsibility, he concludes, were "the original medical officers, indifferent generals, and politicians, a mediocre profession, and rural regiments hitherto unexposed to infections and unfamiliar with the rudiments of hygiene."[30]

In this quagmire of medical inefficiency, nurses to assist these doctors, especially in the field hospitals, were more likely to be disabled soldiers than females. Though mistaken notions of Clara Barton and her work often fostered the legend that women nurses played an important role on Civil War battlefields, the number who functioned in field hospitals, probably one in five, was actually never large, according to Adams.[31] Nevertheless, George Augustus Sala, a British journalist, described the Civil War as "a woman's war,"[32] a war that utilized women's talents and capitalized on their patriotism and domesticity.

Most women worked for the multitudinous and successful aid societies, especially the US Sanitary Commission and the Christian Commission in the North, by sewing, scraping lint for bandages, preparing food packages, and raising money. However, about 9,000 did serve specifically as Union nurses and 1,000 as Confederate nurses. In 1890, after bills had been proposed in Congress for back pay and pensions for female US Army nurses, Samuel Ramsey, chief clerk in the Surgeon-General's office, attempted to clarify various issues surrounding the legislation and, in estimating these numbers, distinguished seven classes of women employed in nursing. The first class included the approximately 3,214 nurses appointed partly by Dorothea Dix and partly by other officials, hired under the Act of August 3, 1861, and receiving salaries of 40 cents and one ration in kind each day. Paid out of Army funds, these nurses had a legal status as employees of the Union.[33]

The second group Ramsey described as "Sisters of Charity [generic name] who received forty cents a day, when paid at all—number uncertain but certainly smaller than the previous class."[34] The third category, estimated at 4,500, were women of all classes who did a variety of domestic chores, such as cooking, scrubbing floors, and washing dishes and were paid "anything that might be agreed on" from "anyone who would take the risk of paying them." "Colored women hired under General Orders in 1863 and 1864 at $10 a month" comprised the fourth class.[35]

A fifth group was composed of those that gave their services without compensation, and a sixth classification were those women "who accompanied regiments," generally called camp followers.[36] Women volunteering through various relief organizations, particularly those of the US Sanitary Commission, the Western Sanitary Commission, and the US Christian Commission, comprised the final group of nurses.

"Was the system of women-nurses in the hospitals a failure?" Union nurse Jane Woolsey, one of a family of seven sisters who served in the war, rhetorically asked. Cognizant of the power of the women and citing examples of the myriad ways in which women came to "nurse" during the war, she concluded, "that the presence of hundreds of individual women as nurses in hospitals was neither an intrusion nor a blunder, let the multitude of their unsystematized labors and achievements testify."[37]

Nevertheless, few of these women possessed actual hospital experience or other qualifications beyond a patriotic desire to serve, or perhaps, in some cases, physical strength to do the chores connected with nursing. As Woolsey explained, these women, usually eight to twenty of them, only slightly educated and without training or discipline, were set adrift in a hospital with no organization or officer to whom to report.[38]

One woman, though, did attempt to provide some organization and structure for these nurses. On the day after Lincoln's call for volunteer soldiers, Dorothea L. Dix, a Boston schoolteacher who had earned a national reputation for two years of work in improving the conditions of the mentally ill, went straight from Trenton, New Jersey, to the War Department in Washington to offer her services to care for the wounded and sick soldiers.[39] She was appointed superintendent of United States Army Nurses on April 23, 1861, by the following order from Simon Cameron, Secretary of War:

The free services of Miss D. L. Dix are accepted by the War Department and that she will give at all times all necessary aid in organizing military hospitals for the cure of all sick and wounded soldiers, aiding the chief surgeon by supplying nurses and substantial means for the comfort and relief of the suffering; also that she is fully authorized to receive, control, and disburse special supplies bestowed by individuals or associations for the comfort of their friends or the citizen soldiers from all parts of the limited states; as also, under action of the Acting Surgeon-General, to draw from the army stores.[40]

Scarcely a week later, floods of women wishing to serve often moved ahead to hospitals without any authorization, compelling Acting Surgeon-General Robert C. Wood to issue a notice telling the women they first needed to contact Dix before starting to work. He further added that the ladies should: "exert themselves to their fullest extent in preparing or supplying hospital shirts for the sick; also articles of diet, as delicacies may be needed for individual cases, and such important articles as eggs, milk, chickens, etc."[41]

In a later attempt to handle the women volunteers, General Order No. 31 came on June 9, 1861, indicating that women nurses were not to reside in the camps nor accompany regiments on a march, and those who applied for service had to have certificates from two physicians and two clergymen of good standing.[42]

Although Secretary of War Cameron reported to Lincoln on July 1, 1861, that the nursing services of patriotic women were entrusted to Dix,[43] the role and duties assigned by the general orders and assumed by Dix as she went about her tasks were not clearly delineated from the beginning. The result was often confusion and misunderstanding on the part of many who dealt with Dix and her nurses throughout the war.

In addition to selecting nurses, Dix was almost immediately called on, because of her prior experience in inspecting hospitals, to give advice and direction in matters of hospital supplies, equipment, and a thousand other details so that her position took on huge but unclear proportions. As her biographer, Helen Marshall, has pointed out, Dix found it hard to realize that no system could be organized overnight and be perfect. "For twenty years, she had been inspecting hospitals, pointing out mistakes, and remedying abuses," Marshall explains, "and it came to her as second nature to ferret out inefficient management, carelessness in attendants, shirking and indifferent physicians," causing antagonism and frustration on the part of many doctors.[44]

Although not a nurse herself, Dix was determined to create admission requirements for the Army Nursing Corps that would screen out women whose conduct might undermine the fragile reputation of the female nurses. Thus, her bulletin stated: "No woman under thirty need apply to serve in the government hospitals. All nurses are required to be plain looking women. Their dresses must be brown or black with no bows, no curls, no jewelry, and no hoop skirts."[45] Her second goal was to bring all unregulated nursing activities everywhere under her control.[46]

In the early days, she had the support of Surgeon-General Wood, who on May 20, 1861, "recommended to all commanding officers and enjoined on all medical officers of the regular and volunteer forces to aid her in her benevolent views."[47] He further ordered:

In reference to the national reputation of Miss Dix as connected with objects of philanthropy and usefulness, she is authorized to exercise a general supervision of the assignment of nurses to the hospitals, general and regimental, occupied by the troops at Washington, and its vicinity, subject to the advisement and control of the Surgeon General's Office in matters of detail, numbers, etc., and excepting such hospitals as already have a permanent organization of nurses.[48]

By October 1863, General Order 351 was issued through the Surgeon-General's office by order of Secretary of War Edwin Stanton in an attempt to clarify the differences existing between the medical staff and Dix. However, the result of the order, which gave the Surgeon-General the right to appoint nurses, undercut most of Dix's authority during the remainder of the war.[49] Doctors who did not want her nurses or preferred other female nurses simply went to the Surgeon-General.

Even before this order, there were ways around the requirements for women who wanted to nurse if Dix rejected the eager volunteers. Cornelia Hancock recalled her experience of going to Baltimore hoping to get to Gettysburg to help the wounded after the battle:

Dorothea Dix appeared on the scene. She looked the nurses over and pronounced them all suitable except me. She immediately objected to my going on the score of my youth and rosy cheeks. I was then just twenty-three years of age. In those days it was considered indecorous for angels of mercy to appear otherwise than gray-haired and spectacled. Such a thing as a hospital corps of comely young maiden nurses, possessing grace and good looks, was then unknown. Miss Farnham [Eliza—a public-spirited woman who also had a pass as a volunteer nurse] explained that she was under obligation to my friends who had helped her get proper credentials. The discussion waxed warm and I have no idea what conclusion they came to, for I settled the question myself by getting on the car and staying in my seat until the train pulled out of the city of Baltimore. They had not forcibly taken me from the train, so I got into Gettysburg the night of July sixth [1863] where the need was so great that there was no further cavil about age.[50]

In addition to Dix's strict view on nurses, many found her personally difficult to get along with. For example, Hancock later wrote to her niece, quoting pioneer woman-journalist Mrs. Jane Swisshelm's comment upon Dix: "[She] is a self-sealing can of horror tied up with red tape." Hancock qualified her judgment somewhat by adding that "Miss Dix's nurses are like all others in my estimation, some excellent, some good, some positively bad. So it would be, let who *would* have charge."[51] Later Louisa May Alcott, whose descriptive account of her service became well known in spite of her brief, six-month length of duty, wrote that Dix was "a kind, old soul, but very queer and arbitrary."[52]

While Dix's reformer reputation and spontaneous offer to coordinate the nursing service gained her an immediate welcome, the difficulties engendered by overwhelming numbers of volunteers and her desire to control all nursing activities herself caused clashes with nurses and doctors. How much of this conflict was due to her personality, how much to the general disorganization of the medical and nursing aspects of the war, and how much was due to general attitudes about women is difficult to determine. These trying circumstances may be some of the reasons why Dix herself said that her Civil War efforts were not the experiences by which she wished to be remembered.[53]

In addition to Dix's nurses and others engaged in direct care of the sick, additional women offered support to the sick and wounded. On April 15, 1861, when Lincoln called for volunteers, some women in Northern cities immediately started organizing relief societies or mobilizing already existing groups to collect supplies, food, clothing, and blankets, and to sew for the men and furnish nurses for the wounded. The first Northern relief society was started at Bridgeport, Connecticut, on April 15, 1861.

Within two weeks after the outbreak of war, there were more than twenty thousand aid societies at work in the Union and Confederacy, but not all were able to continue throughout the conflict, and many in the South were compelled to disband because of invasion, civilian displacement, and scarcity of supplies.[54] Early in the war, these local societies supplied items only for men from their own community or state, and in the Confederacy this generally continued to be the situation throughout the war. In the North, however, many local groups were coordinated under the supervision of the US Sanitary Commission.

In reflecting on the background of the US Sanitary Commission, Dr. Elizabeth Blackwell recalled that at the outbreak of the war, an informal meeting of the lady managers of the New York Infirmary for Women and Children was called on April 25, 1861, to "see what could be done towards supplying the want of trained nurses felt after the first battles." Out of that meeting, the National Sanitary Aid Association and the Ladies' Sanitary Aid Association were formed. The associations worked during the entire war, receiving and forwarding contributions and comforts for the soldiers, but their special work was the forwarding of nurses to the battlefront. Blackwell noted, however, that because of the extreme urgency of the needs, all that could be done was to sift out the most promising women from the multitudes that applied as nurses, to put them in training for a month at New York's Bellevue Hospital, which consented to receive relays of volunteers and send them on for assignment to Dix.[55]

From that meeting, too, came a delegation headed by Reverend Dr. Henry Bellows, pastor of the First Unitarian Church of New York, which discussed with Lincoln and Acting Surgeon-General Wood a proposal for creating a government-approved sanitary association that would "consider the general subject of the prevention of sickness and suffering among the troops."[56] The proposed organization was to operate separately from the Medical Bureau. Lincoln dismissed the plan calling it "the fifth wheel to the coach."[57] However, a new plan was drawn up that resulted in an order, signed by Lincoln on June 13, 1861, creating the US Sanitary Commission, whose purpose was to care for the wounded without duplicating government activities.[58] These early efforts of the Sanitary Commission were strongly influenced by the experiences of Florence Nightingale, who noted that the great loss of life in the Crimean War was due to lack of cleanliness, proper nourishment, and nursing care.

Summarizing these endeavors of the Sanitary Commission, William Maxwell, a twentieth-century historian, concludes that in spite of Elizabeth Blackwell's influence, she found herself hampered by traditional prejudices. Under Sanitary Commission auspices, only a limited number of women received instruction for a period of weeks before turning to help the army. Further, dislike of this assistance was reportedly more pronounced in the medical corps of the East than in the West. Finally, in October 1862, the Sanitary Commission dropped its training program, though it continued to supply nurses.[59]

Unlike the North, the Confederacy, unfortunately, did not have a similar organizer or agency to coordinate the nursing or aid work. However, through real sacrifice and effort on the part of individuals, particularly when their cities were overrun and transportation systems ruined, Southern groups were quite successful in providing some assistance. That the Southern women's efforts were not coordinated as they were in the North was not so much the fault of the women as of the state and of the Confederate officials who often refused to cooperate for the common good.[60]

The Confederate States set up an act in September 1862 to "better provide for the sick and wounded of the Army in hospitals."[61] However, prior to that time, there was notable civilian relief work on a large scale in which Southern women played a major role.[62] Many Southerners were wounded in the first battles, and many more became ill with measles, typhoid fever, dysentery, camp fever, and the other diseases that usually developed among soldiers experiencing the close quarters of camp life for the first time. Even less equipped than the Union government for dealing with the large masses of casualties, the Confederate government had to rely on these various women's relief societies then springing into existence. Food (both luxuries and staples), drugs smuggled in the folds of their gowns, bandages, and bedding were all collected and distributed by these groups.

The founding of hospitals to care for the wounded was also undertaken by groups such as the Southern Mothers' Society. However, the resources of the women were soon inadequate to handle the treatment of all the disabled of the Confederate armies. There were no trained nurses among the Southern women, and the hospitals needed the discipline of skilled experts with the authority of the government behind them. During the last months of 1861 and the first months of the following year, therefore, the Confederate government assumed the control and partial support of all soldiers' hospitals in the South. The change from voluntary to official management did not result, however, in women disappearing from the hospital scene. The hospital relief societies continued to supply these institutions with food and clothing. [An important and able group of lay women found work as matrons, and a few women of exceptional ability, such as Sallie Tompkins and Ella King Newsome, remained as managers. In fact, Southern historians Francis Simkins and James Patton conclude that the services of women continued to be so varied and extensive that the significance of their efforts was in "no sense lessened by the fact that the managerial phases of hospital work largely passed into masculine hands."[63]

The September 1862 act concerning the hospitalized sick and wounded of the Confederate army also provided for a financial allotment to each hospital, for pay with rations based on responsibility, and for suitable places of lodging for those caring for the sick. Two matrons, two assistant matrons, other nurses and cooks as might be needed, and a ward master for each ward were specifically designated. In all cases, preference was given to "females where their services may best subserve the purposes."[64]

[Confederate medical historian Cunningham, citing the low mortality rates in many of the hospitals set up by Southern women, points out that this convincing proof of feminine superiority in nursing caused the Confederate government to believe that many women would now come forward as hospital attendants. However, Cunningham concludes that the prevailing belief that full-time service in the hospitals was not respectable work for women acted as a deterrent in keeping many from taking up this needed work.[65]

[In the South, it was generally held that nursing, which involved such intimate contacts with strange men, was unfit for self-respecting women to pursue, especially for young and unmarried women. The majority of surgeons shared this contemporary prejudice against the service of women in the hospitals. The effects of this belief were to reduce the number of women who were willing to ignore or flout public opinion to a level far below the actual needs of the hospital service, and it tended to drive the "better class" of women away from the hospitals and throw the positions open to women of "indifferent" character and training.[66]

Not every Southerner held these views, however. In response to the argument concerning a lady's modesty, Confederate nurse Kate Cumming responded:

As far as my judgment goes, a lady who feels that her modesty would be compromised by going into a hospital, and ministering to the wants of her suffering countrymen, who have braved all in her defense, could not rightly lay claim to a very large share of that excellent virtue—modesty—which the wise tell us is ever the companion of sense.... There is scarcely a day passes that I do not hear some derogatory remarks about the ladies who are in the hospitals, until I think, if there is any credit due them at all, it is for the moral courage they have in braving public opinion.[67]

But the presence of women in crowded conditions with strange male patients and primarily male nurses, doctors, and other assistants did continue to raise issues of motivation and propriety. A typical situation involving all these concerns was described by Confederate diarist Mary Boykin Chestnut. In her diary, Chestnut recounted the struggles of a Mrs. Louisa Susanna McCord, an author who also ran a military hospital. Though McCord "gave her whole soul to the hospital," there was insufficient medical aid; good nurses were needed, as those she hired ate and drank the food provided for the sick and wounded.[68] Chestnut sympathized with McCord's troubles, saying "a nurse who is also a beauty had better leave her beauty with her cloak and hat at the door." After hearing about a "lovely lady nurse" who had asked a "rough old soldier" what she could do for him," she received the reply, "Kiss Me." The nurse, who apparently did not kiss him, but told the story, was the cause of McCord's fury since she brought the "hospital in disrepute," "and very properly," as Chestnut concluded. Chestnut said that McCord wanted nurses to come dressed as nurses—as Sisters of Charity—not as fine ladies. If they did, there would be no trouble. When McCord saw women coming in angel sleeves, "displaying all of their white arms, and in their muslin, showing all of their beautiful white shoulders and throats," she felt disposed to order them off the premises: that was no proper costume for a nurse. On the other hand, one woman who was praised by McCord was a Mrs. Bartow, who came in her "widow's weeds."[69]

The attitude that a woman must sacrifice her modesty, if not her virtue in order to care for the sick, though more dominant in the South, was hardly confined to the Confederate states. Dr. Samuel Howe, husband of Julia Ward Howe, refused to let his wife do any war work more unconventional than the making of lint and bandages and, toward the end, some hospital visiting, even though it was he who, many years before, had encouraged the young Nightingale to take up a nursing career. When charged with this inconsistency, he justified his stand by saying that it was Nightingale's not being married that made all the difference. He told his wife that "if he had been engaged to Florence Nightingale, and had loved her ever so dearly, he would have given her up as soon as she commenced her career as a 'public woman.' " By "public woman," Dr. Howe seems to have meant any female who had any activities outside home and church.[70]

Because of these attitudes expressed by many doctors and other male medical assistants, such as male nurses and ward masters, Dix and other women who tried to run hospitals generally had to set rigid standards if they expected to overcome the prejudice against them. Even those who saw some value in female nurses had differing views on who should care for the sick.

But the women themselves, although untrained and motivated by a variety of intentions, came with a combination of ideas about women's maternal calling, their mission as homemakers, and their responsibility for bringing refinement, tenderness, and gentility to a male-dominated society. Because of these qualities, the patients usually appreciated the nurses, even if the doctors often disliked them. The soldiers were often young men who were homesick and grateful for motherly ministrations. Thus, the women's attitudes were normally reinforced, rather than refused. Indeed, the titles of many of the famous nurses were "Mother," "Sister," or "Angel."

Louisa Alcott, describing her care of a soldier, explained, "And now I knew that to him, as to so many, I was the poor substitute for mother, wife, or sister, and in his eyes no stranger, but a friend who hitherto had seemed neglectful."[71] "The soldiers talk much of their mothers and sisters, as all men do now," recalled Cumming, alluding to the same attitudes. " 'Home, Sweet Home,' is the dearest spot on earth to them, since they are deprived of its comforts, and mother, wife, and sister seem to be sweeter to them than any words in the English language," she added.[72]

In caring for their patients in the wards, then, women emphasized the familiar domestic virtues, including religious observance, abstinence from alcohol, and familial concern. Yet, while anxious to alleviate the soldiers' suffering, they sometimes grew overly enthusiastic about their maternal role. "The doctors do not like the wives of the men to come and nurse them; they say they invariably kill them with kindness," remarked Cumming. But she added, "There are some ladies who come to take care of their relatives, who seem to understand nursing, and are a great help, not only to their own folks, but to others around them; those the doctors do not object to."[73]

Among the duties assumed by these women, concern for the quantity and quality of the food for the men was paramount. Jane Woolsey wrote from a general hospital in the North:

I have one hundred men in my ward, all in bed. The surgeons appear to give very little care to the diet, but are down on any one else who does. The food is very poor and insufficient. The cooks [male] seem to have it all their own way. The ladies are not allowed to superintend in the kitchen or have anything to do with it. For thirty-eight of my men the ward surgeon orders, in general terms, milk and eggs. It is grimly amusing to hear him say day after day, 'milk and eggs for thirty-eight.' One egg apiece, each meal is all I can ever get from the.

cooks, and for two days there have been no eggs at all. The milk rations are always short.... All this wears upon one infinitely more than the hard work.[74]

Appalled at the sidetracking of food supplies for the men,[75] Annie Wittenmyer, who became famous for the development of special Union diet kitchens, found that "no part of the army service was so defective, during the first two years of the war, as its cooking department in the U.S. government hospitals."[76]

Ordinarily, conditions in the South for patient and nurse were worse. Cumming, though usually complaining about the "sameness of the diet," does recount that sometimes things "improved" temporarily. An improvement for the nurses consisted of "batter-cakes made of the mush left over from the previous meal, rice, and stale bread, (I do not mean what the men leave as nothing is used which has been in the wards,) hash made out of soupmeat, toast, mush, milk, tea, coffee, and beefsteak. Our batter-cakes never have eggs in them; they have a little flour and soda and are very nice."[77]

Besides concern for the food, the other duties of the nurses varied depending on the particular hospital, the attitude of the surgeon in charge, or battle conditions. For example, Alcott, responding to someone who wondered if nurses were obliged to witness amputations as part of their duty, said,

I think not, unless they wish; for the patient is under the effects of ether, and needs no care but such as the surgeon can best give. Our work begins afterward when the poor soul comes to himself, sick, faint and wandering; full of strange pains and confused visions, of disagreeable sensations and sights. Then we must sooth and sustain, tend and watch; preaching and practicing patience, till sleep and time have restored courage and self-control.[78]

In spite of her limited length of service, Alcott, unlike many women, did witness several operations because, as she explained: "The height of my ambition was to go to the front after a battle, and feeling that the sooner I inured myself to trying sights, the more useful I should be." Echoing what was often a criticism of the female nurses, Alcott remarked that some of her friends avoided such sights, "for though the spirit was wholly willing, the flesh was inconveniently weak."[79] She went on to describe "one funereal lady" who said she fainted at the sight of blood, was nervous about infections, couldn't take care of delirious persons, and so was dismissed. "I hope she found her sphere," Alcott concluded, "but [I] fancy a comfortable bandbox on a high shelf would best meet the requirements of her case."[80]

In contrast to this woman, Union nurse Woolsey devoted a chapter in *Hospital Days*, her detailed and insightful account of wartime experiences, to the duties of being a superintendent. Requisitioning and deploying supplies for the wards; supervising the preparation of the food in the kitchen; overseeing the "wittles train";[81] listening to and responding to complaints about the food; handling paperwork related to obtaining supplies; receiving reports from the women nurses; taking care of visitors; talking with the men as they came for their supplies and tobacco—all these activities made up the "Superintendent's day—with its digressions," as Woolsey described her demanding work.[82] All matrons did not necessarily have her abilities, her concern, nor her access to the resources of the Sanitary Commission; nonetheless, the duties of a matron or superintendent were similar and the frustrations uniformly the same.

Southern conditions were more spartan, and Confederate nurse Cumming, who performed duties similar to Woolsey's, recalled her typical day's work:

Mrs. Williamson and I live like Sisters of Charity; we get up in the morning about 4 o'clock, and breakfast by candle-light, which meal consists of real coffee without milk, but sugar, hash, and bread; we eat it in our room. Unless we get up early, we find it impossible to get through with our duties. Mrs. Williamson prepares toddies and egg-nogs; I see that the delicacies for the sick are properly prepared. After the duties of the day are over, we then write letters for the men, telling their relatives they are here, or informing them of their decease; other times mending some little articles for them. Mrs. Williamson is up many a night till 12 o'clock, working for her "dear boys," as she calls them.[83]

The female nurses, whether cook, nurse, or superintendent, often felt they knew how to run the hospital better than the military or medical administrators, and saw many regulations, which were standard military procedure, as tedious or obstructive, to be ignored if possible rather than obeyed. Accordingly, whether out of maternal solicitude or moral superiority, nurses were usually not hesitant to openly criticize medical officers, characterize their treatment of patients as cold and unfeeling, and view the hospital system as in need of women's guidance. Drunkenness was the commonest charge against the surgeons, and the women especially noted "drunken carousals" and resulting neglect and mistreatment of patients, though the major complaints concerned rough handling and the dressing of wounds.[84]

Thus, their understanding of their position and tasks sometimes brought the female nurses into conflict with the hospital authorities. It was unthinkable to the majority of these women that professional medical men could exert the kind of benevolent and healing effect upon the sick and wounded that they, with womanly understanding and gentleness, could. As John Brumgardt explains, these beliefs came from the fact that, first, they were women, and second, they believed that the doctor's work proceeded either from obedience to military duty or a contract for pay, not from real concern for their patients.[85]

The nurses' perception that surgeons were unfeeling toward their patients was not without some foundation. However, as Brumgardt concludes, objective, scientific regard for the patients could hardly be personal, and this tendency of the doctors to have a clinical perspective was reinforced by an order from the surgeon-general that all doctors had to file reports on cases treated as part of the project to compile a medical history of the war.[86]

Assessing the activities of these women and the attitudes displayed toward them has resulted in two twentieth-century views. Nina Bennet Smith, in her dissertation on the Union Army nurse, has suggested that ↙ the women who went to war were not seeking to establish careers in nursing, nor were renouncing relations with men, since most were married or expected to be. Neither were they feminists, however that word is defined, but rather saw their nursing as a local and charitable extension of their home duties; thus, they saw themselves as morally and practically superior to men. Smith argues that the doctors who found fault with them were objecting to a challenge to their authority rather than to the idea of female medical assistants, since the doctors approved of Catholic nursing orders.[87]

On the other hand is a view of women's participation that is more confrontational to male medical authority. Ann Douglas Wood, in an article on Union nurses, proposed that:

Basic to these women's complicated urge to make the front truly a home-front, to replace the captain with the mother, the doctor with the nurse, and even to out-soldier the soldiers, was their sense that they were being kept out of medicine, of war, of *life itself*, by a complicated professional code that simply boiled down to men's unwillingness to let anyone—including themselves—know what a mess they had made. . . . In bringing home virtues to witness against "professional" methods, they did not so much make the world a home, as they helped to make themselves at home *in the world*. Nursing the troops in the Civil War had not only offered them a chance to criticize the imprisoning professional code of the military medical corps from the perspective of their maternal natures; it had also given them the opportunity to make a profession, and a competitive one, out of their maternity.[88]

While Smith's conclusions are based on a larger study of sources than Wood's, the truth may be less definitive than either writer holds. The sources for both positions come largely from more than one hundred volumes and many more articles published between 1865 and 1914, based on women's own experiences as nurses, as Sanitary Commission workers, as teachers of freedmen, and on other adventures such as soldiering and spying. These largely white, middle-class or upper-class women often kept both journals and published memoirs. They went to war primarily out of patriotism, and in their accounts spoke largely of their duties, their difficulties with the system, and their often romanticized concern for the soldiers "who had been reared as tenderly as girls, and who were just from under their mothers' wing...silent heroes, whose gentle patience and uncomplaining fortitude glorified the rough wards."[89] Nonetheless, in spite of some similarities, these accounts are individual views, expressed in nineteenth-century ideology, and not a collective experience of women with twentieth-century perspectives. Thus, Smith's less definitive but more comprehensive view is more valuable in understanding these women than Woods'.

In spite of their efforts in the hospitals and in a multitude of other situations, female nurses did not receive much public praise and recognition during the Civil War itself. Massey suggests the causes for this lack of recognition are complex, but underlying other reasons was the nurses' "inability to overcome in only four years the long-standing, deep-seated prejudice of the general public and the military officials."[90]

Four years was a short time in which to change many of the general medical and surgical understandings, practices, and facilities, let alone specific ideas about the place of female nurses. By the end of the war, the Union army did have twelve thousand doctors, organized into seven ranks, and a system of over two hundred hospitals.[91] Further, knowledge about disease, infection, and surgical procedures learned in crisis situations was in the process of being gathered into written reports that would educate doctors in the future. Clearly, the energies of the doctors and officers, besides dealing daily with the wounded men, were devoted to increasing their medical corps, constructing hospitals, and developing information on the medical and surgical situations with which they were faced. The lack of medical knowledge and the limited number of doctors and hospitals that characterized the early years of the war understandably made these concerns top priority.

In addition, recognition of the value of trained women as nurses was complicated by their lack of training, frequent disorganization, relatively small numbers, and the traditional prejudices against them. Patriotic good will simply did not overcome the lack of experience and skills on the part of many women, even when they fed patients, dressed wounds, and sometimes organized whole hospitals. Individual dedicated and efficient female nurses, such as Cumming and Woolsey, were sometimes appreciated. Nevertheless, even the efforts of Dorothea Dix and of the US Sanitary Commission in the first years of the war were insufficient to mobilize individual women into some kind of trained nurse corps, whose concerted strength might serve to break down the doctors' prejudices.

However, by the war's end, one group of female nurses did gain recognition and earned praise: the Catholic sisters. They, too, were initially viewed with suspicion and suffered the additional prejudices associated with their religion and lifestyle. Unlike other female nurses, however, their services were in demand because they offered nursing skills, hospital experience, and predictable, orderly service arising from their religious commitment and community purposes. Against a background of weak medical staffs, confusion of nursing efforts, and the often negative attitudes of doctors about women, the multitude of requests for sisters to serve in the war can be readily comprehended.

NOTES

1. Walt Whitman, *Memoranda During the War*, (n.d., rpt. Bloomington: Indiana University Press, 1962), pp. 4–5.

2. Thomas L. Livermore, *Numbers and Loses in the Civil War in America* (Boston: Houghton, Mifflin, 1901), pp. 5–8.

3. Stewart Brooks, *Civil War Medicine* (Springfield, IL: C. C. Thomas, 1966), p. 76.

4. George W. Adams, *Doctors in Blue: The Medical History of the Union Army in the Civil War* (New York: Henry Schuman, 1952), p. 14.

5. Richard Shryock, "A Medical Perspective in the Civil War," in Shryock, *Medicine in America: Historical Essays* (Baltimore: Johns Hopkins University Press, 1966), pp. 94–95.

6. Brooks, p. 41.

7. Adams, p. 4.

8. Adams, p. 49.

9. Horace H. Cunningham, *Doctors in Gray: The Confederate Medical Service* (Baton Rouge: Louisiana State University Press, 1958), p. 10.

10. See Adams and Cunningham.

11. Cunningham. p. 20.

12. Cunningham, pp. 11–13.

13. Adams, pp. 54–55.

14. Whitman, pp. 37–38.

15. John Hill Brinton, *Personal Memoirs of John H. Brinton, Major and Surgeon USV 1861–1865* (New York: The Neale Publishing Co., 1914), p. 47.

16. Stevenson, p. 910.

17. Adams, p. 151.

18. Shryock, pp. 92–93.

19. See Adams. The accidental discovery that maggots cleaned out the wounds was made by Confederate doctors who were prisoners and were denied medical supplies to treat their men (p. 129).

20. Isabel Stevenson,"Medical Literature of the Civil War," *CIBA Symposia* 3 (July 1941): 918.

21. See National Archives (NA), John Brinton papers. Brinton kept innumerable small notebooks, in which he drew sketches of various surgical wounds and wrote descriptions and statistics for medical and surgical cases. His material

was used in the official *Medical and Surgical History of the War of the Rebellion.* 1875.

22. Adams, p. 150.

23. John Billings, *Hardtack and Coffee or the Unwritten Story of Army Life* (Boston: George M. Smith, 1887), pp. 300–302.

24. Billings, pp. 304–315; Adams, pp. 59–83.

25. Adams, p. 153.

26. Brooks, p. 48.

27. *Circular No. 4. Reports on the Extent and Nature of the Materials Available for the Preparation of a Medical and Surgical History of the Rebellion* (Philadelphia: J. B. Lippincott, 1865), p. 152.

28. Whitman, pp. 37–38.

29. Shryock, p. 95.

30. Shryock, pp. 95–96.

31. Adams, p. 69. See also Brooks, p. 31.

32. George Augustus Sala, as quoted in Massey, p. 25.

33. Samuel Ramsey, quoted in Julia Stimson and Ethel Thompson, "Women Nurses with the Union Forces During the Civil War," *Military Surgeon* 62 (Feb. 1928): 222.

34. Ramsey in Stimson and Thomas, 222.

35. Ramsey in Stimson and Thomas, 222.

36. Ramsey in Stimson and Thomas, 222.

37. Jane Woolsey, *Hospital Days* (New York: D. Van Nostrand, 1868), p. 41.

38. Woolsey, pp. 41–42.

39. Helen Marshall, *Dorothea Dix: Forgotten Samaritan* (New York: Russell and Russell, 1967), p. 202.

40. US War Dept., *The War of the Rebellion: A Compilation of the Official Records of the Union and Confederate Armies* (Washington, D.C.: U.S. Government Printing Office, 1880–1901), Series III, Part I, p. 107. Hereafter cited as *Official Records.*

41. Joseph K. Barnes et al., *The Medical and Surgical History of the War of the Rebellion, 1861–65,* vol. 1 (Washington, D.C.: Government Printing Office, 1875), pp. 139–140.

42. Barnes, p. 262.

43. Barnes, p. 308.

44. Marshall, p. 219.

45. Marshall, p. 206.

46. Agatha Young, *The Women and the Crisis: Women of the North in the Civil War* (New York: McDowell, Obolensky, 1959), p. 98.

47. Barnes, p. 217.

48. Barnes, p. 217.

49. Marshall, pp. 225–226.

50. Cornelia Hancock, *The South after the Civil War* (New York: Thomas Y. Crowell, 1956), p. 6.

51. Hancock, p. 131.

52. Louisa May Alcott, quoted in Ernest Earnest, *The American Eve in Fact and Fiction, 1775–1914* (Urbana: University of Illinois Press, 1974), p. 170.

53. Marshall, p. 207.

54. Mary Massey, *Bonnet Brigades: American Women and the Civil War* (New York: Knopf, 1966), p. 32.

55. Elizabeth Blackwell, *Pioneer Work in Opening the Medical Profession to Women* (London: Longmans, 1895), pp. 235–236.

56. Charles Stille, *History of the United States Sanitary Commission, Being the General Report of its Work During the War of the Rebellion* (Philadelphia: J. B. Lippincott, 1866), pp. 528–530.

57. William Maxwell, *Lincoln's Fifth Wheel: The Political History of the United States Sanitary Commission* (New York: Longmans, Green, 1956), pp. 1–30.

58. Stille, p. 529.

59. Maxwell, p. 63.

60. Massey, p. 33.

61. *Official Records*, Series VI, Part 2, p. 199.

62. Francis Simkins and James Patton, "The Work of Southern Women Among the Sick and Wounded of the Confederate Armies," *Journal of Southern History* 1 (Nov. 1935): 475.

63. Simkins and Patton, p. 479.

64. *Official Records*, Series IV, Part 2, pp. 199–200.

65. Cunningham, p. 73.

66. Simkins and Patton, pp. 484–85.

67. Kate Cumming, *Kate: The Journal of a Confederate Nurse* (Baton Rouge: Louisiana State University Press, 1959), p. 178.

68. C. Vann Woodward, ed. *Mary Chestnut's Civil War* (New Haven: Yale University Press, 1981), p. 386.

69. Woodward, p. 414.

70. Young, p. 61.

71. Louisa May Alcott, *Hospital Sketches* (Cambridge: Harvard University Press, 1960), p. 52.

72. Cumming, p. 18.

73. Cumming, p. 93.

74. Woolsey, pp. 154–155.

75. Annie Wittenmyer, *Under the Guns* (Boston: E. B. Stillings, 1895), pp. 193–201.

76. Wittenmyer, pp. 259–267.

77. Cumming, pp. 94–95.

78. Alcott, p. 86.

79. Alcott, pp. 86–87.

80. Alcott, pp. 86–87.

81. Woolsey, p. 29.

82. Woolsey, p. 37.

83. Cumming, p. 94.

84. Adams, pp. 54–55.

85. John Brumgardt, ed. *Civil War Nurse: The Diary and Letters of Hannah Ropes* (Knoxville: University of Tennessee Press, 1980), p. 33.

86. Brumgardt, p. 35.

87. Nina Smith, "The Women Who Went to the War: The Union Army Nurse in the Civil War," Ph.D. Diss., Northwestern University, 1981.

88. Ann Wood, "The War within a War: Women Nurses in the Union Army," *Civil War History* 18 (Sept. 1972): 197–212.

89. Mary Livermore, *My Story of the War* (Hartford, CT: A. D. Worthington, 1887), p. 325.

90. Massey, p. 64.

91. Brooks, p. 43.

4

Catholic Sisters Respond to Requests for Nursing in the Civil War

"All the country was hospital, save space for cemetery," a Daughter of Charity concluded, surveying the battlefield the day after the Gettysburg massacre on July 1–3, 1863.[1] This observation accurately described most of the battle-blighted country during the Civil War as public and private hospitals, churches, schools, public buildings, warehouses, homes, and barns near the sites of the battles were quickly converted into service as military hospitals.

A major result of turning much of the country into an extended hospital was the emergence of thousands of women offering to care for the soldiers in these various buildings. However, in contrast to the numerous Union and Confederate women who individually volunteered their services for nursing, generally the Catholic sisters as communities were specifically requested by various authorities to assist the sick and wounded. To understand the unique work of the sisters in the war, it is important to focus first on the communities that became involved in the war, then on the various categories of authorities who requested them, and finally on the arrangements under which they served.

In the course of the war, at least 617 sisters from twenty-one different communities, representing twelve separate orders, nursed both Union and Confederate soldiers. The largest number of sisters, estimated at 232 serving in approximately thirty geographic areas throughout the course of the war, was the Daughters of Charity, whose headquarters was in Emmitsburg, Maryland.

Next to the Daughters, the Holy Cross Sisters from South Bend, Indiana, whose works had not included nursing prior to the war, formed the second largest group of sisters, with sixty-three, serving in at least ten different institutions. In the South, at least eighteen Sisters of Charity of Our Lady of Mercy (then called Sisters of Mercy) in Charleston, South Carolina, and eighteen Sisters of Mercy of Vicksburg, Mississippi, provided sisters throughout the course of the war.

Of other communities of Sisters of Charity, thirty-six Sisters of Charity of Cincinnati, thirteen Sisters of Charity of New York City, and thirty-seven Sisters of Charity of Nazareth, Kentucky—all separate orders— provided nursing care for extended periods. The Sisters of Mercy also were represented with eleven sisters from Cincinnati, twenty-two from Baltimore, fifteen from New York, thirty-four from Pittsburgh, and ten from Chicago. While the city of origin of these sisters identifies the community, often their geographic place of service during the war was elsewhere. The actual locations are not easily identifiable as the temporary hospitals often moved from place to place with the soldiers, or the sisters only served a limited period of time.

Several other communities, with both nursing and teaching backgrounds, also nursed. Of the nursing groups, the Sisters of St. Joseph had ten sisters throughout the war in their own hospital in Wheeling, (West) Virginia, while the Sisters of St. Joseph of Philadelphia had fourteen who nursed in the area around that city. Ten Sisters of the Poor of St. Francis from Cincinnati served in hospitals there and in Columbus. In addition, at least eleven Sisters of Providence, whose motherhouse was in St. Mary of the Woods, Indiana, served in two hospitals in that state for most of the war. Sixteen Dominican Sisters nursed in hospitals in Memphis, Tennessee.[2] These latter communities were not engaged in hospital work before the war, though they, like the Holy Cross Sisters, have remained in hospital work to this day.

Some communities provided only limited help. The smallest group encompassed six Ursuline Nuns in Galveston, Texas, who served in their own convent, which was twice turned into a hospital. Nine Sisters of Our Lady of Mt. Carmel in New Orleans, twenty-four Dominican Sisters in Perrysville, Kentucky, and eight Sisters of Mercy in Little Rock, Arkansas, responded to immediate and short-term battle needs in their own geographic area. These latter three were actually teaching communities that served in the war for only a matter of weeks.

Though statistics are difficult to reconstruct, these sisters probably represented about one-fifth of all the sisters in the United States at the outbreak of the war. In regard to nationality, 320 have been identified as Irish-born or of Irish descent; approximately 200 were American-born, and the rest were mainly French- or German-born.[3]

In general, requests for the use of buildings and institutions under the control of these women's religious communities, and especially for the services of sisters, who often were all called "Sisters of Charity" or "Sisters of Mercy," regardless of the specific name of the religious community, came first from the governmental and political leaders of the Union and Confederacy at national, state, and local levels. Shortly after the start of the war, Surgeon Generals of the various states or of specific hospitals requested sisters, as did various citizens' groups or other organizations. Often, there is no clear record of who actually made the request, and seemingly, oral requests were passed through some combination of the above sources. In a few cases, as will be seen, the requests were more a demand for the use of a building to which the sisters often willingly complied while also offering services where and when they could. Sometimes the requests went to the primary administrators of the religious community and sometimes to the local unit of the community in charge of a specific hospital or usable building. In addition, the requests frequently came through the bishop of the diocese in which the sisters were located, or the bishop offered the services of the sisters under his jurisdiction.

In many cases, documentation on the specific reasons for requesting the sisters does not exist; nevertheless, the availability of sisters in a hospital in a given area, or their willingness to take on the work, must have been a strong determining factor. The general attitudes of those requesting the sisters can be illustrated by part of a letter of Brigadier General John F. Rathbone of Albany, New York. He wrote to Bishop John McCloskey on June 1, 1861, from the military depot there requesting the services of the Sisters of Charity:

Nevertheless, there are now over one hundred men in our Hospital, and the number of nurses employed is quite insufficient to ensure their comfort and proper treatment. The superiority of the Sisters of Charity as nurses is known wherever the names of Florence Nightingale and the Sisters who accompanied her to the Crimea have been repeated, and these soldiers, most of whom have had woman's tender hands to minister to their want before leaving home to engage in their country's battles, would feel encouraged by their kindness and care. I should esteem it a personal favor, should they be able to comply with my request.[4]

One sister did go to the depot from St. Mary's Hospital.[5]

The early requests for sisters followed a pattern that continued throughout the war. The first such request came to the community of the Daughters of Charity, which had a hospital in Norfolk, Virginia. When the Norfolk Navy Yard was destroyed by Confederates on April 20, 1861, the hospital was emptied and the Marine Hospital, in nearby Portsmouth, was prepared for the Union sick. According to the sisters' annals, the "northern authorities" asked for sisters to attend the soldiers, which they promptly did.[6]

The second request involved the recently built City Hospital in Indianapolis, which had been offered and accepted by the medical authorities for sick soldiers in April 1861. Records indicate that management was unsuccessful due to a lack of proper help and organization, which distressed the doctors and authorities. Thus, they turned to the nearby Sisters of Providence, who had no previous nursing experience but had visited sick in their homes. The sisters, known mainly for their schools, quickly took charge by the end of April.[7]

Due to an epidemic, the next request came from Cincinnati. Sr. Anthony O'Connell, a Sister of Charity of Cincinnati at that city's St. John Hospital, recounted that on May 1, 1861: "The most Rev. Archbishop [John] Purcell and Mayor [George] Hatch called upon me at the desire of Governor [William] Dennison, and requested that a colony of the Sisters be sent to Camp Dennison to attend the sick soldiers, the worst form of measles had broken out among them and they needed immediate attention."[8]

By May 16, 1861, the Confederate medical authorities at their headquarters in Richmond, Virginia, had asked the Daughters of Charity to admit sick soldiers to the Infirmary of St. Francis De Sales, which they ran.[9] Within a month, this was too crowded, and the government took over several houses in the city, intending that male nurses would care for the wounded. However, the sisters' annals record: "Within a few days, the Surgeon and Officers, in charge, came to the Sisters of the Infirmary and [orphan] Asylum begging them to come to their assistance as the poor men were in much need of them."[10] Thus, throughout the war, variety characterized the kinds of requestors, and spontaneity generally typified the sisters' responses to the requests. Even in these first four requests at the beginning of the war, a predictable pattern was already apparent: three religious communities that already had hospitals were asked to take in the wounded, though one was asked by the Union government to serve in a hospital other than its own Catholic institution; a mayor requested one community to serve in a camp where an epidemic had broken out; another group of sisters, responding to a general's request, took soldiers into its own hospital; the fourth community had never nursed, except perhaps its own sisters, and yet was asked by civil and medical authorities to take over a city hospital. To these early requests, the response of all these sisters was immediate, and no particular conditions of service were negotiated by the sisters or those asking their services. Throughout the war, requests for sisters would follow a similar pattern of some official aware of critical war needs initiating a call for sisters. Only as the war continued were any kinds of specific agreements sometimes worked out between the sisters and those who asked for them.

While the requests came from a variety of categories of people and groups, the absence of detailed documented reasons given for requesting the sisters probably implies that most people took it for granted that the sisters would and could help. The question was simply whether or not they would be able to take on a specific hospital or nursing task. For example, Dr. John Brinton, well-known for his outspoken attitude against the "terrible, irritable, and unhappy"[11] women generally plaguing the office of the medical director, typified the attitude of most doctors who had experience with any order of sisters. Disgusted with the lay "female nurse business," which "was a great trial to all the men concerned" and to himself, he determined to try to get rid of them from the Mound City, Illinois, Hospital. He explained:

In answer to my request to the Catholic authorities of, I think, North and South Bend, Indiana, a number of Sisters were sent down to act as nurses in the hospital. Those sent were from a teaching and not from a nursing order, but, in a short time they adapted themselves admirably to their new duties. I have forgotten the exact title of the Order. . . . I remember their black and white dresses, and I remember also, that when I asked the Mother, who accompanied them, what accommodations they required, the answer was 'one room, Doctor,' and there were in all, I think fourteen or fifteen of them. So I procured good nurses for my sick and the whole tribe of sanitary "Mrs. Brundages" passed away. The sick patients gained by the change, but for a few days, I was the most abused man in that department, for the newspapers gave me no mercy.[12]

To determine exactly who specifically called for the sisters' services in any instance is difficult. The phrase "the Union government in Washington" or the "Confederate governmental officials" might imply that Abraham Lincoln or Jefferson Davis requested the sisters. However, there is no direct evidence that either man personally requested the sisters' services, though both later graciously acknowledged their efforts. However, South Carolina Bishop Patrick Lynch, in writing to New York Bishop John Hughes on December 15, 1861, said that Davis did invite the Sisters of Charity of Our Lady of Mercy to go to Greenbrier White Sulphur Springs, which they did.[13] This may have reflected the fact that Lynch was a strong Confederate supporter who was often in contact with Davis, especially when arrangements were being made for Lynch to represent the Confederacy at the Vatican.

On the Union side, the highest ranking official to request sisters was Secretary of War Edwin Stanton. He made several requests, perhaps prompted by other people, for at least two Sisters of Mercy communities and for the Daughters of Charity. The request for Sisters of Mercy in New York was made by Major General Ambrose Burnside through the Vicar General of the New York diocese in 1862. Brigadier General John G. Foster reported to Stanton, who facilitated the request, on July 21, 1862: "At the request of Major General Burnside, nine Sisters of Mercy have arrived from New York to take charge of the hospital at Beaufort [North Carolina] and under their kind and educated care I hope for a rapid improvement in the health of patients."[14] The Sisters of Mercy in

Pittsburgh, in charge of Mercy Hospital since 1847, also received a request from Stanton in November 1862 through Bishop Michael Domenec.[15]

Although requests sometimes originated at the top levels of government, the battles were local, and governors and mayors, faced with their local needs and sometimes more familiar with the religious communities, also asked for sisters. For example, a Daughter of Charity in charge of City Hospital in Mobile, Alabama, recounted, "During the first year of the war, the Confederate Governor asked for sisters to take charge of their sick and wounded. About the second year of the war, we had to take in our Hospital the Confederate sick besides the city patients and occasionally Federal Prisoners were sent to us."

The willingness of these sisters to serve was attested to by the superior who remarked that she only had two sisters to give, leaving only herself and two remaining sisters to continue their own hospital. Yet, she concluded, "I gave them freely knowing our Lord would help us in time of need which He did most amply."[16]

Union officials also took care of local needs. For example, after the battle of Shiloh on April 6–7, 1862, Cincinnati Mayor George Hatch, aware of the earlier response of the Sisters of Charity of Cincinnati to help at Camp Dennison, appealed to Archbishop John Purcell for more nursing sisters to look after the Ohio wounded. Cincinnati philanthropist Mrs. Sarah Peter had already taken the Sisters of the Poor of St. Francis on a transport boat to get the wounded from the battlefield. The Mercies also responded with three sisters, one-third of their community. Fortunately, two of the three had nursing experience in Ireland during the plague, and all were connected with the Mercy Sisters who had gone to Crimea and thus were acquainted with the practical nursing methods employed there.[17]

Unlike the Mayor of Cincinnati, the Mayor of New York, though not opposed to sisters, was reluctant to initiate any care for the wounded in his city. In September 1862, the Central Park Commissioners had offered old Mt. St. Vincent's school to be used for a hospital. The building was on property that had been purchased for the park from the Sisters of Charity of New York prior to the war. Mayor Fernando Wood, however, did not want a hospital started because he felt the city would have to pay for it; he believed the federal government or the state should pay.[18] Nevertheless, after Edward Pierpont made a specific request to Secretary of War Stanton, a hospital was finally established there and the Sisters of Charity served until 1866.[19]

In addition to governmental authorities, generals or other top officers concerned for their men frequently made requests for the sisters, often through circuitous channels. For example, General Lew Wallace made a special request for twelve Sisters of the Holy Cross through Governor

Oliver P. Morton of Indiana, who relayed it to Fr. Edward Sorin, founder of Notre Dame. Sorin then rode across the road to the sisters at South Bend, on October 21, 1861. Though not a nursing community, the Holy Cross sisters eventually served in several military hospitals, and finally on the hospital boat "Red Rover" as the first Navy nurses.[20]

The Daughters of Charity were likewise requested by military authorities. A Daughter of Charity, who served the Military Hospital House of Refuge in St. Louis, recounts that the sisters went there on August 12, 1861, at the request of Major General John C. Fremont, commander of the West. She recalled that he "desired that every attention be paid to soldiers who had exposed their lives for their country, visited them frequently, and perceiving that there was much neglect on the part of the attendants, applied to the Sisters at St. Philomena's School for a sufficient number of sisters to take charge of the hospital, promising to leave everything to their management."[21] Since their ecclesiastical superior, Father J. Francis Burlando, had foreseen the possibility of this request a few months earlier, the sisters were aware of the conditions under which they would and could curtail their educational efforts and take on hospital work.[22]

Similar requests by military officials were made to the Daughters of Charity in Mobile, Alabama, and to the Sisters of Mercy of Chicago. The former went to take care of the Floridians and Alabamians with fever, measles, and other diseases.[23] The situations these sisters faced were sometimes perilous. For instance, the Sisters of Mercy of Chicago, were originally requested by Col. James A. Mulligan of the Illinois Irish Brigade, who in 1861 asked them to go to Lexington City, Missouri, to care for the wounded. The sisters, however, were forced by Confederate fire on the ship "Sioux City" to return to Jefferson City, Missouri. Once there, Mother Mary Francis Monholland and several of her sisters were invited by the US Sanitary Commission to take charge of the Jefferson City Hospital, where they stayed until it closed in April 1862.[24]

A more difficult experience comes from an account from the Daughters of Charity. Three days after the bombardment of Natchez, Mississippi, in 1861, three Daughters of Charity were to be sent from St. Mary's Asylum in Natchez to Monroe, Louisiana, at the request of Confederate General Albert Blanchard. According to the sisters' account, Blanchard, commander of the military in Monroe, was "a good Catholic who wished his soldiers to be treated with every care and attention."[25] He had a matron and nurses employed in the hospital; however, he discharged the former and made arrangements for the sisters to take charge the day after their arrival.

The sisters left Natchez immediately because of a report of the imminent arrival of the Federal gunboat, the "Essex," which would have prevented their departure the next day. Accompanied by the Bishop of

Natchez, William Elder, who was concerned for their safety, they crossed the Mississippi River in a small skiff in the middle of the night. After landing, they traveled two days over "a very rough and dangerous road," to get to their destination. [26]

Others faced danger closer to home. The Sisters of Mercy of Vicksburg, Mississippi, and the Dominican Sisters in Kentucky, facing battles in their own towns, offered their services for the wounded. In Vicksburg, the inhabitants fled into the surrounding country. Those who could not find houses camped out in the woods and lived in caves, which they dug in the sides of hills during the siege of the city in 1862. With the town under siege, the Sisters of Mercy were "solicited to preside" at a hospital in Mississippi Springs.[27] They were originally all teachers, but their school of one hundred pupils had gradually broken up as the war progressed and the city was shelled. Thus, the sisters took up nursing, moving with the Confederate army as it retreated along the railroad line into Alabama. At one point, the sisters, anxious about whether they would be able to continue their nursing work, were invited by Dr. Warren Buckell, through their ecclesiastical superior, Father Francis Xavier Leray, to take a house hospital in Jackson, Mississippi.[28]

Similar to the Mercy sisters in Vicksburg, the Dominican sisters found themselves in the middle of the battle at Perrysville, Kentucky, on October 8–9, 1862. Immediately, they offered their convent to care for the wounded. The sisters' annals record:

St. Catharine's Convent was hastily transformed into a military hospital. The dormitories with their rows of snowy white beds and long corridors, the class rooms, the recreation room were all filled with men who had been carried from the field of strife in every kind of available farm vehicle, which served as crude ambulances. Long after midnight of that memorable October 8 and 9, 1862, wagon loads of bruised and shattered heroes were still being brought to St. Catharine. There some Sisters were on duty receiving the soldiers, while others remained for additional service on the battlefield, helping to lift the sick and wounded onto the wagons. When each rumbling cart had its full quota, it started out for the convent hospital. The last seat was reserved for a Dominican Sister who sat there, the embodiment of mercy.[29]

The major battles of 1862, including the Seven Days' Battle, Second Bull Run, Harper's Ferry, Antietam, and Fredericksburg, increased the number of patients and strained the already overcrowded medical facilities and the overworked personnel. Thus, as the reputation of the sisters spread, requests for their services increased, especially from doctors. For example, on June 14, 1862, Surgeon General William A. Hammond at Washington asked for one hundred Daughters of Charity to be sent to the "White House," General Lee's former home in Virginia, which was now in the possession of Union troops. The sisters related that "too many were already among the war-stricken soldiers to admit of that number being sent, but sixty sailed from Baltimore for this place."[30] After some difficulties getting settled there, however, the sisters received another request from Hammond asking them to go on to Fortress Monroe, Virginia, where there was a greater need.[31]

In the spring of 1862, efforts were made to bring the Union wounded and sick from the southern battlefields to the larger northern cities. The medical authorities felt better care could be provided for the men in specially built hospitals, rather than in the field tent hospitals or makeshift facilities. This necessitated frequent trips on hospital transport ships, which were basically river boats fitted up with supplies and personnel and operated by various military and governmental groups.[32]

Sisters, as well as female nurses of the US Sanitary Commission, worked on these boats at various times throughout the war. In one case, several doctors, including Dr. George Blackman, a surgeon at St. Mary's Hospital, Cincinnati, requested the help of the Sisters of the Poor of St. Francis. With the encouragement of Mrs. Sarah Peter, who accompanied them, five sisters set sail for Pittsburgh Landing on the steamer "Superior," which towed several large barges that were really three-story barracks. During the trip the sisters and Mrs. Peter prepared bandages, lint, and straw mattresses.[33]

Requesting six, but getting five sisters for the "Commodore" and the "Whillden" boats operating from Fortress Monroe, Surgeon General Smith of Philadelphia again requested six more Sisters of St. Joseph to take with him on boats going to Richmond. Smith promised the trip would be "pleasanter" than a previous trip to Yorktown. Despite his promise, when a southern gunboat was about to open fire, the officers had the sisters appear on deck to prove that their errand was peaceful; nonetheless, a flying bullet just missed Mother Monica.[34]

Once the sick were in the northern cities, the sisters were then requested to work in these hospitals as well. For example, on May 28, 1862, a requisition was made by Surgeon General William Hammond through Dr. I. J. Hayes for twenty-five Daughters of Charity to nurse the sick and wounded soldiers in the West Philadelphia Hospital, afterwards known as the Satterlee Hospital. The hospital, ultimately to have 3,500 beds and become the largest Union hospital, was not quite finished. However, Dr. Hayes wanted the sisters "on the spot to make preparation" and set the date for the 9th of June. Accordingly, twenty-two sisters arrived at 10 A.M.[35] By the war's end, about ninety Daughters of Charity had worked there.

Geographic proximity to the battlefields was the reason Washington, D.C., with its sixteen hospitals and others in the nearby areas, led all other cities in bed capacity.[36] By 1862, the city of Washington had been turned into a huge hospital, with every building substituting for a medical facility; tents also were erected. Thus, both the Daughters of Charity and the Sisters of Mercy were asked by Hammond to attend the sick and wounded in Washington. The Daughters of Charity, in addition to serving at Providence, Eckington, and Cliffburn Hospitals, also went to Lincoln Hospital in 1862,[37] and the Sisters of Mercy of Pittsburgh went to Stanton Hospital in 1862.[38]

In addition to these many hospitals previously established or erected by the Union medical authorities, the sisters' own institutions were asked to become official government hospitals. A typical instance of this occurred at Wheeling Hospital in Virginia (West Virginia after 1863). The hospital, in existence since 1850, had been run by the Sisters of St. Joseph since 1856. When the battle of Harper's Ferry in September 1862 brought two hundred wounded soldiers into Wheeling, Mother De Chantel, faced with a military request to turn over her entire hospital, sent the orphans housed in the north wing of the building to a farmhouse. Beds or pallets of blankets were set up there within a few hours' time.[39] On April 23, 1864, the Federal government took over the hospital as a post hospital, added field tents on the grounds when the situation demanded, rented the hospital for $600 a year from the sisters, and hired five of them at government pay as nurses.[40] The sisters were supported in this cooperative action by Bishop Richard Whelan of Wheeling.

While the previous examples have illustrated primarily situations in which requests came from official governmental, military, or medical authorities, doctors who had previously worked with the sisters sometimes made their own requests either directly or indirectly through others. For example, Dr. E. Burke Haywood, in charge of the State Hospital at the Fairgrounds, Raleigh, North Carolina, called on Father Thomas Quigley, to find out how he could get three Sisters of Mercy to aid him in nursing the sick. He promised them a large room in a house, where, he said, they would be free from all intrusion and from insult, since the place was guarded by military law and there was a chaplain there.[41] Unfortunately, there were no sisters available to go, even after Father Quigley wrote to Bishop Lynch.

Dr. Henry Smith, Surgeon General of Pennsylvania troops, had more leverage. He was the personal physician of Mother Monica, of the Philadelphia Sisters of St. Joseph. She had also been superior of St. Joseph's Hospital. Thus, he could make his request for Sisters of St. Joseph directly to the superior of the community, Mother St. John Fournier, who consulted with Bishop James Wood. Smith himself explained that though he was "beset by applicants," he had "refused every female applicant being unwilling to trust any but his old friends, the Sisters of St. Joseph."[42] Hoping the sisters would not disappoint him in his requests for their services at Camp Curtin, outside Harrisburg, Pennsylvania, and at Church [Methodist] Hospital in the city, Dr. Smith promised, "There is waiting . . . a large field of usefulness, but it is to be properly cultivated only by those whose sense of duty will induce them to sacrifice personal comfort. The living is rough, the pay poor, and . . . nothing but the sentiments of religion could render any nurses contented."[43] The Sisters of St. Joseph went in early 1862. When the camp closed several months later, Surgeon General Smith again requested sisters for the floating ships going to Fortress Monroe and to Philadelphia. The sisters ministered on these hospital ships for several months until Camp Curtin opened again.[44]

The fact that so many doctors, ranging from Union Surgeon General Hammond to an ordinary doctor in charge of a small general hospital, asked for the sisters is of greater significance than the status of the other requesters. The national and local governmental officials and heads of citizens groups, who often felt the need to do something quickly about frequent crisis situations, might understandably overlook any specific concerns about quality of care and just request any available nursing help. However, the doctors, though equally hard-pressed for assistance, were often prejudiced against women nurses, most of whom they found more of a hindrance than help. Thus, the doctors were probably more careful in seeking out those they considered suitable helpers. Thus, previous personal experience with the sisters, as in the case of Dr. Smith, or awareness of their reputation played a significant part in the doctors' decision to request the sisters.

Perhaps a more predictable source of requests were the petitions for the sisters' service that came through the Catholic bishops. In 1861, there were seven archbishops and thirty-seven bishops, three-fourths of whom were located in dioceses in Union territory, and some of whom were far from the actual battlefront. The eleven Confederate states comprised eleven dioceses. Though there were some Southern-born bishops serving in Union territory, none of the bishops in the Confederate territory were born in the seceded states; many had been born in Ireland or France.[45]

In spite of varying political differences of the bishops and of the general strain among Catholics in the various territories, the Catholic church took no official position on the war and thus was saved from splintering.[46] Whatever the political opinions of the bishops, though, all were concerned mainly with supplying chaplains for the soldiers and generally were supportive of sisters from their various dioceses being involved in the war. Both actions reflected their concerns for the spiritual needs of the men. The bishops of the dioceses in which sisters had hospitals or other institutions, including their central headquarters (motherhouse), were often involved in facilitating the requests for services. However, an atypical reaction was that of a strong Union sympathizer, New York Archbishop John Hughes. In a May 1861 letter to Archbishop Francis Patrick Kenrick of Baltimore, he said that although the Sisters of Charity of his diocese were willing to volunteer from fifty to one hundred nurses, he strongly objected, saying, "They have as much on hand as they can accomplish."[47] Hughes may have been referring to the needed work of education and care of the orphans in his immigrant-crowded New York diocese. In any case, as the war went on, sisters from his diocese became actively involved in nursing, and he apparently did not object.

On the other hand, Bishop Martin John Spalding, from border state Kentucky, had offered the services of the Sisters of Charity of Nazareth, Kentucky, to Federal General Robert Anderson. This offer was made without any reference to the political questions—to nurse all sick or wounded "on both sides." Spalding recorded in his diary that "now in December [1861] three hospitals are graciously attended by 18 Sisters, six in each. Few of the sick, more than a thousand in number, are Catholics but many who were dying were baptized and sent to heaven. The Sisters are very devoted and zealous and are doing much good."[48]

Following the Confederate victory at Manassas, July 21, 1861, Bishop James Whelan of Nashville, Tennessee, offered his cathedral for hospital purposes and the services of the Sisters of St. Dominic of Memphis. By August of 1861, he wrote to South Carolina Bishop Patrick Lynch requesting sisters for Tennessee,[49] which had seceded on June 8, 1861. Sixteen Sisters of St. Dominic of St. Agnes Convent, Memphis, accepted his request to visit hospital homes in Memphis and to take over the City Hospital there.[50] When Sherman took over the city on July 24, 1862, he pitched his tents on their convent grounds, but promised the sisters safety and allowed them to visit the Federal hospital.[51]

Like Bishops Spalding and Whelan, Bishop Maurice de St. Palais of the Vincennes, Indiana, diocese took the initiative in offering buildings and the services of the sisters. The Sisters of Providence related that at the camp formed to receive recruits near Vincennes, some of the men fell sick of a "virulent disease," which made it necessary to care for them apart. Bishop de St. Palais offered a college building and asked for two sisters to take charge of the stricken soldiers. Community records indicate that there were no sisters at Saint Mary-of-the-Woods, Indiana, who could be spared for that purpose. So, in order to respond to the request, Sisters Saint Felix and Sophy were called from their respective establishments to Vincennes to be employed.[52] This emergency hospital opened about the middle of April 1861 and closed the end of July. One sister wrote that while the time of service was brief:

Those three months of service...were equal to as many years, or more, of ordinary hospital work, on account of the hardships endured. An epidemic had broken out; the contagion created a panic, and it was only with greatest difficulty that supplies could be obtained. ... The hired help fled at the approach of danger, leaving the Sisters alone to care for the stricken. The lives of the Sisters were often in danger from delirious fever patients, as well as from the epidemic. Defenseless and isolated, the Sisters still remained at their post; even washing the linen at night, and cutting wood for the fires.[53]

After the battle of Fort Donelson, in February 1862, Indiana soldiers, according to the policy of Governor Morton, were brought home to be cared for. This time the bishop of Vincennes offered the use of the Catholic seminary for the sick, and again he offered the assistance of Sisters of Providence in caring for them, thus demonstrating the co-operation of the church authorities and the willing service of its sisters for war needs.[54]

In early 1864, the Sisters of the Poor of St. Francis at St. Francis Hospital in Cincinnati, Ohio, were requested by Cincinnati Archbishop John Purcell to visit the soldiers at Camp Chase to provide both spiritual and material support to the men. Apparently, due to a prejudice against Catholic clergy on the part of some of the officers, priests were not allowed to visit the camp. This made the archbishop concerned about the spiritual needs of the soldiers; he felt, however, that the sisters might be accepted since they were women and by now were known for their generous and impartial service to the soldiers.[55]

Certainly, by war's end, the bishops were cognizant of the value and impact of the sisters' visible service, which contributed to a favorable view of Catholicism. Since the communities ordinarily were directly un-der their bishop or his representative, especially in the dioceses in which the motherhouses or main administrative headquarters were located, some contact between the sisters and the bishops over their service in the war is presumed, though there is little remaining documentation detailing that contact.

While generally the sisters were involved in some kind of discussion with ecclesiastical authorities, or at least with their own religious com-munities, sometimes time and circumstances did not allow the sisters to check with various community and church authorities before accepting requests for service. For example, Sisters of Charity of Nazareth from St. Mary Academy, Paducah, Kentucky, closed their academy and nursed both Union and Confederate soldiers in the early winter of 1861. In September of that year, Confederate General Leonidas Polk had moved from Tennessee and had occupied Columbus, Kentucky. Federal forces under General Ulysses S. Grant responded immediately by occupying Paducah and building Fort Anderson to protect their position. Thus, before the end of the year, many wounded and sick soldiers were brought to Kentucky, and Union General C. F. Smith requested that the Sisters of Charity nurse these men. Communication with the Nazareth moth-erhouse was impossible; hence, Sister Martha Drury, the superior of the

academy, acted on her own responsibility in closing the school and com-
plying with the request.[56]

Often, the sisters initiated offers of service themselves as they saw the
needs. After the Infirmary in Washington burned to the ground, for
instance, the "Sisters [of Mercy of Baltimore] barely escaped with their
lives having risked them in trying to save the patients." Immediately,
Mother Alphonsus "hastened to Washington to bring the sisters supplies." Responding to the continued need for medical facilities, the War
Department shortly took possession of three senatorial residences near
the Capital and transformed them into a military hospital known as the
Douglas, after Senator Stephen Douglas. The sisters immediately responded, as their annals record:

Not being satisfied with the good being done in the "Old Armory" [where the
patients had been taken after the fire] Mother Alphonsus wrote the government
officials offering the Services of the sisters to nurse in the military hospital where
the wounded had been arriving daily. The offer was gratefully accepted ... and
at once the sisters took up their residence at the Douglas, full charge being
assigned them by the Government.[57]

Another offer on the part of the sisters was that of the Holy Cross
Sisters. In June 1862, Mother Angela offered the services of the sisters
for a "hospital boat" and Flag Officer Charles H. Davis, commanding
the Western Flotilla, wrote to Fleet Officer A. M. Pennock to make
arrangements for their coming. While Navy records indicate no conclu-
sive evidence that women served as nurses on the "Red Rover" prior to
the time that she was fitted out and commissioned as a US Navy hospital
ship at the end of the year,[58] the Holy Cross archives do indicate that
these sisters had earlier been on board "Red Rover." [59] While at this
point in the war, the Holy Cross Sisters, originally all teachers, had
become experienced in nursing, the discrepancy might be explained by
the fact that the boat was first an army vessel after it was captured by
the Union authorities. Thus, the sisters may have been on it under army
auspices.

On occasion, the sisters' generous offer to nurse caused them difficulty
once the town was captured by opposing forces. For example, in Arkansas, the only sisters were Sisters of Mercy, who were teachers. However, when the Confederate hospitals became overcrowded, they freely
opened a building in Little Rock to serve the wounded. In spite of their
generosity, after the capture of the city by General Frederick Steele on
September 10, 1863, a local Arkansas historian recounted that the "position of the sisters became almost unbearable, on account of the rude
behavior of federal officers, who resented the kind treatment which the
sisters were giving the Confederate sick."[60] The sisters, however, con-

tinued their same impartial treatment by opening their school building in Helena, Arkansas, to care for both Union and Confederate soldiers.[61]

However, government officials did not always look kindly on offers of assistance. The Cincinnati Sisters of Mercy had their offer to serve refused by the government. When the local military was looking over every building for possible use, they asked for the Sisters' House of Mercy in October 1861. The sisters rented the building to the government, which officially rechristened it "McLean Barracks" and reopened it as a "receiving depot for prisoners of war and state prisoners, deserters, and stragglers."[62] The House of Mercy was compressed into the convent above it. The first impulse of the sisters was to come to the assistance of the men being moved into the sealed-off House of Mercy, but when they offered nursing services to the "wretched" inhabitants, the officials, for unknown reasons, were not interested. Finally, under the influence of Mrs. Sarah Peter, sisters were permitted to at least visit the unfortunate soldiers, many of whom were prisoners from the Southern army, even though the military persisted in refusing nursing privileges. The sisters visited the men regularly until the last prisoner was freed or removed, some time around November 1, 1865.[63]

In addition to requests from specific, individual authorities, petitions for the sisters' services also came from various combinations of aid groups, officials, donors, or involved citizens. Because the aid societies largely confined their work to providing clothing, bandages, and small comforts for the soldiers, which they often distributed themselves, they sometimes saw other needs, which they directed to the sisters. For instance, on March 4, 1864, Mother De Chantal of the Sisters of St. Joseph in Wheeling was requested by the Soldiers' Aid Society to take care of all the military patients in the Athenaeum, the city jail. The sisters had been visiting the jail, in addition to their work at Wheeling Hospital, so they were acquainted with the men. However, this added forty-seven ill and disabled soldiers immediately to the already filled hospital, though the sisters willingly took them in.[64]

Though most of the requests for sisters' services came in the first year of the war, and some terms of service were only of a few months, the changing nature of the war created new demands, especially in the South. As the Daughters of Charity in Richmond reported near the end of the war, "The Southern Confederacy seeing their cause likely to fail resolved to concentrate their hospital facilities in or near Richmond. Upon arrival there we were immediately called upon, they begging us to take the hospital under our care and charge."[65]

The existing data on requests indicate that the sisters were asked to serve primarily in the first two years of the war. However, lack of documentation for the last two years does not indicate that the sisters were no longer wanted; rather, it reflects the fact that most of these sisters or their communities were still serving and thus had no more sisters to send. Too, in the North, the men were moved to large governmental or other stable hospitals, and those sisters that could be spared were in such places as Satterlee or Point Lookout, as well as working on the transport boats bringing soldiers to these and similar places.

On at least one occasion, requests for service or the sisters' desire to serve caused difficulties within the sisters' own communities and among church or governmental authorities because their privacy or cloistered protection would be invaded. In August 1861, Ursuline Mother St. Pierre offered the new convent building in Galveston, Texas, to the Confederates for a base hospital. The sisters' own annals record, "This act, prompted by the generosity of the nun's heart, opened the flood gates of much criticism. Reverend Father Chambodut, [ecclesiastical superior at the time] an impetuous man himself and the only priest who is thought to have pulled the lanyard of a cannon on the side of the Confederacy, reprimanded Mother Saint Pierre severely."[66]

The action was criticized by some of the sisters, as well as the chaplain, all of whom wrote to Bishop John Odin about her. Others, however, supported her. One priest wrote, "The Sisters seem fearless with the yellow flag flying above their convent."[67] Mother St. Pierre herself was aware of the controversy surrounding her actions and recorded in the annals: "Unfortunately, this act—the offering of the house as a hospital—seemingly good, was praised by some and blamed by others. Dearly did my heart pay for having been too hasty in following my natural disposition on this occasion."[68] She had to contend with the sisters in her community. Some complained about the "invasion of their privacy," saying, "The Chapter should have been consulted before the offer was made; not afterwards. If seculars are admitted into our house, what becomes of the cloister?"[69]

Nevertheless, Dr. Oaks, the surgeon, took possession of the convent building in the name of the Confederacy and designated the place as a "Confederate Hospital." Perhaps in an effort to recognize the concerns of some of the sisters, Father Anstaedt obtained permission for only older nuns to act as nurses in order that the entire convent life and the younger sisters would be protected.[70]

While there may have been controversy among the Ursulines, they did use their buildings for the wounded. One community of sisters, though, was not willing to give up their buildings for use as a hospital. Archbishop Francis Kenrick of Baltimore recounted to Bishop Patrick Lynch that "the Sisters of Georgetown (Visitation) were called on by Dr. Lamb in the name of the public purveyor to give a portion of their buildings for an hospital for soldiers, but were excused on appealing to General Winfield Scott, whose daughter died within their convent, though the Jesuit fathers next door had a regiment quartered in their college."[71] This refusal can probably be explained by the fact that the sisters were a cloistered, rather than an active order.

Although some active communities did have hospital experience, or at least experience in caring for the infirm members of their own communities, many sisters were teachers or in charge of orphans. Nonetheless, the spirit and attitude in which they, the superiors, and the bishops engaged in the work is well summed up by the ecclesiastical superior of the Daughters of Charity, who wrote the following to the Paris motherhouse shortly after the war ended:

Called for the first time to exercise their services on the field of battle, our Sisters were without practical experience; for this reason I did not hasten to acquiesce to the desires and solitations of many, who pressed me to offer to the Government the assistance of the Sisters for the work of the ambulances. It was to be feared moreover that they were apt at this kind of services, might they not stray from the spirit of regularity which seems incompatible with camp life. However, the will of God was manifested through the medium of superiors, and I cast aside these fears to count more assuredly upon the succor of God as we confronted the designs of his Providence.[72]

In addition, this opportunity to serve in the war was seen by at least one nonteaching community as a real opportunity to expand services. As the Sisters of Providence remarked, "To have a hospital has long been desired; a choice has come at last to have one. We have a fine opening to commence that branch of our vocation."[73]

Although care of the sick and wounded was the major service that the sisters were asked to do, visiting prisoners was also a requested service, or a service they took on voluntarily. The route was often circuitous; governmental officials, eager for sisters of any community, usually went to the bishop of the area, who then went through the religious community. For instance, Colonel Ware, in charge of Illinois prisons, applied to the Bishop of Alton, Illinois, Reverend Henry Juncker, for some Daughters of Charity. He, in turn, applied to the superior of St. Philomena's School, who secured permission from Father Francis Burlando, who was actual superior of the sisters' community.[74]

With less complication, other communities visited prisoners in both the South and North. For example, the Sisters of Charity of Our Lady of Mercy in Charleston, South Carolina, visited prisoners of war at four locations there: the jail yard, the work house, Roper Marine Hospital, and the Race Course (Fair Grounds Prison).[75] After caring for the seriously ill prisoners in the Union Military Hospital in Indianapolis, Providence Sister Athanasius Fogerty was allowed by military authorities to visit the men when they were transferred to Camps Morton and Carrington.[76] Generally these sisters became involved in visiting prisoners either because the soldiers had been first their patients or because the sisters were viewed as "neutral" or equally attentive to both Union and Confederate men in need.

Responding readily to the myriad requests for serving the sick and wounded of both Union and Confederate forces, the sisters did not generally seem to draw up formal agreements, except in the case of the Daughters of Charity and of the Sisters of Charity of Nazareth. However, the sisters did have specific, nonnegotiable needs of a religious nature. For example, the opportunity for church services on Sunday and sometimes throughout the week, an obligation and practice all communities of sisters observed, was generally a stated expectation on the part of all the sisters or their male ecclesiastical superior or bishop who was serving as an intermediary. However, chaplains of any denomination were often scarce during the war,[77] even though efforts were made by the governmental and military authorities, individual denominations, or through the efforts in the North of the US Christian Commission, to supply them to the troops.[78]

Among Catholic chaplains, it has been estimated that only thirteen priests were appointed hospital chaplain by Lincoln on May 20, 1862; there were only forty chaplains in the volunteer regiments of the Union Army; only about twenty took care of the spiritual needs of the soldiers in their geographic area; and only about twenty-eight who were Confederate chaplains in hospitals and in regiments.[79] Thus, obtaining priests for soldiers or sisters was not an easy task.

The records sometimes reveal attempts to place a chaplain or make provisions for one. Lincoln himself wrote a memo in September 1862, after a visit from a Daughter of Charity working in a Washington hospital, asking that Father Joseph O'Hagan, a regimental chaplain, become a hospital chaplain. The Catholic chaplain already appointed, she explained, could not handle all the Catholic soldiers.[80]

This scarcity of chaplains was similarly noted by some bishops. Baltimore Archbishop Francis Patrick Kenrick wrote to New York Archbishop John Hughes in 1862 asking for sisters from the New York diocese and explaining that, though the Surgeon General wanted more sisters, the Daughters of Charity could not provide any more. Kenrick pointed out the difficulties in getting chaplains appointed:

The Sisters may experience difficulty in regard to their spiritual duties unless some arrangement be made for chaplains. These are generally Preachers [Dominicans?]. It is hard for the Sisters to hear Mass even on Sundays. The Surgeon General asked me some months ago to designate a priest for them, and took no notice of my request to have him appointed and provided for. The Jesuits will no doubt look to those who will be in charge of the St. Aloysius' Hospital in Washington. Public notice has been given that no new chaplains will be appointed. If a moderate addition were made to the allowance for the Sisters, it might be the least invidious mode of providing for the priest in attendance.[81]

In a similar vein, Bishop McGill of Richmond, Virginia, writing in 1862 to Bishop Patrick Lynch of Charleston, South Carolina, said he could have any sisters from his diocese provided he could "either fund or furnish a chaplain for them."[82]

If there were no chance of having a chaplain for services for both the sisters and the Catholic soldiers, this sometimes was a reason for sisters not going to a specific location or for pulling out. For example, Father Francis Burlando ordered the Daughters of Charity to leave shortly after they had begun working on hospital transport boats. As Burlando explained to his superiors in France:

Those floating hospitals were, however, very frightful: more than four or five hundred sick and wounded lay heaped on one another; the bottom, middle and hold of the ships were filled with sufferers. Willingly would we have continued our services, but our Sisters were deprived of all spiritual assistance; no mass or communion even when they entered the port, it was hard for them to go to church, either because they did not know where there was one, or because the distance would not allow them. We were therefore obliged to remove and place them in the organized hospitals on land, where they can at least rely on the assistance of a priest. It is true, some were promised me, but their number is too small.[83]

Other communities, though, who worked on the transport ships seemed to adjust to the situation in other ways. For instance, the Sisters of Charity of Cincinnati served on the transports and at least did not record any particular concerns about participating in services on Sunday. They may have been able to dock along the way, as the Holy Cross Sisters seem to have done on two occasions at Natchez, Mississippi, as recorded by Archbishop Elder in his diary.[84]

Similarly, St. Joseph superior Mother St. John anticipated the possible difficulties of fulfilling religious duties and made arrangements before the sisters went. Writing to her sisters who were about to set out on floating boats, she commented:

The Bishop [James F. Wood] has already given the necessary dispensations.... Go to Holy Communion when you have that favor.... Make your Meditation in the morning after your prayers and be not troubled if you can say no other prayers of the community, not even if you are deprived of Mass on Sundays. In the meantime, I recommend you all to unite yourselves to the prayers of the community, and often times through the day to make short ejaculations and never give a short answer to a Sister or any one else.[85]

Perhaps aware that there were possible difficulties, Holy Cross Superior Mother Angela in corresponding with Mississippi Fleet Surgeon Ninian A. Pinkney, said:

I hasten to inform you that I have not the slightest inclination to remove our
Sisters from the Red Rover [Navy Ship]—provided they are enabled to attend
Mass (as they do at present)....It was a deep source of regret to me when I
feared we might have to do it—mainly because the nature of the boat's movement
would continue to prevent the fulfillment of one of our essential duties. But as
this obstacle is removed I am rejoiced to have them stay as long as their services
are needed.[86]

While working on the transport ships understandably posed problems
for obtaining the services of a chaplain, there were other kinds of service
which also had to be refused on religious grounds. For instance, after
work among measles patients at Camp Denison was finished, the Sisters
of Charity of Cincinnati planned to return to St. John's Hospital in the
city. Some of the Ohio regiments, however, desired the sisters to continue
their services with the army as it marched southward. The Mother Superior granted the permission, but she withdrew it when she learned
that a Baptist minister, and not a Catholic priest, was to accompany the
troops from Camp Denison.[87]

In spite of these requirements for spiritual services, as well as the
desires of the sisters, the realities of the war and the urgency of caring
for the wounded often took precedence over the kind of regularity of
religious exercise observed in the quiet of the prewar convent days. A
Daughter of Charity reported that on their return to Richmond:

We had at once a pious chaplain and the Holy Mass four days in the week. For
the first three years of the war, we had Mass only on Sunday and very, very
often had only time for vocal prayers, then read meditation, and hurried to the
dying men. Thus passed the day and after heavy battles, we could not retire
until ten or eleven o'clock. We were called during the night short as it was; but
we always rose at four o'clock. When the condition of our sick would admit it,
our blessed exercises were resumed with renewed fervor.[88]

The difficulties surrounding Mass attendance were specifically noted by
two communities working in the South. A Daughter of Charity working
in Marietta, Georgia, recounts, "Five weeks without Mass. At last, two
sisters went to Atlanta where there were two priests—did get one to
come for Mass on Easter."[89] The Sisters of Charity of Our Lady of Mercy
from Charleston, serving at the Confederate hospital in Montgomery
White Sulphur Springs, Virginia, were without a chaplain for six weeks
while Bishop Lynch attempted to find a replacement and get him commissioned.[90]

Concern for the sisters' inability to perform their religious duties was
also expressed by others besides the bishops and the communities. A
letter appeared in the Indianapolis *Sentinel* on February 25, 1862, in
which the writer called for public attention to the problem.

I consider it as fact worthy of notice that the Sisters of Providence who have charge of the Military Hospital, are not furnished with a conveyance to and from the city, but are obliged to wade through mud and mire on foot. A carriage is furnished them on Sundays, it is true, but the religious duties of the Sisters make it necessary that they should come in town every day, and it is a crying shame that they should be allowed to walk. I can safely say that the greater part of the way to the Hospital the mud is knee deep. A small one-horse spring wagon would be of infinite use; and where so much money is spent, why not a little be invested to this good purpose? The Sisters are uncomplaining, and for that reason, their comfort should be more carefully looked after.[91]

In a few cases, the sisters recalled being able to perform all their religious exercises as well as attend Mass, much the same as they had been in their convents in prewar times. For example, the Galveston Ursulines, not a nursing community, remarked, "Our new vocation, which sad circumstances forced on us, won for us the sweet title of 'Sisters of Charity,' whose vocation we so awkwardly fulfilled. Having charge of the hospital did not interfere in the least with our religious observances; neither did the war prevent us from giving the holy habit to our two postulants."[92]

In addition to the requirement of a chaplain for fulfillment of spiritual duties, the Daughters of Charity, probably under Father Burlando's specific direction, laid down the following conditions under which they would nurse:

1. In the first place that no *Lady Volunteers* be associated with the Sisters in their duties as such an association would be rather an encumbrance than a help;

2. That the Sisters should have entire charge of the Hospitals and ambulances;

3. That the Government pay the traveling expenses of the Sisters and furnish them board and other actual necessities during the war. Clothing also in case it [the war] should be protracted.[93]

The Sisters of Charity of Nazareth, Kentucky, had a similar arrangement, though worded somewhat more tactfully, which they worked out with General Robert Anderson. A copy went to Bishop Martin Spalding of Kentucky, who later sent a copy to Bishop Purcell.[94]

1. The Sisters of Charity will nurse the wounded under the direction of army surgeon without any interference whatsoever;

2. Everything necessary for the lodging and nursing of the wounded and sick will be supplied to them without putting them to expense; they will give their services gratuitously;

3. So far as circumstances will allow they shall have every facility for attending to their religious devotional exercises.[95]

The only other formal arrangements were made by the Sisters of Mercy of New York when they took charge of the military hospital at Beaufort, North Carolina. They required that a chaplain was to be appointed, paid, and maintained; private apartments allotted to the use of the sisters; and provisions, medicines, and utensils supplied for the patients and themselves.[96] Records indicate the chaplain was so appointed.[97]

Precise reasons why some communities had written regulations and some did not is difficult to determine because of limited evidence. Because the Daughters of Charity were the largest group of sisters serving in the war, and their ecclesiastical director, Father Burlando, was active in most of the arrangements for the sisters to nurse, it is understandable that they would develop these regulations at some point in the war. However, exactly when and where the Daughters' requirements were developed, implemented, or even whether they were always written down is not known. The one extant penciled copy may just be a written version of oral agreements.

Nevertheless, Bishop Martin Spalding, writing to Archbishop John Purcell of Cincinnati, probably summarized the prevailing cooperative attitude of the authorities toward the regulations of the communities who had them. Spalding said, "We have the Sisters here at the Military Hospital, and they are not annoyed but treated as well as could be expected. The spirit of my agreement with General Anderson seems to have been at least substantially carried out, and I apprehend but little difficulty in the future."[98]

The reasons behind these stipulations, particularly on the part of the sisters, included the need of the sisters, especially those who had hospital and nursing experience, to control those conditions that would make for good nursing care as well as the primacy with which they and their advisers saw the need and importance of fulfilling spiritual desires and obligations. For example, ability to enforce standards of cleanliness, proper nutrition, and suitable order in the wards for the comfort of those recovering or dying were all aspects of proper care. In addition, disabled soldiers put to work nursing other soldiers, completely untrained ward masters and medical assistants in the field and general hospitals, hordes of well-meaning but often interfering women visitors, and other untrained female nurses were all sources of complaints by many doctors and by the other more experienced and organized female nurses. Thus, the sisters' need to be in complete charge, as they were in their own institutions, without being hampered by female volunteers, can be understood. The requirements, then, though seemingly stringent, were probably appropriate at the time, even if some of the stipulations were occasionally met with strained relations within the hospital setting or became the source of critical attitudes from others.

Whether communities had formal agreements or not, other issues, particularly remuneration, were handled in a number of ways. The standard pay for female nurses hired by the Union through Dorothea Dix was forty cents a day plus rations; however, the sisters were not under her jurisdiction. Thus, they generally were not listed on the official records and rolls of the army records, so determining their actual pay is almost impossible. Payment policies for the sisters serving the Confederacy are equally unclear.

For example, internal evidence from the Sisters of Charity of Our Lady of Mercy in Charleston shows that they received no remuneration from the Confederate army. As proof, a letter from Sister De Sales to Bishop Lynch comments on a visit from a Dr. Archer, who said that the Daughters of Charity at the Alms House Hospital in Richmond received $330,000 from the Surgeon General in charge. The doctor was surprised to learn from the Sisters of Mercy that they received no remuneration.[99] However, the $330,000 in Confederate money may well have been the food and clothing allowance stipulated in the Daughters of Charity written agreement. Similarly, Sister M. Ignatius Sumner, a Vicksburg Mercy Sister describing conditions as they traveled with the fleeing Confederate army eastward through Mississippi to Alabama, said, "From the beginning we had refused all compensation, but fortunately we had a little money left to buy what provisions we could find.[100] These same sisters did receive in 1862 "in recompense for their services [in Oxford, Mississippi]... sufficient means from the Confederate government to rent a small cottage of four rooms which they formed into something like a convent home complete with chapel."[101]

The Holy Cross Sisters who served on the Navy boat "Red Rover" received fifty cents a day, ten cents more than army nurses, though no actual total of monies earned can be determined.[102] Even if records had been kept, the frequency of payment may have been erratic. For example, Mother Angela of the same community noted on January 1, 1862, in the fragment of what appears to be the Mound City Hospital account book: "The paymaster is generally very tardy, leaving an interval of several months between his appearances."[103]

Though the Daughters of Charity may have asked for "no remuneration," certainly the "provisions" would have been in keeping with the regular female nurse pay. Since only the Satterlee Hospital account book remains from any of the places where the Daughters served and the actual sources of income are not clear, the various expenditures for the sisters' clothing items may or may not have been paid for by the government. On the other hand, in Lynchburg, each Daughter of Charity was paid $18.50 per month for nursing at General Hospital #3, which incorporated the college building, Division #1, and Fergusan's (Tobacco) Factory, Division #2.[104]

Of particular interest is the fact that in December 1864, Sister Ann Simeon Norris, the head of the Daughters of Charity, made a petition to the Congress of the United States, at the recommendation of Lincoln, that the material for the habit worn by the sisters, which was manufactured only in France, be admitted duty free. In her petition, she referred to her contact with Lincoln, saying, "His Excellency, the President kindly replied: that in consideration of the Services the Sisters had rendered the Union soldiers in the different Hospitals of the United States, he would most willingly grant this favor, but that the law required an act of Congress."[105] However, the Daughters have no record this was ever done. Records of Congress indicate only that a bill was introduced in 1864 and then referred to the finance committee.[106]

This last example underscores the fact that the written or oral agreements for the sisters' services that still exist relate not to any demands or requirements of the requestors, but rather to issues the sisters or their ecclesiastical authorities wanted clarified. Because few of these agreements are in existence, only tentative conclusions can be drawn.

These stipulations, dealing primarily with the fulfillment of religious obligations or clarification of authority lines in the hospital setting, seem to originate directly from the male ecclesiastical authority over the community, rather than from the sisters themselves. While this is probably a reflection of the nineteenth-century dependency of women religious on male hierarchical structure or of the practices of certain communities, some of the issues seem to represent the sisters' desire to have necessary control over certain areas of the hospital or the care in order to do a good job.

While not all nursing communities had such regulations, those agreements that still exist are only from nursing communities. It might be concluded that experiences in dealing with issues of control of the hospital or the nursing setting, as well as the anticipated difficulty of fulfilling their religious duties in a non-Catholic setting, may have caused these communities to develop such "conditions of services" as the war went on.

That over six hundred sisters from twenty-one different communities of twelve orders responded in some way to the many requests underscores two important points. First, in responding, the sisters demonstrated a willingness to adjust their lifestyle to the needs of their country and its wounded. Second, they had a flexibility that enabled them to exercise their nursing skills in new and difficult situations or to learn nursing skills quickly on the job. Only the lack of sisters in the many small religious communities, or in a few cases the inability to fulfill their religious duties, caused a difficulty in the sisters' response. Rather, in cases where the sick and wounded were in the immediate geographic vicinity, sisters responded with whatever services, buildings, and supplies they could offer. Those communities who had the largest number of sisters and the most experience, like the Daughters of Charity, who supplied over one-half of the sisters who served in the war, were in the greatest demand. Nevertheless, even though ten of the twenty-one communities who served were teaching orders, they willingly took up the tasks of nursing.

Thus, prior reputation and experience, as the Civil War began, and visibility, respectability, willingness to serve, and flexibility in adjusting to new situations as the war continued were the key strengths of the sisters. Yet, primary to the sisters as they exhibited these qualities in their specific nursing duties on battlefields, transport boats, and in hospitals, was the opportunity to continue their own religious commitment and to extend the values of religion to those they worked with and cared for, especially the wounded and dying. Significant, too, was the fact that those who requested the sisters were willing to permit the sisters to carry out the religious duties that sustained their own commitment and service during the Civil War.

NOTES

1. Archives of the Daughters of Charity, Emmitsburg, Maryland (ADC), *Annals of the Civil War*, vol. I, p. 47.

2. Statistics taken from Ellen Jolly Ryan, *Nuns of the Battlefield* (Providence, RI: The Providence Visitor Press, 1927). She cites twenty communities; however, the Sisters of Mercy in Arkansas appeared to have served for a limited time. Jolly's statistics for the number of sisters from each community came from figures supplied to her. In some cases, the figures now seem slightly different, perhaps reflecting increased attention to records in these intervening years. Jolly also indentified the nationality of sisters.

3. The figure of one-fifth is an estimate based on figures supplied by those communities that had data and extrapolating for those that did not have data. There is no way to accurately determine the figure for the historical period. For additional figures, see Eileen Mary Brewer, *Nuns and the Education of American Catholic Women, 1860–1920* (Chicago: Loyola University Press, 1987), p. 15.

4. Archives of the Daughters of Charity, Albany, New York (ADC-Albany), Letter of Brig. General John Rathbone to Bishop McCloskey, June 1, 1861.

5. ADC-Albany, "St. Mary's Hospital and the Civil War," p. 5.

6. ADC, *Annals of the Civil War*, vol. I, p. 14.

7. Sr. Mary Theodosia Mug, *Lest We Forget: The Sisters of Providence of St. Mary of the Woods in Civil War Services* (St. Mary of the Woods, IN: Providence Press, 1931), p. 17.

8. Archives of the Sisters of Charity of Cincinnati (ASCC), "Memoirs of Sr. Anthony O'Connell," n.p.

9. ADC, *Annals of the Civil War*, vol. II, p. 58.

10. ADC, *Annals of the Civil War*, vol. II, p. 58.

11. John Brinton, *Personal Memoirs of John H. Brinton* (New York: The Neale Publishing Co., 1914), p. 294.

12. Brinton, p. 199.

13. Charleston Diocesan Archives (CDA), H361 (old numbering), Letter of Patrick Lynch to John Hughes, n.d.

14. US War Department, *The Wars of the Rebellion: A Compilation of the Official Records of the Union and Confederate Armies* (Washington: Government Printing Office, 1880–1901), Part I, Vol. IX, p. 411 (hereafter cited as *Official Records*).

15. *Official Records*, Part I, Vol. IX, p. 411.

16. ADC, *Annals of the Civil War* (handwritten copy), pp. 478–481.

17. Mary Ellen Evans, *The Spirit Is Mercy* (Westminster, MD: The Newman Press, 1959), p. 90.

18. Sr. Marjorie Walsh, *The Sisters of Charity of New York, 1809–1959*, vol. I (New York: Fordham University Press, 1960), p. 198.

19. Archives of the Sisters of Charity of New York City (ASCNYC).

20. Congregational Archives of the Sisters of the Holy Cross, Saint Mary's, Notre Dame, IN (ACSC), Civil War, "Red Rover" file.

21. ADC, *Annals of the Civil War*, vol. II, p. 111.

22. ADC, *Annals of the Civil War*, vol. II, p. 111.

23. Michael Gannon, *Cross in the Sand: The Early Catholic Church in Florida* (Gainsville: University of Florida Press, 1967), pp. 175–176.

24. Jolly, pp. 231–233.

25. ADC, *Annals of the Civil War*, vol. II, p. 105.

26. ADC, *Annals of the Civil War*, vol. II, p. 105.

27. Archives of Sisters of Mercy, Vicksburg (ARSMV), Sr. M. Ignatius Sumner, "Register of the Events from the Foundation of the Convent of the Sisters of Mercy, Vicksburg, Miss.," pp. 6–7.

28. ARSMV, Sumner, p. 10.

29. Archives of the Sisters of St. Dominic, St. Catharine, KY, (AOPK), Sr. Margaret Hamilton, "In My Times," typescript, pp. 53–55.

30. ADC, *Annals of the Civil War*, vol. I, p. 19.

31. ADC, Letter of Fr. Francis Burlando to Mother Ann Simeon Norris, June 23, 1862. For another point of view on the difficulties of the sisters' getting settled, see Frederic Law Olmsted, *Hospital Transports* (Boston: Ticknor, 1863), pp. 113–114, 134. See also Anne Austin, *The Woolsey Sisters of New York* (Philadelphia: American Philosophical Society, 1971), p. 57.

32. George W. Adams, *Doctors in Blue: The Medical History of the Union Army in the Civil War* (New York: Henry Schuman, 1952), p. 82.

33. Betty Perkins, "The Work of the Catholic Sister in the Civil War," Masters thesis, University of Dayton, 1969, p. 89.

34. Sr. Maria Kostka Logue, *Sisters of St. Joseph of Philadelphia* (Westminster, MD: The Newman Press, 1950), p. 128.

35. ADC, *Annals of the Civil War*, vol. I, pp. 19–20.

36. Adams, p. 152.

37. ADC, *Annals of the Civil War*, vol. I, p. 11.

38. Sr. Jerome McHale, *On the Wing: The Story of the Pittsburg Sisters of Mercy, 1843–1968* (New York: The Seaburg Press, 1980), p. 111.

39. Sr. Rose Anita Kelly, *Song of the Hills: The Story of the Sisters of St. Joseph of Wheeling* (Wheeling, WV: Sisters of St. Joseph, 1962), pp. 216–217.

40. Kelly, p. 215.

41. CDA, 27D4, Father Thomas Quigley to Bishop Lynch, May 10, 1862.

42. Logue, p. 121.

43. Logue, p. 121.

44. Logue, pp. 125–129.

45. Benjamin J. Blield, *Catholics and the Civil War* (Milwaukee: Bruce, 1945), pp. 36–52, surveys the bishops of the Northern states; pp. 53–69, surveys the bishops of the Southern states.

46. See Willard Wight, "War Letters of the Bishop of Richmond," *The Virginia Magazine* 67 (July 1959): 259–270; Wight, "Bishop Verot and the Civil War," *Catholic Historical Review* 47 (May 1961): 153–163; Wight, "Bishop Elder and the Civil War," *Catholic Historical Review* 44 (Oct. 1958): 290–306; Wight, ed., "Some Wartime Letters of Bishop Lynch," *Catholic Historical Review* 43 (April, 1957): 20–37.

47. Archbishop John Hughes quoted in Walsh, p. 198. For a life of Hughes's see Richard Shaw, *Dagger John* (New York: Paulist Press, 1977). For Hughes's relationships with the Daughters of Charity, see Joseph Code, *Bishop John Hughes and the Sisters of Charity* (n.c.: Miscellaneous Historical reprint, 1949).

48. Archives of Sisters of Charity of Nazareth, KY (ASCN), reference taken from Diary of Martin Spalding, n.p.

49. CDA, 26 H4. Letter of Bishop James Whelan to Bishop Lynch, Aug. 22, 1861.

50. AOPK, "Activities of St. Agnes," manuscript, p. 9.

51. Jolly, p. 97.

52. Archives of Sisters of Providence, St. Mary of the Woods, IN (ASP), "Extracts from the Annals of the Sisters of Providence re: Civil War," typed sheet.

53. Mug, pp. 64–65.

54. Sr. Eugenia Logan, *History of the Sisters of Providence of St. Mary of the Woods*, vol. II (Terre Haute, IN: Moore-Langen, 1978), p. 73.

55. Perkins, p. 91.

56. Sr. Mary Agnes McGann, *The History of Mother Seton's Daughters: The Sisters of Charity of Cincinnati*, vol. III (New York: Longmans, Green, 1917), p. 47.

57. Archives of Sisters of Mercy, Baltimore (ARSMB), "Baltimore Interests," p. 2.

58. E. Kent Loomis, "History of the U.S. Navy Hospital Ship *Red Rover*," typescript, 1961, p. 3.

59. ACSC, Civil War, "Red Rover" file.

60. J. M. Lucey, "Arkansas Sisters of Mercy in the War," in *Confederate Women of Arkansas in the Civil War* (Little Rock: J. Kellogg, 1907), pp. 135–136.

61. Lucey, pp. 135–136.

62. Evans, p. 87.

63. Perkins, p. 88.

64. Kelly, p. 214.

65. ADC, *Annals of the Civil War*, vol. I, p. 51.

66. Archives of Ursuline Nuns of Galveston, TX (AUNG) "Account taken

from the Annals of the Ursuline Community of Galveston, Texas," typescript, p. 1. See also the Archives of the University of Notre Dame, South Bend, IN (ANDU), papers of Bishop John Odin, New Orleans, VI–2-e. Letters of Louis Chambodut to Odin; Mother St. Pierre Harrington to Odin; Joseph Anstrett to Odin; Napoleon Perché to Odin; Mother St. Pierre Harrington to Stephen Rousselon.

67. ANDU, VI–2-e, Letter of Father Louis Chambodut to Bishop John Odin, October 8, 1861.

68. AUNG, "Account taken from Annals," p. 1.

69. AUNG, "Account taken from Annals," p. 1.

70. AUNG, "Account taken from Annals," pp. 1–2.

71. CDA, 26D3, Bishop Kenrick to Bishop Lynch, May 12, 1861.

72. ADC, "Annals of the Civil War," manuscript, Letter of Fr. Francis Burlando to Fr. Etienne, April 10, 1868, preface, n.p.

73. ASP, "Journal of Mother Cecilia," typescript, n.p.

74. ADC, *Annals of the Civil War*, vol. I, pp. 3–4.

75. Perkins, p. 131.

76. Logan, p. 68.

77. See Rollin Quimby, "The Chaplain's Predicament," *Civil War History* 8 (Mar. 1962): 25–37.

78. The Christian Commission was formed Nov. 15, 1861, by the Young Men's Christian Association, to publish religious tracts, supply nurses, and aid the soldiers.

79. Blield, pp. 107–116; 122–23; see also Aidan H. Germain, "Catholic Military and Naval Chaplains, 1776–1917," *Catholic Historical Review* 15 (July 1929): 172–174.

80. ADC, photocopy of original memo of Abraham Lincoln, Sept. 22, 1862.

81. "Notes and Comments," *Catholic Historical Review* 4 (1918): 387.

82. CDA, 27R4, Letter of Bishop McGill to Bishop Lynch, Sept. 2, 1862.

83. ADC, *Lives of Our Deceased Sisters, Reports of 1862*, p. 29.

84. Elder, pp. 110, 120.

85. Logue, p. 126.

86. ACSC, Civil War, Letter of Mother Angela to Surgeon Pinkney, typescript, Aug. 11, 1863.

87. ASCC, "Memoirs of Sr. Anthony O'Connell," n.p.

88. ADC, *Annals of the Civil War*, vol. I, p. 51.

89. ADC, *Annals of the Civil War*, vol. I, p. 49.

90. Sr. Anne Francis Campbell, "Bishop England's Sisterhood, 1829–1929," Ph.D. Diss., St. Louis University, 1968, pp. 122–123.

91. ASP, Copy of letter of Feb. 25, 1862, in *Indianapolis Sentinel*, n.p.

92. AUNG, "Account Taken from Annals, p. 2.

93. ADC, in *Annals of the Civil War*, manuscript, p. 503. Penciled note, no date, no sender/receiver given.

94. ASCN. See also ANDU, Purcell papers, II–5-a, Letter of Bishop Spalding to Bishop Purcell, Oct. 29, 1861.

95. ASCN. See also ANDU, Spalding to Purcell, Oct. 29, 1861, enclosure of copy of memo of General Robert Anderson to Martin Spalding, Sept. 24, 1861.

96. Archives of the Sisters of Mercy of New York (ARSMNYC), "From the Annals," n.p.

97. *Official Records*, Series I, Vol. IX, pp. 410–411.

98. ANDU, Letter of Bishop Martin Spalding to Bishop John Purcell, Oct. 29, 1861.

99. CDA, 28S2, Letter of Sr. De Sales to Bishop Lynch, Mar. 12, 1863.

100. Mother Bernard McGuire, *The Story of the Sisters of Mercy in Mississippi* (New York: P. J. Kennedy, 1931), p. 20.

101. McGuire, p. 17.

102. ACSC, Civil War, "Red Rover" file.

103. ACSC, Civil War, Mound City account book, manuscript.

104. Cornelius Buckley, *A Frenchman, a Chaplain, a Rebel: The War Letters of Père Louis-Hippolyte Gauché, SJ* (Chicago: Loyola University Press, 1981), p. 166.

105. ADC, Letter of Mother Ann Simeon Norris to the Senate and the House of Representatives, Dec. 8, 1864.

106. *Congressional Globe* Dec. 21, 1864, p. 95; Jan. 5, 1865, p. 127.

5

Catholic Sister Nurses in the Civil War

The key to understanding why military and medical authorities so desired the values brought by the sisters to the Civil War health-care needs lies in the very nature of religious life with its emphasis on community life and charitable service to others as expressed by public, lifelong vows of poverty, obedience, and chastity.

For the sisters, there was an underlying religious and theological basis for a life of service to others. As Jesus Christ gathered apostles and disciples around him, gave them a commandment to love all people, and sent them out to teach, preach, and heal, so did Roman Catholic sisters live in community and engage in various services in order to be faithful to Christ's example. The three vows, which were customarily pronounced for life, were simply a public declaration of the sister's commitment to this life. Thus, a willing sacrifice of one's will, one's material possessions, and one's desire to marry and have children was done in imitation of Christ, who was obedient to God's will, poor in order to share His life with all, and chaste so that His love might be given to all. Admittedly, the authorities generally did not understand the religious lifestyle nor consciously refer to the structure of religious life in requesting the sisters. Rather, they focused on the sisters' nursing experience or on a general impression that the sisters could and would learn to do what was needed. Nevertheless, it was these inherent, underlying qualities of religious life that caused the sisters to be able and willing to respond quickly to the requests, to move to a variety of locations and situations, and to assume the multitude of duties loosely classed as "nursing."

Living out the vow of obedience meant being willing to mobilize oneself or the community to respond to needs of others as articulated through

the requests of legitimate religious authority, usually the superior or
bishop. Poverty was expressed by a simple life style, the sharing of goods
in common, and often, in the mid-nineteenth century, rigorous physical
and material hardships. Chastity, though largely understood in the negative sense of not being married, also implied an attitude of inclusiveness
of all people in a sister's or a community's love and service. In addition,
the constitutions and regulations of the various communities, which provided commonsense wisdom and basic rules for caring for the sick, enabled the sisters to know what to do or to easily learn from one another
once they arrived at the various medical facilities.

Thus, while other female nurses sometimes did serve in comparable
battlefield, transport ship, and hospital situations and performed similar
duties, the sisters were often preferred as nurses because the special
characteristics of their lives enabled them to function as a cohesive group,
to accept difficult physical and material circumstances, and to relate to
the soldiers in a nonsexual, even-handed manner. From the sisters' perspective, the hardships of the Civil War experiences were not minimized.
However, they willingly took on the different situations and duties as
an expansion of their main purpose, which had always been to instruct,
to care for the homeless, and to comfort the sick and dying in imitation
of Jesus Christ, "Amen, I say to you as long as you did it to one of my
least brethren, you did it to me."[1]

While no sisters or lay women are recorded as having been assigned
as nurses to any regiments, sisters did serve in every other place where
there were wounded and sick soldiers. Battlefields, hospital transport
ships, field hospitals, hastily established hospitals in various buildings,
tent hospitals, and their own or other private, already established hospitals were all scenes of the sisters' services, especially in the first two
years of the war. During the last two years, they served in general hospitals specifically built by the Union. These locations varied, but conditions for the soldiers and for themselves were invariably depressing,
dirty, and demoralizing.

Just as the general experiences and functions of the few thousand
female nurses in the Civil War constitute a relatively unknown chapter
in the history of the rebellion, so too, the variety of places the sisters
served and the duties they performed comprise a similar, obscure historical record. Yet, careful examination of extant archival sources shows
that sisters were hardly confined to Catholic hospitals, caring only for
religious needs of soldiers, as might be presumed. Rather, they were
engaged in an amazing number of situations accomplishing a wide variety of duties. The cumulative effect of these accounts shows not only
the sisters' willingness to respond, but also their ability to nurse or quickly
learn to nurse under trying circumstances; their flexibility in adjusting
to constantly changing conditions; and, above all, the underlying reli-

gious commitment that enabled them to respond to these many envi-
ronments and duties.

The display of these qualities and the typical response they elicited in
others is illustrated by the experience of Cincinnati Sister of Charity
Anthony O'Connell. On a transport boat holding 700 men, that was
caught on the shoals at Louisville after the battle of Shiloh in 1862, the
captain told the sisters they would have to leave the ship if they wished
to live. However, Sister Anthony explained, "None would think of doing
so. All expressed their willingness, their determination to remain." The
doctor, seeing the sisters' firm resolve, said, "Since you weak women
display such courage, I, too, will remain."[2]

In their obedient response to requests, sisters were to be found following the movement of men from battlefield to transport ship, to field
and general hospital, and eventually to permanent hospital. A common
practice in the North was to go to the battlefield in order to bring the
men back on Army or US Sanitary Commission transport ships to general
hospitals. At least six communities recorded the horrors of the battlefield
and of the transport ships and of the heroics of the sisters' work. In
almost every instance, the evidence documenting the sisters' activities,
directly or indirectly, includes an awareness of the values of religious
life that initiated and animated their work.

For example, the annals of the Holy Cross Sisters of South Bend,
Indiana, indicate that the sisters' custom was to go out on the battlefield
to "succor the wounded and dying" after the battles, but it was not an
easy task. The "sight of a macerated face and stench of his wounds
dreadful" caused one of the doctors' wives, who traveled with the sisters,
to suggest they "turn to other soldiers." Yet one sister, conscious of the
religious motivation that enabled her to endure the situation, gently
reminded the woman of the Scriptural passage, "Whatsoever you do to
the least of mine, you do to Me." The willingness of the sister to share
her own motivation helped the doctor's wife. The annals record that the
wife remained, and, after that, "could never do enough for wounded
soldiers."[3]

Another battlefield experience attesting to the sisters' willing response
and quick mobility was that of the Daughters of Charity after the Battle
of Gettysburg. The property of the Daughters of Charity in Emmitsburg,
Maryland, a scant ten miles south of Gettysburg, had been the scene of
a Union encampment and General George Meade's headquarters days
before the tragic battle. Confederate scouts moved in as the Union troops
marched toward Gettysburg. Though spared the fighting on their own
land and property, several Daughters of Charity and their priest superior
traveled under a flag of truce to the battleground, reaching it on the
morning of July 5, 1863. They tended some wounded on the field and
then were directed into the town, where all available buildings had been

turned into makeshift hospitals. St. Francis Xavier Catholic Church and the Methodist church, hastily set up with boards across the pews for operating tables, were among the sites of the sisters' work during the next several days as all of Gettysburg turned out to tend the wounded.[4]

A major task after battles was moving the wounded and dying men from the battlefield onto transport boats of the US Sanitary Commission, which went up and down the Ohio, Mississippi, and other rivers. According to eyewitness reports, the horrors of the screams and the sights on the transport ships were compounded by the overcrowding. One of the most graphic descriptions of this experience was that of a Daughter of Charity:

When men, sisters, provisions, horses, etc. were all on board, we were more like sinking than sailing. . . . Here misery was in her fullness and her victims testified to her power by the thousand-toned moans of bitter waves. . . . Here our sisters shared with their poor patients every horror except that of feeling their bodily pains. They were in the lower cabins; the ceiling low, and lighted all day by hanging lamps or candles; the men dying on the floor with only space to stand or kneel between them.[5]

Obviously, most of the wounded, who already may have waited for days on the battlefield, needed attention long before the boats reached an established hospital. "At one time our boat deck looked like a slaughter-house, wounded everywhere," described Cincinnati Charity Sister Theodosia. "I have seen Dr. Blackman cut off arms and limbs by the dozens and consign them to a watery grave. Accompanied by Miss Hatch [Daughter of Mayor Hatch of Cincinnati] or a Sister I would pick my steps among the wounded bodies to follow the doctor, dressing the wounds of those brave boys. . . . The groans of those poor boys as they lay on deck in that pool of blood would rend the stoutest heart."[6]

Of unique interest among sisters serving on transport boats were the four Sisters of the Holy Cross who served on the "Red Rover," a captured Confederate ship, after it was refitted by the Federal Army.[7] Along with five Black female nurses working under their direction, they are considered the pioneers or forerunners of the US Navy Nurse Corps because the "Red Rover" eventually became a Navy vessel in late 1862, carrying over 200 patients.[8] While accounts by the sisters on board the ship are rare, *Harper's Weekly* in May 1863 carried three drawings by Civil War artist Theodore R. Davis, one depicting the "Red Rover" and two showing sisters in the wards moving from soldier to soldier. Part of the caption reads, "The sister is one of those good women whose angelic services have been sung by poets and breathed by grateful convalescents all the world over."[9]

Though not equally eulogized, the Sisters of the Poor of St. Francis of Cincinnati also served on a transport, the "Superior," gathering the wounded Union soldiers from southern battlefields.[10] In addition, the Sisters of Mercy of Cincinnati and the Sisters of St. Joseph of Philadelphia spent time on the hospital transport boats,[11] the former spending the time on the way to Pittsburgh Landing "sewing ticks, folding bandages and preparing supplies."[12]

This battlefield and transport work offered perhaps the greatest challenge to the sisters. The immediacy with which they had to respond when battle occurred, the difficulties of attending to the sick because of the cramped and crowded quarters, the uncertain length of the trip, and the probable lack of any privacy all reflected the sisters' commitment to being flexible.

While battlefield and transport ship conditions were grim, work in the hospitals was almost as difficult since many were makeshift facilities. Even if there was a building, the situation was almost always primitive. For example, in the Cumberland, the Sisters of Charity of Cincinnati recalled that accommodations were poor because hotels and warehouses had been converted into temporary hospitals. In addition, the weather was cold, and the twelve hospitals were some distance from one another, which made it impossible for the sisters to give proper attention to the sufferers. One of the sisters pointed out that crowded into these hospitals at one time were 2,200 soldiers suffering from typhoid fever, pneumonia, scurvy, erysipelas, and other diseases.[13]

The Southern experiences were even more difficult, and sisters laboring there rarely had a chance to stay long even in a makeshift hospital. This situation undoubtedly added to the sisters' work as well as to their frustrations. For example, arriving at Mississippi Springs, Mississippi, to hastily set up a hospital for the sick soldiers being hurried out of Vicksburg, the Sisters of Mercy found that the assigned house was dirty, neglected, and entirely unfurnished. Further, the mattresses had been burned on the railroad cars coming out because they were contaminated, and the sisters lacked the necessary equipment or supplies for cooking. After describing their plight, the sister recorder added, with the characteristic compassion of all sisters, that "the sisters suffered much in seeing the sick suffer."[14]

These primitive conditions taxed the sisters' energies. Nevertheless, previous experience in preparing old houses for schools and hospitals, and working long hours cleaning and scrubbing their own institutions and convents, were familiar tasks for the sisters. Thus, their particular attention to cleaning was a needed and valued skill that contributed to the overall care of the wounded.

Even though the sisters may have been able to restore some cleanliness and order to the temporary medical facilities, the constantly changing nature of the battles brought new challenges to their compassion and ingenuity. Frequently, seriously wounded men were brought hastily to the hospitals on the boats and in ambulances, leaving the sisters no time to get beds and supplies ready. For example, Sister of Charity of Our Lady of Mercy Agatha wrote to South Carolina Bishop Patrick Lynch about the sisters' exhaustion caused by a large crowd of badly wounded men brought in without "one moment's warning." The wounded were carried in on litters, she wrote, and "left before my ward until my heart grew sick and I was compelled to whisper to myself again and again during the day your salutary advice, 'Take it easy.' "[15] She added that these men with broken legs and arms and other dreadful wounds had not tasted a morsel for fifty-two hours and were nearly exhausted.[16]

Writing after the Battle of Fort Donelson, February 16, 1862, Holy Cross Sister Calista recorded one of the more graphic descriptions of the condition of the wounded men. "Many had to be neglected on the field; frozen fingers, ears and feet were the result, but the cooling of the blood must have saved many from bleeding to death. Sometimes men were brought in with worms actually crawling in the wounds. Some were blind, their eyes being shot out."[17]

The difficulties of handling horribly wounded men brought on short notice after the battles was compounded by the fact that there was a limited number of sisters to nurse hundreds of men. As one sister explained, "After one battle there were seven hundred in the hospital and only four sisters to wait on them. It was a heartrending sight to see the poor men holding out their hands to the sisters to attract their attention for many were not able to speak."[18]

No Union hospital had more men crowded in it than the Satterlee Hospital in Philadelphia. A unique handwritten journal kept by the Daughters of Charity at Satterlee Hospital had entries for July 5, 7, 8, 1863. The account indicates that a "great commotion was created throughout the hospital by the arrival of several hundred of the wounded" after the Battle of Gettysburg. This continued for several days until "the hospital [was] filled in every hole and corner with those who have been wounded...and nearly all are from Pennsylvania." The sisters recorded that those who came in on July 7th had been wounded since the 1st. These soldiers told them that other men who were more dangerously wounded were still on the battlefield, since there was no means of removing them. The sisters received orders, then, to "prepare for two thousand more which will make nearly five thousand patients." By July 8, the sisters explained that four rows of beds were in each ward, with the two rows in the center pushed together. Again, demonstrating their willingness to serve where needed and to be attentive to the most critical soldiers, the sisters assisted as much as possible in dressing the wounds since there were few attendants in the wards, and watched the most dangerous cases as many of the soldiers' wounds would frequently bleed during the night, causing death.[19]

Often the sheer numbers of sick and wounded required tents to be set up on the grounds of a general hospital. This was the situation for the Sisters of Mercy from Pittsburgh who, besides being at Stanton Hospital in Washington, also served at West Penn Hospital, Pittsburgh. There, the increased number of wounded and convalescent soldiers caused the erection of the "City of Tents," which one sister said sheltered thousands who had been brought to Pittsburgh from the battlefield, encampments, and prisons.[20] The Sisters of Saint Joseph of Philadelphia also served briefly at two different times at the tent hospitals at Camp Curtin in Pennsylvania, which were opened and closed as the needs dictated.[21]

What is clear from the cumulative archival accounts of the sisters is that their nursing was hardly confined to one place or even to one type of medical facility. While the sisters certainly took the wounded into their own hospitals, in most cases, these were not near the battlesites, and so they went wherever they were asked for, primarily places of immediate need. Nothing in their previous experience, though, could have prepared them for the thousands of men, seriously wounded and ill, who crowded into the hastily converted building or huge government hospitals. Even those communities which had hospitals had never dealt with the numbers of sick and wounded brought in by the war. In addition to the unpredictability of the numbers, the sisters had to face the problems related to evacuating the men when opposing forces moved in. This, too, required both flexibility and ingenuity.

The ingenuity is illustrated well by three Sisters of Mercy, who were with a group of seriously ill Confederates who had been evacuated to several sites at the rear of the line near Pensacola Bay, Florida, in 1861. Faced with the possibility that Union soldiers from Fort Pickens would believe the hospital was deserted and shell it, the sisters paraded back and forth all day in front of it.[22] When the expected Union attack failed to materialize, the evacuees were quickly moved back to the hospital from the hastily constructed open shed in which they had been placed. By then, many of the men had already died from exposure, and the sisters were anxious to get the living back into the hospital. However, as one of the returning sisters wrote, "We were merely settled when too [sic] our astonishment they [Union troops] opened fire on the hospital without the least warning." Frantically, the sisters worked to remove the patients while three shells crashed into the building, one nearly killing a sister.[23]

Another group of sisters who risked the possibility of being shelled was the Ursuline Sisters in Galveston, Texas, after the Battle of Galveston on January 1, 1863. Shells were falling around the convent-turned-hospital when a Confederate courier, dispatched by General John Magruder, came dashing up, yelling for a yellow flag to be immediately put up to keep the building from being hit. As the sisters' annals record, "A search for the desired article was immediately begun, but yellow flags are not easily come by at anytime. Finally, after what seemed an eternity of bursting shells and shuddering earth, someone produced a bit of cream-colored flannel, in reality a sister's old and well-washed winter petticoat."[24]

Even if the evacuation efforts as a result of enemy occupations did not threaten the lives of the sisters or their charges, the confusions and hardships involved in moving with the men were traumatic enough. A typical experience was that of the Vicksburg Sisters of Mercy. They, along with a doctor and wounded Confederate soldiers, moved in boxcars from Meridian to Demopolis to Selma in Mississippi, and then finally to Shelby Springs, Alabama, "boiling coffee by the side of the road." Settling at Shelby Springs in what had once been a resort, the sisters quickly converted the ballroom into a surgical ward. "We had found," Sister M. Ignatius Sumner recalled, "whole rations not too much, we were now put on half rations, until the sick came. The dirt as usual [was] in melancholy ascendancy, and one of the sisters not yet recovered from the jaundice, [and] from exposure."[25] Nonetheless, they made do with limited food, cleaned the building, and readily began the nursing tasks again.

Though the living quarters of the sisters, at least in the North, were improved after the hospital complexes were built, the sisters' personal living conditions in the early years mirrored conditions of the buildings used for hospitals. From Frederick, Maryland, a sister wrote,

When we reached the hospital, we were received by an orderly who showed us our room in an old stone barrack. . . . On entering, the sisters looked at each other and smiled, for it seemed quite too small for the number of occupants. There were ten beds jammed together, at the end of which was an old table and two or three chairs, the only furniture in the room with the exception of an old rickety wash stand and two affairs that seemed to be fixed up to ornament the place. [Yet], . . . we had enough when we saw the condition of the poor wounded soldiers who were without food and nourishment enough, and even that was ill-prepared.[26]

A similar experience is recorded by the Holy Cross Sisters who, arriving in Mound City, Illinois, found Mother Angela "scrubbing the floor . . . and a very miserable barracks of a place, an unfinished warehouse with out even the common necessities of life. One bed and one chair had to do service for five sisters. Mother Angela and I slept on a table on some clothes which had been sent to be washed."[27]

The willingness of the sisters to put up with these difficult physical conditions in their own living quarters stemmed from their general orientation toward simple living and enduring hardship without complaint, as well as from a certain recognition that whatever their own personal hardships, the men they were caring for were in worse condition. This contrasted with the attitude of many of the lay female nurses, who, as Dr. John Brinton remarked, wanted a room and a looking-glass for themselves.[28] Whatever the legitimacy of such requests by the women might have been, the demands were impossible, and even ludicrous, in wartime. Thus, the sisters' demonstrated ability to adjust to the ebb and flow of wounded men, to the physical constraints of the boats and hospital buildings, and to the dangers of the shelling during occupation, combined with their uncomplaining acceptance of cramped and uncomfortable physical quarters for themselves, all caused them to be preferred to other female nurses. Clearly, the qualities inherent in their religious commitment enabled them to make these adjustments.

As has been seen, battlefields, transport boats, tent hospitals, and other temporary facilities were the sites for service by nearly half the communities of sisters. A greater number of sisters, however, nursed in the various buildings designated as hospitals by the Union and Confederate governments. Some, like the Sisters of St. Joseph in Wheeling, West Virginia, nursed in their own hospital when it was leased to the Union government for a military hospital.[29] The Daughters of Charity in New Orleans and Richmond continued to use their own institutions. The same was true for the Daughters of Charity at St. Mary's Hospital in Albany, New York, which had a government contract from March 1863 to the end of the war.[30]

Later, as the Federal Government built huge army hospitals on the "Pavilion" plan,[31] the Daughters of Charity served at hospitals at Point Lookout, Maryland; Lincoln General Hospital in Washington; and Satterlee Hospital in Philadelphia. The sisters' service in some of these newly built government hospitals is clear not only from their own archival sources, but, more significantly, from several official descriptions of the physical layouts of the buildings, which made special provisions for female nurses in general and sisters in particular.

Under Stanton's order of July 20, 1864, instructions for building all general hospitals were to include "quarters for female nurses" and a "chapel."[32] The standard plan provided quarters that were to be a "detached building containing lodging-rooms, dining room, and kitchen for the female nurses."[33] The chapel was to be a "detached building, fitted for the purpose of religious services, so arranged as to be used also as a library and reading room."[34] While this multipurpose room was constructed primarily for the soldiers' use, the fact that it was required presumably made it easier for the sisters to participate in religious services. Thus, the sisters' ability to serve in these permanent army hospitals was enhanced.

As the Union government began to construct various hospitals according to these instructions, some plans made specific provisions for sisters' quarters, notably at Point Lookout, Maryland, and Lincoln General Hospital in Washington (two types of pavilion-constructed hospitals) and also at Satterlee Hospital in Philadelphia. The hospital at Point Lookout, Maryland, was described as arranged like the spokes in a wheel, with about 1,400 beds serving large numbers of Confederate prisoners as well as Union soldiers.[35] Corporal Bishop Crumrine, in his letters, gave a description and map of Point Lookout, corroborating the sisters' presence both in the location of their living quarters and in their work in the kitchen and storerooms.[36] In addition, in circular #4 of the Surgeon General concerning hospital organization and construction, Surgeon J. J. Woodward described the sisters' quarters at Lincoln General Hospital as follows, adding a personal note that was atypical of the rest of his precise description of every other part of the hospital:

The building is 23 by 51 feet, with a wing 16 by 28, forming a letter "L." It is divided into chapel, sitting room, kitchen, etc. Twenty-eight Sisters of Charity were on duty, and I must bear evidence to their efficiency and superiority as nurses. The extra-diet kitchen is under the care of a sister and one is detailed by the superior for each ward. They administer medicine, diet, and stimulants, are under the orders of the ward surgeon, and are responsible to him alone. They have been beloved and respected by the men.[37]

A similar description and personal comment is also provided in the official *Medical and Surgical History of the War of the Rebellion*. Surgeon I. I. Hayes, in charge of Satterlee Hospital, West Philadelphia, said he was "fortunate in being able to engage, as directed when the hospital was first opened, forty Sisters of Charity whose labors have been unceasing and valuable."[38] In describing the elaborate building, he said, "These corridors terminate at the eastern end each in a storehouse, which is two stories high; the second story furnishes quarters for the Sisters of Charity. . . . At the end of the ward which joins the corridor are two rooms, one on either side, ten by eight feet, one of which is used for a wardmaster, the other for a female nurse (Sister of Charity)."[39]

These unusual personal testimonies included in official reports add two important facts to the history of sisters serving in the Civil War. First, through official governmental documentation, the statements establish the accuracy of the record of the sisters' presence. More importantly, the highly unusual nature of words of praise and gratitude inserted in the otherwise very factual accounts supports the view that the sisters were very highly regarded. Thus, the medical authorities wished to make special note of their contribution in official records. No similar comments exist in regard to any other personnel, let alone other female nurses.

Whether on battlefields, transport ships, or in temporary or permanent hospitals, whether serving Union or Confederate soldiers, the sisters took on a multitude of duties subsumed under the title "nurse." During the Civil War, the word "nurse" for both the lay woman and the sister encompassed different activities than the common understanding of the word does today. In general, the sisters, like their lay counterparts, provided services in the areas of administration, direct nursing, housekeeping, cooking, and other support staff functions. For example, sometimes sisters were in charge of the whole hospital, with the sisters' superior assigning sisters and others to various duties within the hospitals, including wards, kitchens, and laundry facilities. More often, however, the sisters nursed in the wards with a doctor or, occasionally, a matron in charge of the hospital. In their nursing duties, the sisters dressed wounds, gave medicines, often tended contagious diseases, and sometimes even assisted with surgery. Cleanliness and nutrition were key elements in preventing disease, keeping infection from spreading, and helping the soldiers regain their strength, so sisters also functioned as housekeepers, laundresses, dietitians, and cooks.

Among documented miscellaneous duties assumed by sisters during the war were obtaining and dispensing the supplies that came from friends, the US Sanitary Commission, and other aid groups. In addition, mediating quarrels among the soldiers, staff, and other personnel, handling special cases such as the female soldiers (usually discovered when they were wounded or sick), and preparing corpses for burial were all tasks that sisters were engaged in. Since the wounded sometimes were prisoners of war, the sisters also cared for them and even visited them later when they were transferred from hospital to prison. Though other female nurses may have assumed most of these same duties, the sisters had a different underlying motivation that sustained them. More importantly, the sisters assumed another major duty consonant with that motivation. Primary in the sisters' view was their desire to be with the dying soldiers, baptizing those who wished it, and encouraging repentance and providing a peaceful atmosphere for all.

A key benefit in having sisters rather than other women work in a hospital was that sisters, because of their religious training, were used to being assigned demanding tasks within the convent and institutional structures, and working and learning easily from each other. Thus, it is valuable to look at the variety and multiplicity of all these tasks in greater detail, especially the sisters' religious duties on behalf of the men.

A typical situation was described by Father Neal Gillespie, brother of Mother Angela of the Holy Cross Sisters, after he had visited Mound

City Hospital, Illinois, where she was in charge, with ten sisters working with her. He explained that each sister had one or two wards for her special care. To assist her was a wardmaster for each ward and a certain number of soldier-nurses from the different regiments. However, in addition to supervising all these, Mother Angela was also the cook for some of the sick as well as the correspondant with various aid societies to get little comforts for the soldiers.[40] In spite of these many tasks, Fr. Gillespie, as a concerned brother, was pleased to say that the doctor in charge tried to provide everything for the sick that the sisters wanted.[41]

Another hospital administrator with a multitude of duties was Charleston Sister De Sales Burns, in charge of the Confederate hospital in White Sulphur Springs, Virginia. Her letters give the most complete account of the sisters' duties in the war. In 1862, for instance, she wrote to Bishop Lynch that they were very much in need of another sister, as the number of patients had increased very rapidly during the previous eight or ten days. She also indicated that she had taken on the duty of staying up with a patient until midnight in order to dispense a special life-sustaining medicine because the doctor needed someone he could count on. She closed the letter by saying that it was late and she still had some eight or ten blisters to dress. In that hospital, as well as in others, the distribution of the medicines was turned over to the sisters because they could be counted on to be conscientious. Willingly, the sisters took on the task, even though they were then almost constantly confined to the wards, barely able to care for all the men they already had.[42]

Since so many more men were sick from disease than from wounds, much of the sisters' work involved nursing men suffering from a variety of diseases. Typhoid, pneumonia, erysipelas (a streptococcal infection), measles, and smallpox were among the contagious diseases frequently encountered. Smallpox was especially dreaded; the Sisters of Mercy of Cincinnati recount that they had the assistance of lay women in getting the wounded on the transport ships "until smallpox broke out. . . . The ladies then fled in dismay, leaving the sisters to continue alone their labor of love and danger."[43]

From November 1862 through the spring of 1863, Sister De Sales was concerned with smallpox, which was first brought in by one wounded soldier and later reappeared among other soldiers in the Confederate hospital in West Virginia. "Employees, patients, and Negroes are all panic stricken," she wrote, as she described the various measures taken to prevent the spread of the disease.[44] The sister, who was to visit a man in the small house in which he was isolated, was told by the doctors "not to protract her visits lest she might take the contagion in her habit to the other patients."[45] For a time, Sister De Sales did assign a sister to the smallpox hospital, but later quarantine regulations caused her to withdraw the sister because there was not a separate room she could occupy.[46]

While the majority of the sister nurses dealt with diseases similar to those described by Sister De Sales, they might also be asked to assume other tasks, especially if there was a shortage of doctors. However, the only recorded instance of a sister assisting with surgery was that of Sister Anthony O'Connell. She did not specifically explain what her responsibilities were, but judging from the surgical practice of the time, she probably assisted by providing surgical instruments and dressings, perhaps administering the chloroform or ether, or holding limbs as the doctors amputated.

She reminisced,

The Sisters of Charity of Cincinnati went to the war, as nurses, but it sometimes fell to their lot to be assistant surgeons. After the battle of Shiloh the young surgeons were off on a kind of lark as they called it, to prevent blue mal. I became Dr. Blackman's assistant in the surgical operations. He expressed himself well pleased with the manner in which I performed this duty and indeed I was well pleased to be able to alleviate in any degree the sufferings of these heroic souls.[47]

Consistently permeating the duties that the sisters performed was an awareness of the soldiers' sufferings and a desire to alleviate them. Though the tasks of administering the wards, dressing wounds, giving medicines, treating diseases, and even assisting surgeons were all duties that even today come under the heading of nursing, cleaning and cooking were also key responsibilities of the sisters. Again, the constitutions of many of the orders spelled out the importance of cleanliness and good food as a major part of proper care of the sick. Thus, the sisters came to their wartime duties with a clear understanding and knowledge of all the needed basic nursing skills.

Whether or not the sisters were officially in charge of housekeeping, generally their first task upon coming to any building designated as a "general" hospital was to make the place habitable. The Sisters of Mercy from Vicksburg recalled going to take charge of Mississippi Springs Hospital, at the time a "fashionable watering place" about forty miles from Vicksburg. The steward had had to whisper something about "smallpox" to get the guests to leave. The frightened inhabitants took flight precipitously, leaving the sisters "such an accumulation of dirt to clean up as they had never beheld."[48]

The Sisters of Providence took charge of the cooking, cleaning, washing, and general housekeeping of the military hospital in Indianapolis, reported the *Indianapolis Daily Journal* in 1861, praising their "unpleasant but noble duty."[49] Clearly, the sisters made a significant improvement, for in 1864, the same newspaper reported that the laundry, under the sisters' direction, was washing and ironing a thousand pieces of clothing and five hundred sheets every week.[50]

At the Satterlee Hospital in Philadelphia, housing 7,000 men after the battle of Gettysburg, Sister Angela, a Daughter of Charity, was in charge of thirty women who did the laundry. A major responsibility was to count and sort the clothes from the various patients and departments and return them when clean. Due to the great influx of patients, Sister Angela had to be reassigned by the sister superior to one of the wards and the surgeon assigned a "reliable gentleman" and several male assistants to do the heavy laundry work, presuming that the work would be done even better with the extra help. However, as the sisters' journal records, "It became in a few days a kind of Bedlam, dancing, singing, quarreling, and fighting constituted a large part of each day's work and at the end of the first week, doctors, druggists, clerks, Ward Masters looked for their clothes in vain. All were mixed together and everything in confusion."[51] After one more week's trial, Sister Angela went back to the laundry, where order was restored. The return to normality attested not only to her ability to keep things clean, but also to her ability to organize things and keep peace.[52]

Besides actually doing the laundry or supervising those who did it, sisters, especially in smaller hospitals, often distributed it, thus ensuring that supplies were equitably distributed and clothing given to the right people. This task was not equally demanding in all hospitals, probably due to the fluctuations in occupancy. For example, just distributing the linen was an "arduous task" for Sister Stanislaus, a Sister of Charity of Our Lady of Mercy, in the Confederate hospital in West Virginia.[53] On the other hand, at Mound City, Illinois, a Holy Cross Sister was placed in the linen room so she would have time to visit the sick and poor in the neighborhood.[54] Clearly, time was not wasted.

In addition to making sure the hospital and the linen and clothing were clean, the sisters were concerned with providing the basic dietary necessities for the soldiers, as well as preparing special meals. An example of this can be inferred from a letter of Frank Hamilton, the surgeon in charge of St. Joseph's Government Hospital, Central Park, New York, to Sister Ulrica, the superior. The sisters must have requested a special dinner for the soldiers because Hamilton wrote that it would give him great pleasure to grant the sisters' request for a Thanksgiving dinner for the men.[55] At the same hospital, the sisters also had been looking for a resident baker so that they might directly supervise the making of special delicacies for the men. Hamilton granted this request as well.[56]

Those outside the hospitals also confirmed the special attention sisters gave to the dietary needs of the soldiers. An article in the Indianapolis

Daily Journal, March 8, 1864, reported on its investigative tour of City Hospital. The editors commented favorably on everything; however, the cooking and the Sisters of Providence were singled out for special mention. The sisters superintended and directed all the domestic arrangements and, the paper noted, "give comfort and cheer to the sick in a thousand kind attentions."[57]

Part of the reason the sisters' efforts were often called "excellent" was due to their ability to assess difficult situations and make appropriate changes. This was as true in dietary areas as it was in the laundry. For example, Sister De Sales, a Sister of Charity of Our Lady of Mercy, recalled that complaints in the dining room caused her to go into there, although it wasn't her area of responsibility, and attend to the men's concerns. She humorously recalled that before opening the dining-room doors for the first meal, the crush of people at the door was indescribable because the men didn't know she was there. She wrote:

The man who opened the door was compelled to close it again per force—as soon as they became quiet, I went to the door. As soon as they saw me, one man called out "boys, it is a lady that is here—fall back." Every man fell back to his place and they walked in two by two in perfect order. When the next meal came round, every man stood in rank at the door, and walked in perfect silence, taking off hats and saying good morning Sister. As one came in he said, "There is no 'storming the battery now' Sister."[58]

Realizing that a shortage of dishes and lack of organization were causes of the complaints, she got permission from the doctors to buy cups and spoons and directed that the ward masters march their men in two by two. No doubt, previous experience with schoolchildren helped her considerably.

Thus, part of the sisters' responsibility in most hospitals was obtaining and distributing food, clothing, and other supplies. These tasks were handled by the sisters partly because provisions and supplies were often connected with particular dietary or housekeeping duties and partly because the sisters sometimes had ingenious ways of obtaining supplies for the hospital and themselves when no one else could. More importantly, the sisters could be trusted with the equitable distribution of the food and medical supplies.

Generally, food and other supplies were scarce, though the sisters did recount provisions' coming from the US Sanitary Commission, various aid societies, and friends. These donations were welcome as conditions were often destitute, especially in the South. For example, in Frederick, Maryland, a Daughter of Charity recalled, "Our food consisted of the soldiers' rations, and not enough of them. It was served . . . on broken dishes, with old knives and forks, red with rust. The patients often amused us at mealtime by saying, 'Sisters, there is no need for the doctor to order us the tincture of iron, three times a day; don't you think we get enough off our table service.' "[59]

A more critical experience was that of the Vicksburg Mercy Sisters, who followed the Confederate sick from hospital to hospital as the Union lines closed in on them. Typical of the sisters' generosity and foresight, they brought their own provisions with them. As Sister M. Ignatius Sumner recalled later, "It was well we did because though there were provisions in the country, little experience and forethought in collecting and distributing them and officers who were 'busy making themselves friends of the mammon of iniquity,' distributing supplies to their friends, left the Sisters trying to meet the needs of the sick."[60]

Although the South did not have a Sanitary Commission, individual benefactors, as well as groups, were organized to assist. For example, Sister De Sales reported that the South Carolina Association sent to the Montgomery Sulphur Springs Hospital, probably in 1864, another large box of clothing; five gallons of brandy, port, and cherry wine; sugar; tea; coffee; and a variety of other staples.[61] Of particular note are the recollections of the Daughters of Charity in Richmond, who reported that Mrs. Jefferson Davis often came to the hospital to see the sick Union soldiers and supplied them with tobacco, cigars, soap, razors, and anything they asked for. She requested the sisters not to let patients know who she was, commenting that the Confederates would be well supplied by the Southerners but that the Union soldiers needed things.[62]

In addition, the sisters often used their own ingenuity in securing provisions. In the fall of 1863, Sister De Sales wrote to Bishop Lynch several times requesting his permission to go to Baltimore to get needed supplies. One of her arguments was that "the Sisters of Charity cross continually and bring over any amount of things"[63] to the sisters in Lynchburg. She promised that since there were two flags of truce each month, she would not be gone longer than two weeks.

Besides getting supplies for the hospital, the sisters, especially in the South, had to devise ways of getting clothing for themselves. For example, the Sisters of Mercy of Vicksburg described the rabbit-skin shoes that Father Francis X. Leray, their chaplain, constructed for all of them, and added, "We sewed our own clothes [black] with white thread, and we made him [Leray] trousers out of a shawl, and a brown delaine shirt from a dress. A calico [dress] for our postulant cost $113, and she was much afraid the Father would covet it as a homespun dress had gone for a shirt."[64]

The experience of these limited supplies and donations had its humorous side. A Sister of Charity recounted a story of the sisters trying to get eggs for their sick Union soldiers from various benefactors. Finally, a large box arrived from the North, and everyone eagerly crowded around to see the opening of the box. Unfortunately, the eggs, long in transit and short in freshness, burst over the spectators when the lid was opened.[65]

The supplies that the sisters received from others or procured themselves had to be carefully distributed, a task that was often entrusted to the sisters. Special placards were printed with words such as, "All articles, donations, etc., for the use of the soldiers here, are to be placed under the care of the Sisters, as also, paper, books, clothing, money and delicacies."[66] Clothing, food, and other supplies intended for the patients, but taken by others or diverted to officers, seemed to be a common difficulty. For example, on November 16, 1862, Surgeon Frank Hamilton, at St. Joseph Hospital, Central Park, reminded the hospital staff that whatever was received as private or public contributions intended for the soldiers must be held sacred for that purpose. No officer or attendant was permitted, under any circumstances, to appropriate them to his own use. Supported by this order, the Sisters of Charity of New York, serving at the hospital, were designated to oversee the contributions. Hamilton believed in their integrity and in their impartial distribution of goods.[67]

The sisters' tasks of nursing, supervision, housekeeping, cooking, and procuring and distributing supplies flowed from the general nature of serving the direct needs of the wounded soldiers and caring for them in some kind of institutional setting. Often these duties were carried out by other female or male nurses and assistants as well. Those working with the sisters, however, generally turned to them for assistance because of the sisters' training and experience, their general religious commitment, or their reputation as women who would be honest and impartial toward all. These qualities, of course, were the direct result of the lifestyle and purpose of the sisters.

In addition to these duties, which might be considered normal "nursing" tasks for the Civil War period, sisters sometimes were called on to engage in two other activities. Their reputation as dedicated women enabled them to respond to specific situations of peacemaking and of attention to female soldiers. Two situations where sisters were called on to resolve arguments illustrated the respect that the men had for the sisters, both as women and as sisters.

One instance was at a hospital in Winchester, Virginia. The Daughters of Charity recounted that after hearing "loud threats and angry jargon" coming from the kitchen, two sisters hurried there and found two "colored men," a cook and a nurse, fighting. The sisters forced them apart by stepping between them and mildly requested each man to calm himself. Acknowledging the sisters' request, the men stopped with no further incident.[68] In a slightly different situation, at Antietam, a Northern steward and a Southern surgeon had a disagreement, and one challenged the other to meet him in a quiet spot. With loud, angry threats, both withdrew to an old shed. At first, no one was willing to interfere; then, one of the Daughters of Charity followed them and after "speaking to them firmly and reproachingly," she persuaded them to separate. Like docile children they returned to their posts.[69]

Quarreling and fighting certainly were expected events among men in the camps and hospitals; however, a much more unusual situation for the sisters was that of caring for women dressing as men. Though female soldiers were not common in the Civil War, over 400 women disguised themselves as men in order to serve in the army, to be with a husband or lover, or to serve as a spy.[70] That women served at all illustrates the inadequacies of the recruitment techniques and physical exams given to any Union or Confederate soldier. Often, the females were not discovered until they were wounded or sick. Thus, in hospitals where there were sisters, such cases were assigned to them and several different communities of sisters noted their care of such women. The records of the Holy Cross Sisters record an incident of a young girl who enlisted with the express purpose of shooting her stepfather. When she became ill, a doctor discovered her sex and her pregnant condition; the sisters cared for her, and their kindness and concern caused the girl to become a Catholic convert.[71] Because of the sisters' experience in the education of young women, a female soldier was brought to the Daughters of Charity in Richmond, Virginia, so that she might be "taught to know her place and character in life."[72]

In another situation in Memphis, a Holy Cross sister wrote about a young orderly, pretty and small, who became very ill and was sent to her ward, wrapped in a shawl. The surgeon in charge sent word to the sister to keep the patient separate and not to have the men wait on "him." The sisters recalled that "he" seemed a "pretty hard case who would curse and swear and scream." The screaming finally gave the soldier away. The sisters cared for her for three weeks until she died and also baptized her before her death.[73] In most situations, if the sick female lived, she was usually sent home immediately, so the sisters' contact with these women was limited. Apparently, however, it was strong enough for the sisters to have the opportunity to discuss religious values with the women.[74]

The opportunity to relate to the soldiers, and sometimes other doctors and staff, in a religious way was the most unique aspect of the sisters' work. This religious dimension was also the quality that motivated and enabled them to carry out the other nursing duties that were often demanding and difficult, even for those sisters who had previous nursing experience. Cincinnati Charity Sister Ambrosia said of her arduous tasks in the Cumberland, "Our duties [were] fatiguing and often disgusting to flesh and blood, but we were amply repaid by conversions, repentances, and the removal to a great extent of certain prejudices to our Holy Faith."[75] Her attitude succinctly expresses the nursing experience of all the Civil War sisters.

Regardless of how the sisters became involved in the war, where they worked, or what activities they engaged in, the written accounts that remain all stress the sisters' overwhelming desire and need to offer spiritual support to the wounded and dying, and often to the doctors and officers as well. Typical of the hagiographic writing of the period, the sisters' archival accounts and the two published accounts that exist recount primarily the conversion experiences and deathbed religious conversations.[76] In retrospect, much of the seeming emphasis on this aspect of the sisters' experience may be due to the fact that most extant material written by the sisters was completed shortly after the war, and they may have wished to emphasize the religious focus of their work. Further, specific questions such as the number of baptisms were asked for in some written accounts.[77] However, given the facts of the sisters' life of religious commitment, the major purposes of their communities, the mid-nineteenth-century Protestant-Catholic tension, and the desire of the minority, immigrant Catholic church for an increase in numbers, the emphasis on conversion stories is probably not just a fact of skewed records.

Even tasks as simple as writing letters for soldiers, a common occupation of women who visited soldiers, was done for a different motive by the sisters. One sister, trying to give examples of difficult situations the sisters sometimes found themselves in, wrote of a dying young man who seemed impervious to the sister's attempts to speak to him about his soul. Finally, he asked her to write a letter to his fiancée, promising that he would then listen to her. The sisters' account records: "The poor sister thinking that the soul was worth too much to stop at any terms asked him what she should say, and wrote accordingly. All the ward was attentive to hear it. When done, it was read to him. He was satisfied now to do as she advised, and being prepared for baptism died with very pious disposition."[78]

Among the corporal works of mercy articulated in the Catholic tradition are the admonitions to heal the sick and to bury the dead; the spiritual works include praying for the living and the dead. Thus, the sisters, in a blend of practical action and spiritual wisdom, often combined religion and the care of the sick and wounded. As a consequence, they frequently had a closer relationship with the men than some visiting clergyman.

For example, in a Washington hospital, a man called out, "I want a clergyman . . . a white bonnet [referring to the head dress of the sisters] clergyman, such as you ladies have." He was not a Catholic but continued to ask for a catechism or any book that would instruct him on the "White

Bonnet Religion"[79] Another instance where the men preferred the sisters to the clergy was at the prison in Alton, Illinois, which was frequently visited by a Catholic priest. While he was there, a sick man asked for baptism, but when approached by a priest, cried out, "No, I want Sister to baptize me!" In an unusual gesture, the priest told the sister, a Daughter of Charity, to baptize the soldier while he stood looking on.[80]

The baptisms, while extremely important to the sisters, were not universally appreciated by others with whom the sisters worked. One sister wrote to Charleston, South Carolina, Bishop Lynch saying that some of the doctors "are frantic at the influence we have over the men and at the number that have been baptized." She recounted that, largely because of the admiration the men came to have for the sisters' work, they were receptive to being baptized Catholics when they were dying. Though the fear of dying may have also contributed to the soldiers' requests for baptism, the sister also recorded at least three other men, not in danger of death, who studied the Catechism and asked for baptism.[81]

Though all communities ministered to the sick and assisted the dying, it is specifically recorded that the Sisters of St. Joseph, Wheeling, also prepared the corpses for burial and made the shrouds.[82] Further, the Indianapolis *Daily Journal* noted that at the City Hospital there, the Sisters of Providence beautifully arranged the dead rooms, hanging them with "white muslin, festooned with crepe, and at the head of each room are the Stars and Stripes also draped in mourning."[83] This special attention to concern for the dead came from the spiritual injunction of the corporal work of mercy that enjoined them to bury the dead.

In spite of the demands of both their physical and spiritual duties, the sisters had occasional moments of respite. For example, from White Sulphur Springs in March 1862, Sister De Sales wrote to her sisters about the beautiful rosebuds and the japonicas given for their altar by a storekeeper in town. After she explored the mountains "before the hospital fills in," she described the scenery as "truly beautiful" even though the sulphur water was "horrid."[84]

More often, however, the sisters' labors caused them fatigue, disease, and sometimes death. A Daughter of Charity recalled that the sisters, hoping for a little rest after the exhaustion of caring for the Confederate wounded, were startled by a terrible noise just as they were settling down in chapel. Running out, they momentarily thought it was the day of judgment as they saw bodies of men and the heavens on fire. The powder magazine had exploded, so: "With a right good will we went to work and we took good care not to console ourselves again with the thought of rest, fearing another catastrophe."[85]

Exhaustion was one consequence of Civil War nursing for the sisters, but sickness had more serious consequences. Confederate nurse Kate Cumming recalled a meeting with her old friend, Mrs. Ella King Newsome, whose health had been ruined by extensive nursing duties in Atlanta. This was the same tent hospital, Cumming recalled, which the Daughters of Charity had left because they, too, could not stand the work or exposure to the weather.[86]

Sisters, too, sometimes fell victim to the diseases to which they were exposed. For example, Sister De Sales wrote to her sisters back in Charleston, South Carolina, in September 1862, saying, "I can scarcely write my little finger is exceedingly sore. I am fearful that I have contracted erisipelas as I have three cases of it in my ward."[87] Clearly, as the records show, the sisters were not sheltered or protected. They were not only fully engaged in various nursing tasks, but also suffered the consequences inherent in those tasks. Some sisters lived to see the monument to the "Nuns of the Battlefield" erected in Washington, D.C., in 1914, but several sisters died in the course of their labors in the Civil War.[88] Sister of Charity of Nazareth Sister Lucy Dosh was given a military funeral as the first sister to die while on duty. Assigned to nurse typhoid fever patients, she died at the Central Hospital in Paducah, Kentucky, on December 29, 1861. Her remains were taken to Uniontown, Kentucky, by gunboat under a flag of truce and then overland to the cemetery near St. Vincent Academy in Union County.[89]

While Mary Ryan Jolly in her research indicates that the only Daughter of Charity who died was Sister Consolata Conlon, who was buried with military honors on the banks of the Potomac,[90] a search of the records at the Motherhouse at Emmitsburg, Maryland, indicates that at least two other sisters also died. The sisters' handwritten account book of their experiences at Satterlee Hospital in Philadelphia indicates that two sisters had died during the time they were there,[91] although the official community records list only a Sister Xavier Lucot.[92] Jolly, on the other hand, does not list this sister at all for Satterlee, but lists a Sister Xavier Van Drome as serving at Satterlee during the war.[93] This is an apparent error, perhaps in last names, because the religious name of the sister—"Xavier" in this case—was not given out until after a sister died. Jolly also lists a Sister Catherine Chrismer as having served at Gettysburg,[94] but the community records list her as dying in 1862 at Mt. Hope Infirmary in Baltimore, an institution not otherwise known to have Civil War soldiers.[95]

The Holy Cross Sisters record the death in 1862 of Sister Elise O'Brien, whose body was given a military escort, at the general hospital in Cairo, Illinois,[96] and of Sister Fidelis Lawler, at Mound City Hospital, Illinois, whose body had to be taken by boat due to flooding at the Ohio River.[97] Sister Gerard Ryan of the Mercy Sisters of New York, serving in North

Carolina, died in 1864 "as a result of hardships."[98] At the Douglas Hospital in Washington, Sister Coletta O'Connor of the Baltimore Mercy Sisters died in 1864 and was buried with the military honors of a major.[99]

Whether death, disease, or exhaustion was the consequence of the sisters' many services, a Daughter of Charity in Richmond eloquently summarized the sisters' approach to their nursing:

Day and night our Sisters constantly administered by turns to soul and body; nourishment, remedies and drinks to the body and as best they could "living waters to the soul." Indeed, as far as possible, our dear Sisters subtracted from food and rest, the dying and suffering state of these poor men, causing them to make all sacrifices to them even joyfully, regarding such sacrifices as only a drop or cipher compared to the crying duties before them. While they were attending to some, others would be calling to them most piteously to give their wounds some relief.[100]

Clearly, the sisters were not the only women nurses functioning on battlefield, ships, and in hospitals, carrying out a multitude of duties, and often suffering from the consequences of hard work. They were but a sixth of such women, who themselves were but a small part of those who cared for the sick and wounded during the Civil War. What set them apart was the entire context of religious life, which consciously and unconsciously shaped the sisters and their actions. The result of this shaping produced a group of women like no other, willing to serve in a variety of places and doing a multitude of jobs in a manner that exhibited dedication and organization. But no matter what others saw as the value of their nursing services, the sisters saw themselves as missionaries promoting religion, not nursing pioneers opening up new areas for themselves or other women. To them the fundamental purpose for serving was to care for the sick and suffering as Jesus Christ would, bringing sick and dying men to think of God in their suffering and to be baptized if they were not. Often, in their memoirs and letters, the sisters seemed cognizant of the hard work needed to accomplish their job, but, they seemed to have no particular awareness that they had a skill that could or should be promoted among other women. Basically, whether the sisters came from hospital service or from teaching, care of children, or some other ministry, the areas in which they served in the Civil War and the duties which they performed simply were viewed as an extension of their ministry of doing good for those in need. As one Holy Cross sister succinctly stated, "We were not prepared as nurses, but kind hearts lent willing hands and ready sympathy and with God's help, we did much toward alleviating suffering."[101]

NOTES

1. Archives of the Sisters of Mercy of Vicksburg, Mississippi, (ARSMV), Handwritten copy of Mother M. de Sales Browne's *Constitution of the Sisters of Mercy*, Chapter II, Section 1, n.p.

2. Archives of Sisters of Charity of Cincinnati (ASCC), "Memoirs of Sr. Anthony O'Connell," n.p.

3. Congregational Archives of the Sisters of the Holy Cross, Saint Mary's, Notre Dame, IN (ACSC), Civil War, "Civil War narrative about Mother Angela," n.p.

4. Archives of the Daughters of Charity, Emmitsburg, MD (ADC), *Annals of the Civil War*, vol. I, pp. 40–47.

5. ADC, *Annals of the Civil War*, vol. I, pp. 19–20.

6. ASCC, "Memoirs of Sr. Theodosia," n.p.

7. Records in the Archives of the Sisters of the Holy Cross seem to indicate some sisters may have been on board the ship earlier than the records of the US Navy indicate (see Loomis below); however, the discrepancy might be explained by the fact that the "Red Rover" was an Army ship for a period of time after it was captured, and the Sisters may have been serving for the Union Army.

8. E. Kent Loomis, "History of the U.S. Navy Hospital Ship *Red Rover*," typescript, 1961, p. 7.

9. *Harper's Weekly* 7, No. 332 (May 9, 1863): 300–301.

10. Ellen Ryan Jolly, *Nuns of the Battlefield* (Providence, RI: Providence Visitor, 1927), p. 118.

11. Sr. Marie Kostka Logue, *Sisters of St. Joseph of Philadelphia: A Century of Growth and Development* (Westminster, MD: The Newman Press, 1950), pp. 127–129.

12. Mary Ellen Evans, *The Spirit Is Mercy: The Sisters of Mercy in the Archdiocese of Cincinnati, 1858–1958* (Westminster, MD: The Newman Press, 1959), pp. 90–91.

13. ASCC, "Memoirs of Sr. Ambrosia," n.p.

14. Archives of Sisters of Mercy, Vicksburg (ARSMV), Sr. M. Ignatius Sumner, "Register of the Events from the Foundation of the Convent of the Sisters of Mercy, Vicksburg, Miss.," p. 7.

15. CDA, 29W6, Sister Agatha to Bishop Patrick Lynch, Nov. 10, 1863.

16. CDA, 29W6.

17. ACSC, Civil War, Archives Narrative, Saint Mary's Convent, Vol. 1, "Memoirs of Sr. Calista," pp. 211–212.

18. ACSC, "Memoirs of Sr. Calista," pp. 211–212.

19. ADC, Satterlee notebook, manuscript, pp. 50–51.

20. Archives of Sisters of Mercy of Pittsburg (ARSMP).

21. Logue, p. 129.

22. Michael Gannon, *Cross in the Sand: The Early Catholic Church in Florida* (Gainsville: University of Florida Press, 1967), p. 176.

23. Gannon, p. 176.

24. Archives of Ursuline Nuns, Galveston Texas (AUNG), "Annals," p. 4. See also Archives Notre Dame University (ANDU), VI–2-e, Letter of Chambodut to Bishop Odin, Oct. 8, 1861.

25. ARSMV, Sr. M. Ignatius Sumner, p. 18.

26. ADC, *Annals of the Civil War*, vol. I, p. 28.

27. ACSC, "Memoirs of Sr. Calista," pp. 211–212.

28. John Brinton, *Personal Memoirs of John H. Brinton* (New York: The Neale Publishing Co., 1914), p. 294.

29. Archives of the Sisters of St. Joseph, Wheeling, West Virginia (ACSJW).

30. ADC, Albany, "St. Mary's Hospital," p. 11.

31. U.S. Surgeon General's Office, *Reports on the Extent and Nature of the Materials Available for the Preparation of a Medical and Surgical History of the Rebellion*, Circular No. 6 (Philadelpia: J.B. Lippincott, 1865), p. 153.

32. Joseph K. Barnes, et al., *The Medical and Surgical History of the War of the Rebellion, 1861–65*, vol. III (Washington: Government Printing Office, 1875), pp. 942–45.

33. Barnes, vol. I, p. 154.

34. Barnes, vol. I, p. 154.

35. Edwin Beitzell, *Point Lookout Prison Camp for Confederates* (Abell, MD: E. W. Beitzell, 1972), p. 22.

36. Beitzell, p. 104.

37. The quoted description by Woodward is from a description furnished by Brevet Lieutenant Colonel J.C. McKeen, Surgeon, USA, surgeon in charge. The hospital was constructed in 1862 and first occupied in January 1863, with twenty pavilion wards and support-services buildings covering thirty acres; it closed August 22, 1865, after handling almost 25,000 patients. Circular No. 6, pp. 157–158.

38. Barnes, vol. III, p. 926.

39. Barnes, vol. III, p. 928.

40. ACSC, Civil War, Letter of Fr. Neal Gillespie to Mrs. Gillespie, Jan. 6, 1862.

41. ACSC, Civil War, Letter of Fr. Gillespie to Mrs. Gillespie, Jan. 6, 1862.

42. CDA, 27C6, Letter of Sr. De Sales to Bishop Lynch, April 15, 1862.

43. Evans, p. 91.

44. CDA, 28C7, Letter of Sr. De Sales to Bishop Lynch, Nov. 14, 1862.

45. CDA, 28C7.

46. CDA, 28Sl, Letter of Sr. De Sales to Dr. Woodville, Mar. 7, 1863.

47. ASCC, "Memoirs of Sr. Anthony O'Connell," n.p.

48. ARSMV, Sr. M. Ignatius Sumner, p. 36.

49. Archives of Sisters of Providence, St. Mary of the Woods IN (ASP), *Indianapolis Daily Journal*, June 18, 1861, typed copy.

50. ASP, *Indianapolis Daily Journal*, June 11, 1864, typed copy.

51. ADC, Satterlee notebook, manuscript, pp. 27–29.

52. ADC, Satterlee notebook, manuscript, p. 29.

53. CDA, 27T4, Letter of Bishop Augustine Verot to Bishop Lynch, Sept. 19, 1862.

54. ACSC, "Civil War narrative about Mother Angela," n.p.

55. Archives of the Sisters of Charity of New York City, (ASCNYC), item 243. Letter of Surgeon Frank Hamilton to Sister Ulrica, Nov. 19, 1862.

56. ASCNYC, item 240, Letter of Charles Devlin to Dr. McDougal, Oct. 30, 1862.

57. ASP, *Indianapolis Daily Journal*, Mar. 8, 1864, typed copy.

58. CDA, 28EI, Letter of Sr. De Sales to Bishop Lynch, Nov. 25, 1862.

59. ADC, *Annals of the Civil War*, vol. I, p. 28.

60. ARSMV, Sr. M. Ignatius Sumner, p. 36.

61. CDA, 30K7, Letter of Sr. De Sales to Bishop Lynch, Mar. 18, 1864.

62. ADC, *Annals of the Civil War*, vol. II, pp. 64.

63. CDA, 29N5, Letter of Sr. De Sales to Bishop Lynch, Sept. 14, 1863.

64. ARSMV, Sr. M. Ignatius Sumner p. 19.

65. ASCC, "Memoirs of Sr. Anthony O'Connell," n.p.

66. ADC, *Annals of the Civil War*, vol. I, p. 10.

67. ASCNYC, Memo from Surgeon Frank Hamilton to "Those in charge," Nov. 16, 1862.

68. ADC, *Annals of the Civil War*, vol. II, p. 57.

69. ADC, *Annals of the Civil War*, vol. II, p. 71.

70. Mary E. Massey, *Bonnet Brigades: American Women and the Civil War* (New York: Alfred Knopf, 1966), p. 17.

71. ACSC, Civil War, Archives Narrative, Saint Mary's Convent, vol. I, "Memoirs of Sr. Placides," p. 226.

72. ADC, *Annals of the Civil War*, vol. I, p. 62. See another example in Mary A. Holland, *Our Army Nurses* (Boston: B. Wilkens, 1895), p. 341.

73. ACSC, Civil War, Archives Narrative, Saint Mary's Convent, vol. I, "Memoirs of Sr. Matilda," p. 227.

74. See ACSC, "Memoirs of Sr. Matilda," p. 227, for another instance at Mound City Hospital, Illinois, where a female soldier was sent home from the cavalry after she became ill.

75. ASCC, "Memoirs of Sr. Ambrosia," n.p.

76. See Jolly; see also George Barton, *Angels of the Battlefield* (Philadelphia: Catholic Art Publishing Co., 1898).

77. ADC, Burlando's outline for writing the accounts of the war.

78. ADC, *Annals of the Civil War*, vol. I, p. 10.

79. ADC, *Annals of the Civil War*, vol. I, pp. 7–8.

80. ADC, *Annals of the Civil War*, vol. I, p. 5.

81. CDA, 27P5, Sr. De Sales to Bishop Lynch, Aug. 27, 1862.

82. Sr. Rose Anita Kelly, *Song of the Hills: The Story of the Sisters of St. Joseph of Wheeling* (Wheeling, WV: Sisters of St. Joseph, 1962), p. 220.

83. ASP, *Indianapolis Daily Journal*, June 11, 1864, typed copy.

84. CDA, 27B3, Letter of Sr. De Sales to Sr. Agatha, Mar. 11, 1862.

85. ADC, *Annals of the Civil War*, manuscript, Account of Sr. Gabriella, pp. 478–481.

86. Kate Cumming, *Kate: The Journal of a Confederate Nurse* (Baton Rouge: Louisiana State University Press, 1959), p. 262.

87. CDA, 27S4, Letter of Sr. de Sales to "My Beloved Sisters [Sister?]," Sept. 14, 1862.

88. See Jolly's introduction in *Nuns of the Battlefield*, pp. viii-ix, and references throughout the text.

89. Sr. Mary Agnes McGann, *The History of Mother Seton's Daughters: The Sisters of Charity of Cincinnati, vol. III* (New York: Longmans, Green, 1917), p. 47.

90. Jolly, pp. 73–74.

91. ADC, Satterlee Record Book, n.p.

92. ADC, Record sheet of Sr. Xavier Lucot.

93. Jolly, p. 83.

94. Jolly, p. 78.

95. ADC, Record sheet of Sr. Catherine Chrismer.

96. Jolly, p. 141.

97. ACSC, Civil War, Notebook of Sister Paula, typescript, "Civil War Narrative," pp. 1–7.

98. Jolly, p. 219.

99. Sr. Mary Loretto Costello, *The Sisters of Mercy of Maryland, 1855–1930* (St. Louis, MO: B. Herder, 1931), p. 48.

100. ADC, *Annals of the Civil War*, vol. I, p. 15.

101. ACSC, Civil War, Archives Narrative, Saint Mary's Convent, Vol. I, "Memoirs of Mother Augusta," p. 216.

6

Contemporaneous Attitudes about the Catholic Sisters in the Civil War

Regardless of how the sisters themselves regarded the inner religious purpose for their external work, what other people actually thought about sisters' nursing in the war clearly served both to define the sisters and to set them apart from other lay women nurses. The range of recorded perceptions and attitudes about them demonstrate that the sisters were definitely not invisible women. In the midst of the chaos of the war, people were aware of their presence and commented on them. These attitudes form the basis for comparing the sisters to other female nurses, for comprehending why the sisters were chosen for the work, and for understanding why the sisters were better known and understood after the war than before. More importantly, a study of the various attitudes toward the sisters reveals whether the religious values motivating the sisters' work were discernible to others.

Praise for the sisters was the typical, though not completely universal, response of those who came in contact with them during the Civil War. The attitudes, as expressed in writing by doctors, other women with whom the sisters worked or interacted, the soldiers themselves, and other military and governmental authorities ranged from apprehension or mistrust—stemming from ignorance about sisters or from religious prejudice—to acceptance, support, and warm appreciation. Though each of these categories of people generally responded in a variety of ways depending on the situation and length of interaction, the responses from each group were fairly consistent, except for those of the female lay nurses.

As has been previously pointed out, doctors, especially in the North, generally did not favor female volunteer nurses because they felt the women had little or no experience, were disorganized, or were too regulated by Dorothea Dix. Thus, doctors felt that female nurses tended to mother the men and disregard orders regarding diet and medicine. In the South, a prevalent view among doctors was that women did not belong at the bedside of strange men.

However, because doctors worked directly with the sisters, whose assistance in caring for the patients and directing various support areas of the hospitals was beneficial, their attitudes toward the sisters were generally positive. The most famous comments came from Dr. John Brinton, whose attitude toward most female lay nurses was direct and negative because of their "inexperienced and troublesome presence."[1] Yet, he decided to replace female lay nurses in his Mound City, Illinois, hospital with the Sisters of the Holy Cross, who were not even nurses, because he believed they would be better nurses for his sick men. These men, he reported, not only improved under the sisters' care,[2] but they grew to love and respect the sisters.[3]

The doctors' attitudes toward the sisters can sometimes be determined through the sisters' correspondence. For instance, at a West Virginia Confederate hospital, the sister superior wrote that everything was getting on quietly and satisfactorily, once a Dr. Woodville "rightly took charge" of the post, because he was always satisfied at any arrangements the sisters made. She added that the doctors and other nurses preferred the sisters to be in charge of the wards since they could "handle the men better," thus ensuring cooperation and good order.[4] She later recounted a visit from the Confederate examining physician from General Jones' staff, who examined the hospital very thoroughly and pronounced it the best kept and the best organized in the Confederacy.[5] Further, the examination indicated that Jones was very fearful of losing the sisters' services and was "determined to do all in his power to retain them."[6]

This positive attitude and desire to retain the sisters was found equally among Union doctors. One example of this occurred toward the end of the war, when the Daughters of Charity at a Washington hospital were completing the inventory of all hospital goods prior to the hospital's closing. As they finished, the sisters recorded that the surgeons and officers in charge expressed much gratitude and confidence in what had.been done by the sisters. The first surgeon, wrote one sister, especially was at a loss to put his satisfaction into words, saying, "The Sisters of Charity were able to lessen the cares and labors of the physicians and surgeons in any hospital they might be placed."[7]

Typifying the attitude of most doctors, Surgeon-General Isaac J. Hayes wrote to the superior of the Daughters of Charity as they terminated their services at the Satterlee Hospital, Philadelphia. Aware that almost ninety sisters had served there during the war, he said:

My most sincere and hearty thanks for the faithful and efficient manner in which you have performed your duties. Joining it [Satterlee] at its foundation under an impulse of true Christian charity you have remained true and stedfast [sic] to the end; suffering discomfort, working early and late, never murmuring. You have won my gratitude and the gratitude of every true soldier, and have confirmed me in the profound esteem which I have always entertained for your noble order.... May the knowledge of the good which you have done to the sick and wounded and weary soldiers of our common country be to you a satisfaction and reward.[8]

The generally positive and supportive attitude of doctors was appreciated by the sisters, especially when it lessened the prejudice of their patients. For instance, the Daughters of Charity in their *Annals of the Civil War* remarked, "Fortunately the corps of doctors then employed in the hospital were in our favor, and occasionally through their means we would be enabled to soften the prejudice of the patients who saw the respect the doctors showed us by the attention they would give to any remarks it was necessary to make; and by degrees we gradually gained their confidence."[9] Besides the doctors, in the actual day-to-day activities of the wartime hospitals, other men, such as orderlies, male nurses, and ward masters probably had direct experience with the sisters. However, because these hospital workers did not generally leave written accounts, their views of the sisters are not known. Thus, in terms of people with whom the sisters worked, the other major group was other women. These women fell into three broad categories: other female nurses, including those selected and appointed by Dorothea Dix; members of various ladies' aid societies and church groups, which visited patients and brought supplies; and members of the US Sanitary Commission, who inspected the hospitals as well as supplied various clothing and food items. Within these categories, there were wives of doctors and officers, who remained with their husbands and sometimes assisted the sisters in the hospital in some capacity; auxiliary helpers in the hospitals, such as laundry, dietary, housekeeping; and nurse's "aides."

Attitudes of other women toward the sisters varied considerably, from that of a nurse "who had registered a vow not to serve with any sisters— or with members of any secret society"[10] to that of Sanitary Commission leader Mary Livermore, who said, "The world has known no nobler and no more heroic women than those found in the ranks of the Catholic Sisterhoods."[11]

The largest group of women with whom the sisters worked were other female nurses. Not all religious communities had a written stipulation in their agreement that they would not serve under a female matron (nurse superintendent) or with other female nurses, but that generally seemed to be the case, and the two groups apparently did not work well

together. The issue seemed to be one of control of the hospital facilities
and services. For instance, from the beginning the Sisters of Charity of
Our Lady of Mercy, Charleston, had difficulty with Miss Emily Mason,
a woman encouraged by Bishop Patrick Lynch to start the Confederate
hospital in White Sulphur Springs, West Virginia, where the sisters went.
In offering one viewpoint for the cause of the difficulty, the chaplain,
Father L. P. O'Connell, wrote confidentially in January 1862 to Bishop
Lynch that the sisters, though justifiably dissatisfied, should be patient
for a time. He concluded that "the bone of discontent consists in their
not having supreme government over the hospitals and the stores connected therewith."[12] Certainly, the sisters were used to being in charge
of their own institutions, and there may have been an initial misunderstanding in this particular situation.

The greatest clashes between sisters and female nurses, however, involved Dorothea Dix and her nurses. It might be thought that Dorothea
Dix, whose nurses were expected to be over thirty, plain-looking, and
wearing black or brown with no jewelry or hoop skirts, might appreciate
or, at least, respect the sisters. However, as Civil War medical historian
George Adams has noted, one of Dorothea Dix's "oddities was the res-
olute anti-Catholic feeling which made her refuse appointment to a
Catholic woman."[13] She discriminated against Catholic nurses, lay or
religious, despite the fact that the doctors preferred the nuns.

The sisters were never under Dix's jurisdiction, and this fact became
even clearer and perhaps more irritating to Dix as the war went on.
Finally, in 1863, attempts were made to respond to some of the doctors'
complaints against female nurses by General Order 351, which limited
Dix's authority. The general order, issued by Secretary of War Stanton,
required that "certificates of approval" be given by Dix to each nurse
approved by her and countersigned by the medical director in whose
department the nurse was to serve. Further, assignment of women nurses
was to be made only by the surgeon in charge through the medical
director to Dix. The final provision stated that the women nurses, while
on duty, were under the exclusive control of the senior medical officer,
who could discharge them when they were considered "supernumerary"
(only one female nurse per thirty beds was allowed), or for incompetence,
insubordination, or violation of his orders. There was one exception:
while no female nurse could serve without a certificate, Surgeon-General
William Hammond could specifically appoint any nurse he wished. On
the reverse side of the copy of the order in the possession of the Holy
Cross Sisters, it was specifically written on Hammond's authority that
"Sisters of Charity" [generic] were not part of the order.[14]

The situations in which this Order was enforced sometimes added to
the conflicts between the sisters and the female nurses. For instance, at
Point Lookout, Maryland, the Daughters of Charity remarked on "a

band of philanthropic lady nurses" who arrived in 1863 and who showed surprise that the sisters were there before them. The sisters, who were the only nurses allowed to attend the newly arrived Confederate prisoners, noted that "the women would have greatly annoyed us, but their duties were sufficiently apart from ours. They were as hostile to Catholicity as was the North and South to each other."[15] When General Order 351 came from Washington stating that no female nurses were to remain at the Point, the sisters made preparations to leave. However, the doctor said, "Remain, sisters, until I hear from Washington for we *cannot* dispense with the services of the sisters." He telegraphed and received the reply, "The Sisters of Charity are not included in our orders; they may serve all . . . at the Point, prisoners and others, but all other ladies are to leave the place."[16] While this response did not endear the sisters to the other female nurses, it certainly demonstrated that the skills and experience of the sisters were in great demand.

Another conflict over this same general order involved the Sisters of Charity of Cincinnati. Vowing not to leave Hospital #14 in Nashville, Tennessee, when General Order 351 was first received, Sister Anthony O'Connell wrote in October 1863 to Cincinnati Bishop John Purcell. "This day I received a copy or certificate which places us under the special direction of Miss Dix. I thought it best to send you mine, which you will pleas[e] return as I could not draw anny [sic] pay without it. I hardly thought you would be willing to leave us subject to Miss Dix's whims."[17] Bishop Purcell apparently encouraged them to stay, for a few weeks later, Sister Anthony again corresponded with the bishop, saying:

I received your letter yesterday and also the one previous both approving my remaining longer with the sisters to care for the sick and wounded Soldiers. I send you a letter, Mr. Read Sanitary Inspector sent me, and also an apiel [sic] from the soldiers. I would not like to lieve [sic] now it would be gratifying to the Presbetarian [sic] Minister and Miss Dix's Delegates for us to get out of the way. We are now so independent, we can stay as long as we plies [sic], there is anny ammount [sic] or rather number, of sick brought in whilst I am writing to you, they appear more like cacis [sic] of starvation than anny [sic] I have ever nursed before.[18]

The *Catholic Telegraph*, diocesan newspaper of Cincinnati, two days later quoted a letter in the Nashville *Daily Commercial*, which took up the sisters' cause:

The thousands of sick and wounded soldiers in the hospitals here, whose wants have been ministered to and whose beds of pain have been smoothed by those devoted women, Sisters of Charity, regret to learn that Sister Anthony and her co-laborers of your city have been recalled from Nashville for other fields of labor. I do not understand the cause of their withdrawal, but it is stated that some rules of restrictions instituted by Miss Dix at Washington, conflicted with, or were unacceptable to the rules of the Sisters, and their recall from this field of labor followed. No humane system during the war has been so successfully and usefully carried out as that of the Sisters of Charity, and whether their labors are recognized and appreciated by the rulers or not, certain it is the soldiers, who are most interested, will miss their kind ministrations and never cease to regret their absence from the hospital.[19]

Whether it was the determination of the sisters, the desire of the doctors, the influence of the bishop, the pleading of the patients, the support of the publicity or a combination of all these influences, the sisters did remain at Nashville.

Others of Dorothea Dix's nurses also remarked with criticism, curiosity, praise, or envy, about additional aspects of the sisters that they observed. One critic was a Mrs. Pomeroy, who recounted her visit to "St. Alyosus [sic] Hospital, under the control of the Sisters of the Sacred Heart." (Actually, St. Aloysius Hospital in Washington, D.C., was under the Sisters of the Holy Cross.) Commenting first on the sisters' clothing and what she perceived was its negative effect on the soldiers, she said, "This order wears black woolen dresses and capes, white muslin caps or bonnets, with black woolen veils hanging negligently graceful over the back; thick boots and checked aprons. A heavy leaden cross, and quite a large leaden heart, are suspended from the neck. What looking objects to wait upon our sick and dying boys!"[20] In addition, Pomeroy, acknowledging that Dix was equally disturbed about the sisters, noted with shame that the surgeons generally preferred Catholic sister nurses to Protestants. Pomeroy did concede, however, that a reason for this preference was the fact that many of the Protestant nurses got married and left. In contrast, with the sisters' vow of celibacy, which publicly acknowledged that they would not marry, and their vow of obedience, which assured their service to the hospital where they had been sent by the community, the sisters were understandably more dependable than female nurses.

A different view was presented by Dix-appointed nurse Sophia Bucklin. She mingled admiration for the sisters with an envy for their working conditions, as well as an observation on their humanness. In her memoirs she told of twenty-five Sisters of Charity at Point Lookout, Maryland, who cared for the freshly wounded from Fredericksburg in newly built quarters. Dix's nurses were in an older section, where, Bucklin recalled, the sisters had charge of the linen room. There she sometimes caught a glimpse of "a sweet placid face from under the long white bonnets which they wore," and she noted that the sisters were ceaseless in the work of mercy amongst those poor suffering soldiers." Yet, as she observed, they did not prove "entirely impervious to the wiles of those passions which belong to this earthly state, for by-and-by one of them was wooed by, and fell in love with a Union officer." Bucklin reported that the sister denounced her faith, went to Seven Pines, Maryland, and was married to the officer.[21]

⌞ Since Dix's biographer Helen Marshall offers no particular reason for Dorothea's anti-Catholicism, the conflict between Dix, some of her nurses, and the sisters may have been due more to issues of control of the hospital and approval by the doctors than to anti-religious feelings, even though the conflicts were often stated in those terms by both parties. Certainly, the earlier anti-Catholic feelings continued during Civil War times. The sisters, many of them immigrants and conscious of such sentiments, understandably would generally not be supportive of efforts by Protestants to move them out of areas where they were. Too, the sisters were used to being in charge of their own schools and hospitals, even though other women may also have worked with them, and probably the sisters did not want to be told what to do by outsiders.

Thus, the conflict may have stemmed more from a power struggle between the doctors and Dix, who (as even her admirers admitted) was a difficult person to work with, than from a problem between the sisters and the nurses. Mary Livermore assessed the multiple aspects of the situation by noting:

Unfortunately many of the surgeons in the hospitals did not work harmoniously with Miss Dix. They were jealous of her power, impatient of her authority, condemned her nurses, and accused her of being arbitrary, opinionated, severe, and capricious. Many, to rid themselves of her entirely, obtained permission of Surgeon-General Hammond, to employ Sisters of Charity only in their hospital, a proceeding not at all to Miss Dix's liking. I knew by observation that many of the surgeons were unfit for their office; that too often they failed to carry skill, morality, or humanity to their work; and I understood how this single-minded friend of the sick and wounded soldier would come in collision with these laggards.[22]

Another reason for the clash between some of the female nurses, especially in the North, and the sisters may have been a strong desire on the part of some female nurses to have the same spirit and prestige that came with an organized group of women working for the public good. For example, reflecting the views of many of these Protestant nurses, Union nurse Jane Woolsey wrote after the war, "The Roman Catholic system had features which commended it to medical officers of a certain cast of mind. The order and discipline were almost always good. The neatness, etc., were sometimes illusory." Though Woolsey offered no specifics, she added that there were great objections to the general introduction of such a system among American volunteer soldiers. Further, she concluded with a desire that Catharine Beecher, Kate Cumming, Mary Livermore and other American and English women had expressed elsewhere, ["There was nothing good in it that we also might not have had; and taking the good, leaving the bad, and adapting the result to the uses of the country and the spirit of the time, we might have had an order of Protestant women better than the Romish sisterhoods, by so much as heart and intelligence are better than machinery."[23]

Nevertheless, as Mrs. Lew Wallace, wife of the Union general, explained in a letter to her mother in December 1861, "Nothing in our churches equals the devotion of these women. When Protestant Sisters [nurses] get tired they go home, but the Sisters of the Holy Cross live among the patients without thought of deserting infected places or avoiding contagion by flight." About Mother Angela of St. Mary's Academy, who had come to Mound City, Illinois, with thirty nuns, Mrs. Wallace said, "A flock of white doves—to nurse in the hospitals, where the stillness is like the silence of death."[24]

Since there were only about one thousand women nurses, and perhaps one hundred sisters in the Confederate states, recorded attitudes there about the sisters were generally positive and did not seem to reflect strong conflicts. This was partly due to the fact that there was no issue of control in the South, because female nurses were not mobilized under any government agency. For example, experienced Confederate nurse Kate Cumming praised the Sisters [Daughters] of Charity, who were at the Cantey Hospital, Mobile, Alabama, saying, "The Sisters of Charity are its matrons, and we all know what they are in hospitals. And, by the way, why can we not imitate them in this respect, during these war times? Here one of them is a druggist; another acts the part of steward; and, in fact, they could take charge of the whole hospital, with the exception of the medical staff."[25]

Perhaps frustrated herself by untrained female nurses, who were often more hindrance than help, Cumming frequently spoke of her desire and that of others that there be a Protestant sisterhood. One time when Cumming and her nurse were at church, the minister

adverted to our having an order of sisterhood in the church; this he seems to have very much at heart. We had our sunbonnets with us, and he wished to know if they were our uniform; we have never worn any, as we cannot afford any clothes but what we may have. We have always made it a rule of wearing the simplest kind of dress, as we think of any other kind sadly out of place in a hospital; calico or homespun is the only dress fit to wear; but to get the former is a real treat.[26]

Previously, the minister had suggested to her that he thought another hospital, started by a clergyman and some Mobile ladies, had been a failure. This, he said, was because the ladies had not been educated in nursing, as were the Sisters of Charity. The minister hoped that some day there would be a sisterhood in the church as there was in the day of the apostles and in many parts of the old country.

Besides Dix's nurses and the other nurses of the North and South, the other large organized group of females often in contact with the sisters was the US Sanitary Commission. Though he gives no specific examples, historian William Maxwell, in his work on the US Sanitary Commission, commented on the rivalry that sprang up between Protestant nurses and Catholic sisters. According to Maxwell, complaints reached the Sanitary Commission that army officers preferred nuns because they were docile and obedient workers who took no notice of the evils denounced by Protestants. In addition, Maxwell said that critics accused the sisters of showing partiality to Catholic soldiers and withholding the consolation of the Bible from men of other faiths. Further, the sisters supposedly lacked warmth, exercised formal discipline, and turned a hospital into a house of reform. However, Maxwell stated that when the champion of Catholic nurses, the non-Catholic Surgeon-General Hammond, was asked why the sisters were numerous in the army hospitals, he replied that the sisters were there because they were good nurses. Hammond further asked where one could find Protestant nurses comparable to the Sisters of Charity in efficiency and faithfulness. Nevertheless, though Hammond deplored any attempt to discharge loyal servants on the basis of religious difference, he agreed to increase the number of Protestant nurses, according to Maxwell.[27]

Both Mary Ann Hoge and Mary Livermore, US Sanitary Commission leaders who inspected the Union hospitals and transport boats serviced by the commission, referred to the prejudice against the "Protestant" nurses and the preference for the Catholic sisters. Hoge found everywhere the greatest prejudice against Protestant women nurses: medical directors, surgeons, and even ward masters, she explained, openly declared they would not have them in the service and that only the "Sisters" of the Catholic church should receive appointments. In trying to find the cause of this attitude, Hoge quoted a surgeon who said:

Your Protestant nurses are always finding some mare's-nest or other, that they can't let alone. They all write for the papers, and the story finds its way into print, and directly we are in hot water. Now the "Sisters" never see anything they ought not to see, nor hear anything they ought not to hear, and they don't write for the papers and the result is we get along very comfortably with them.[28]

Hoge, herself, felt it was futile to combat the prejudice of the doctors. She decided to content herself with refusing to fill the hospitals and boats with Catholic sisters, as she had been entreated, or consenting to do anything to discourage the detailment of Protestant nurses.

Later, Hoge's coworker Mary Livermore met a group of Protestant nurses, all "women of experience, carefully examined, and properly detailed" by Dix. The Protestant nurses were determined to appeal to Secretary of War Edwin Stanton if the medical authorities employed Catholic sisters instead of them. "The Protestant nurses," Livermore reported, "carried the day, chiefly because of their good sense and worth, and hundreds went to the front before the end of the war, welcome by both surgeons and patients, and rendering invaluable service."[29]

Nevertheless, she and Hoge were both lavish in their praise of the Holy Cross Sisters in the general hospital in Cairo, Illinois,[30] and Mound City, Illinois.[31] "It is not necessary here to say more than that we were satisfied that the sanitary stores were wisely appropriated, under the supervision of Mother Angela, at Mound City," wrote Hoge.[32] Livermore praised Mother Angela as "a gifted lady, of rare cultivation and executive ability, with winning sweetness and of manner." Further, Livermore noted that the sisters had nearly broken up their famous schools at South Bend, Indiana, to answer the demand for nurses. She concluded, "If I had ever felt prejudice against these sisters as nurses, my experience with them during the war would have dissipated it entirely."[33]

Later, Hoge and Livermore's excellent report on the "Brick Hospital" in Cairo, Illinois, noted:

Here the "Sisters of the Holy Cross" were employed as nurses, one or more to each ward. Here were order, comfort, cleanliness, and good nursing. The food was cooked in a kitchen outside the hospital. Surgeons were detailed to every ward, who visited their patients twice daily, and more frequently if necessary. The apothecary's room was supplied with an ample store of medicines and surgical appliances and the store-room possessed an abundance of clothing and delicacies for the sick.[34]

The recorded reaction of female nurses and Sanitary Commission workers fell into three consistent patterns. They respected the sisters completely, or they admired their work without necessarily favoring the aspects of Roman Catholic religious life that permeated the sisters' services, or they resented them. However, other women also came in contact with the sisters, and there are scattered reactions and comments from them.

Accounts, both positive and negative, from various women's church and aid societies differed, but not necessarily because of any religious affiliation of the women. Sometimes women praised the sisters because they were Catholics or conversely felt they were suspect because of their religion. Some thought it admirable that the sisters took care of Union or Confederate soldiers and prisoners; others saw this action as the sisters treating the "enemy." Further, sisters were both praised and criticized because they established a certain order and atmosphere or enforced various visiting and food distribution regulations for the good of the hospital and patient. In other words, they praised or blamed the sisters because of what they did or did not do, not because of religion. Nevertheless, the sisters and the hospitals they served in were often the grateful recipients of food and supplies from various religious aid groups, even if comment or criticisms came along with the supplies.

For example, the Daughters of Charity in St. Louis Military Hospital recounted that the Ladies of the Union Aid Society, who visited the hospital twice a week, became jealous of the good that the sisters were doing. The women feared, the sisters said, that everyone would become a Catholic. The ladies even tried to make the patients call them sisters, telling the soldiers they were charitable ladies who went about doing good. However, as the sisters noted, the women could not succeed because "the poor patients knew how to distinguish between real merit and big talk." In spite of the fact that the ladies could not see or understand how the sisters could have so much influence over the patients, they showed the sisters the greatest respect. The sisters recalled the women would often say, "How happy the sisters look! and they make all around them happy, too, I wish my presence could be a sunshine somewhere."[35]

Although the ladies in St. Louis may have been irritated by the sisters' attempts to keep good order and provide care to all, diarist Mary Boykin Chestnut, who often visited Confederate hospitals, appreciated the sisters' efforts. In discussing the care given to officers of both sides, she recorded in her diary that in the hospitals with the Sisters of Charity, the Union prisoner officers were better off than the Confederate men at other hospitals without sisters as nurses. That care, she said, she "saw with her own eyes."[36]

Sometimes the women visiting the soldiers became themselves the subject of amusing stories. For example, a Vicksburg Sister of Mercy remarked, "Many persons from the country round visited the hospital; at first from curiosity or prejudice, but after some time, with better feeling, often bringing food to the patients."[37] Nonetheless, she noted, they generally selected the "handsome fellows" for the distribution of favors. The sisters humorously observed that this caused the male nurses to sometimes jump in bed with their boots on, so that some sentimental lady would bestow upon them preserves and the gentle motion of the fan.[38]

In contrast, those soldiers who were too sick or too repulsive to attract "a dainty notice received the tenderest care of the sisters in charge." Because of this, one time, a soldier not ill enough to require much attention, "complained to some bigoted women that he was not treated well." The women then went to the sister, took her by the arm and shook her saying, "Woman, how dare you treat a sick man so." The memoirs of these Vicksburg Sisters of Mercy observed that the actions were noted by the soldiers who were there day in and day out. A truly ill man, appreciative of the sister's efforts, said, "Never mind, sister, you do the best for all."[39]

This was the usual reaction once the soldiers got to know the sisters. However, the soldiers were initially perplexed or frightened by the sisters, either because of the sisters' strange garb or by what they had heard about Catholics. "Great heavens!" shrieked one suffering soldier to the Sister of Mercy that bent over him, "are you a man or a woman? But your hand is a woman's hand; its touch is soft, and your voice is gentle—what *are* you?."[40] Some soldiers called them "holy Marias,"[41] and another group thought that the nine black-robed sisters making their way along a narrow wharf to a hospital in Beaufort, North Carolina, were "lone widows" coming for their husbands' bodies.[42] Someone thought they might be Freemasons.[43]

The sisters themselves recounted many stories that amused them about the reaction provoked by their strange garb, especially the various headdresses. Cincinnati Charity Sister Ann Cecilia recalled:

We were frequently asked why we dressed so different from other ladies. One boy told us that the girls up at his place, wore low necks and short sleeves—adding—"you know them dresses make you look so funny." Another—quite young and innocent desired to play with my beads—thought they would make a pretty watch chain; but how different were his ideas regarding my "Rosary" after he was instructed and baptized in our holy religion. Oh! with how much ignorance did we not meet.[44]

Once the soldiers got used to the sisters, they sometimes tried to show their appreciation for their care by trying to buy clothing for the sisters, not realizing their garb was made by them and not available in stores. At the Satterlee Hospital in Philadelphia, one soldier asked if the government provided the sisters' "uniforms" while they were in service. Another proposed to buy a silk dress for a sister after pay day,[45] and a third wandered the streets of Washington all day "to buy one of your white bonnets but did not find a single one for sale."[46]

The amusement, perplexity, and curiosity that the sisters' clothing caused was not confined just to the soldiers. The Sisters of Charity of Cincinnati, going to the Cumberland, recalled that as they marched in procession through the streets to the hotel where they were to lodge one night, the streets were crowded with men, women, and children wanting to see the sisters. Later, while the sisters were waiting for supper, "The windows were besieged from without by children, white and black, peeping in to see the curiosity."[47]

The headdress, especially, was strange and often terrifying, particularly the spread-eagled, white cornette of the seventeenth-century

French peasant worn by the hundreds of Daughters of Charity. US Sanitary Commission leader Mary Livermore said she often sympathized with some of the sick men who frequently expressed a wish for a reform in the "headgear" of the sisters. " 'Why can't they take off those white-winged sun-bonnets in the ward?' " asked one man. " 'Sun-bonnets!' " sneered another of the irreverent critics, Livermore reported, " 'they're a cross between a white sun-bonnet and a broken-down umbrella and there's no name that describes them.' "[48]

Some other sisters remembered that new patients continued to cover their heads with blankets while the sisters were in the wards. The soldiers were frightened—or "skerte," as they used to say—by the sisters' appearance. The Confederate soldiers were anxious to know to what regiment the sisters belonged or if they had been engaged in any battles. They thought the sisters should go to battle because the Yankees would be more afraid of them than any gun the boys could show them.[49] Though a soldier who had never seen a sister before might say, "I do not want to stay in this ward for I do not like the looks of that woman who wears that Bonnet," he would usually be answered by another who said there was nothing to fear, for she was a Sister of Charity.[50]

"The general prejudice toward Catholics was, at least initially, displayed toward the sisters though this often changed after the soldiers watched the sisters," recalled a Daughter of Charity. "Many of our sick, who seemed to fear and hate us on their arrival, soon showed they had been mistaken and would even place money in our hands when they received it, and would try to find out what we would like to have, that they might get it for us."[51]

In Norfolk, Virginia, hospital after a Union takeover, the sisters remembered in particular one very sick man who seemed to hate them. He refused his medicine, and tried to strike the sisters and spit upon them when they would offer it to him. After often acting in this manner and finding that the sister still hoped he would take it, for his life depended on it, the man said: *Who* or *what* are you anyway?" The Annals record that the sister said, " 'I am a Sister of Charity.' 'Where is your husband?" he said. 'I have none' said the sister, 'and I am glad I have none.' 'Why are you glad?' he asked, still very angry. 'Because,' she replied, 'if I had a husband, I would have to be employed in his affairs, and consequently could not be here to wait on you.' As if by magic, in a subdued tone he said, 'that will do,' and turning his face from her, he remained silent."[52] Later, he took his medicine and asked about instructions in religion. "He was very soon a true friend of the sisters, but so ignorant of religion in every way that he hardly knew he had a soul,"[53] the sisters recalled.

Generally, then, the sisters had to overcome initial prejudice related to their clothing or to their religion. Nevertheless, their care and concern almost always disarmed those who were in close contact with them. For example, the Daughters of Charity were in the hospital in Frederick, Maryland, only a few days when they realized that they were in the midst of a prejudiced community that did not want their services. The sisters felt the townspeople had embittered the patients' minds against them so much that the soldiers often would not look at them or even speak to them. "We had no delicacies to give them," the sisters wrote, "the ladies had all. Therefore, we could do little for the poor soul, while we had not means of nourishing the exhausted body."[54]

Yet later in this same hospital, a sister was unexpectedly stopped one day by a convalescent soldier. She had often noticed that he viewed her with a surly countenance and only reluctantly took from her whatever she offered him. She wrote that he said:

Sister, you must have noticed how stiffly I have acted toward you . . . but I could not help it as my feelings were so embittered against you, so much so, that your presence always made me worse. I have watched you closely at all times since you came to the barracks; but when you came in last night with the doctor to see the patient who lay dangerously ill, I noticed particularly that you did not come alone, but in company with a sister; and when you did all that was necessary for the patient, you returned. It was then my feelings became changed towards you, as I saw how clearly, how differently you acted from the female nurses.[55]

This soldier apparently felt the female nurses spent too much time alone with the men, especially at night. Thus, the other nurses were viewed with suspicion by the men. However, after reflecting on the actions and care of the sisters, this soldier changed his attitude.

Ultimately, among most soldiers, the sisters were highly respected largely because of their motivation, self-sacrifice, and skill. The sisters even recorded many instances of men who stopped swearing in their presence,[56] or that oaths or disrespectful words were not heard in the hospital in the years that they were there.[57] The Cincinnati Charity sisters, in fact, once overheard the remark, "Surely these ladies are working for God. Money is not the motive here!" The sisters felt that the great respect that some people held for them was remarkable, and even the "more ignorant never forgot themselves in the presence of the 'good ladies.' "[58]

One aspect of this admiration and respect was that the soldiers frequently gave credit to the sisters, rather than to the doctors, for curing them. The patients believed there was nobody like the sisters. They would often say, "Indeed it was not the doctors that raised me, it was the sisters."[59] A Daughter of Charity in a St. Louis hospital recalled that the soldiers would generally go to a sister rather than to a doctor, when given a choice. Thus, the sisters had to encourage them to have confidence in doctors. For example, every evening one sister visited a man whose hand had been amputated at the wrist. The man complained that the doctor had ordered hot poultices that morning, and he still hadn't gotten them. The sister, calling the nurse and wound dresser to find out what happened, discovered that no poultice was available. The sister immediately sent across the yard to the bakery and got some hops and had the poultice put on. The man was surprised and said, "The sisters found ways and means of relieving everyone and those who made profession of the business did not even know where to look for them."[60]

It was these direct, specific, and practical actions of the sisters, who were often carefully observed by the men lying on their beds, that resulted in a change from indifferent or negative attitudes to positive attitudes. In addition, the sisters' willingness to work with smallpox victims did not go unnoticed by the men. For example, Sister De Sales at the Confederate hospital in West Virginia wrote to Bishop Lynch to explain her action in quarantining a sister with the smallpox victims.[61] She wrote, "But things turned out such a way that I could not await your replies and consequently did what seemed to me right *under* the circumstances. Had not sister been *there*, two men would have died without baptism last week. The fact of a sister having gone there when those poor men were abandoned by the physicians has done more for religion at large and our community than all we have done since we left home."[62]

Because so many of the soldiers were young, the ministrations of the sisters, as well as those of other mature women nurses, tended to call forth in the soldiers memories of their own mothers. This also enhanced the positive feelings toward the sisters. Write to my mother," said a young soldier to a Daughter of Charity, "and tell her I was cared for in my suffering by a band of ladies who were as tender to me as mothers."[63] As a result of their experiences, the soldiers developed a loyalty to the sisters. If the men were wounded again and returned to the same hospital, they sometimes cried out, "I want to go to Sr. Frances's ward—I want to go to Sr. Helena's ward, I want to go to Sr. Agatha's ward."[64]

In addition, the condition of dying men and the horrors of the war put many of the soldiers in a receptive frame for religious instruction from the sisters. One Daughter of Charity recounted that often the men, when questioned concerning their future welfare, would reply, "I have not been of your religion, but wish to become what you are. The religion of the sisters must be the true one." "The religion of the sisters" became a common phrase among the men.[65]

In another incident, a Cincinnati Sister of Charity recalled a very young man in a bed at the extreme end of a ward who was suffering from a deep wound in the shoulder. The sister assisted the surgeon in dressing the wound, but the man closed his eyes, wouldn't speak, and avoided her every look. The sister realized "he had no love for the

Catholic Church or her children." Nevertheless, she observed that he noticed every word and every action of priests and sisters. Finally, after listening to the instructions and watching the baptisms, he was convinced by what he saw and asked for baptism.[66]

The soldiers' attitude and response toward the sisters was a reflection of the sisters' own care and concern for the soldiers. The men were often little older than the boys some of the sisters taught in their schools or cared for in their orphanages. Speaking for many sisters, one wrote, "It was heartrending to see those young fellows die hourly, often from fright, being too young to bear the hardships of a soldier's life or to withstand the scenes of battle; they seemed to me to be dazed and to die ere the scene passed their vision."[67]

Cincinnati Sister of Charity Agnes, returning to Cincinnati to assist in caring for the soldiers at St. John's Hospital after three months in Cumberland, was struck by the appalling sights of men without arms or legs. They were pale, haggard, and worn out with fasting and marching, and many died of broken hearts, she remembered. Long after the war, she wrote:

Faces and voices haunt me yet, calling for home and dear ones whom they were destined never again to behold on earth. The streets of Cincinnati . . . witnessed extreme suffering and misery. Frequently fine young men, seated on their own coffins, passed through them [streets] on their way to execution on some neighboring hillside. We cared for Unionists and Confederates alike. We knew no difference and made no difference.[68]

It was this attitude of impartiality toward Union and Confederate soldiers, whether a prisoner or a compatriot, that enabled the sisters to pass through the blockades and lines, getting supplies and sometimes attending to community matters. For example, discussing the need for an Ursuline Sister from Columbia, South Carolina, to go to Florida for health reasons, Bishop Verot wrote to Bishop Lynch that it would be safe. "The Yankees seem to be willing to do anything for the Sisters of Charity of Our Lady of Mercy," he said, "who have been so kind to their wounded soldiers in Charleston."[69]

A similar experience was that of a Daughter of Charity on duty in Mobile, Alabama, in 1864 who needed to go to New Orleans for clothing and also to take a sister for some community business. She obtained a pass from the Confederate soldiers without difficulty. Apparently, by this, the third year of the war, sisters were visibly established in many people's minds as nurses. The sister superior reported that the sisters were objects of excitement at every stopping place; the people even believed that there was going to be another battle because they thought the sisters were there to nurse. In one effort to test the sisters' neutrality, a woman on the train with them demanded to know what side they were on. "Now Sisters, I know you are for us, you know our cause is right, just say it is," she said. The sisters replied, "Madam, we are neutral and wheather [sic] the cause be just or not, it never gives us a thought, we devote our life to the suffering members of Jesus Christ and wheather [sic] they be Confederate or Federal, when placed in our charge, they are alike cared for by us." That response seemed to quiet the woman and she troubled the sisters no more.[70]

However, on the sisters' arrival at the Federal line, they found it more difficult to obtain a pass. The Union soldiers wanted the sisters to take the oath of loyalty to the Union. The sisters replied that they never took the oath because while they were nursing the sick and wounded Confederates, their sisters in the North were nursing the Federals. After some deliberation, the Federals allowed the sisters to pass with the greatest courtesy. When the sisters reached the Confederate line on their return to Mobile, the Federal officers sent for the Confederate officers and asked them to see the sisters safely home, which they did. This prompted a response from some refugee ladies traveling with them, who said, "How is it, sisters, that you are treated with so much courtesy by both parties while we are totally neglected."[71]

The sisters' reputation for impartiality to all soldiers was further confirmed by the Confederates when they had to evacuate Mobile in 1865 and were concerned about what to do with their sick and wounded who could not be removed from the city. After some deliberation, they decided to send them to the City Hospital, assured that "they would not be molested while in the charge of the Sisters of Charity." Though the hospital was already crowded, the men were sent, fully supplied with provisions. Somehow, the sisters made room for them.[72]

In the treatment of the soldiers, then, the sisters certainly seemed concerned about Union and Confederate soldiers alike. The most common attitude was that expressed by a Daughter of Charity who said she tried to impress on her sisters the necessity of "observing the greatest prudence in not manifesting partiality in any way whatever for either side but looking on them all as the wounded members of Jesus, which they did most faithfully I am happy to say." She added that it was "a beautiful and sad sight to look on those poor men, beautiful to see the union that existed among them in our Hospitals, sad to think that if they recovered they would be perhaps mortal enemies."[73] On the other hand, in 1862, Mother Angela Gillespie of the Holy Cross Sisters, wrote to Orestes Brownson, editor of *Brownson's Review*, remarking, "The bitter hatred expressed by Southerners without being able to express any other reasons except 'we hate the North' has entirely destroyed the highest sympathy I ever felt for the South and my heart now agrees with the article in the October issue on Slavery & War."[74] No other political reactions are recorded from her, however, and this may well have been an isolated remark. The only other known partisan comment was that of a Southern Mercy sister, originally from Charleston, who remarked in her diary that the sisters in Savannah were "heart and soul for the Confederacy."[75]

In general, however, the sisters maintained their reputation for impartial and excellent care of the soldiers, bringing them praise from officers and other high-ranking military officials. For example, the history of Charity Hospital, New Orleans, credits the presence of sisters with averting a disaster when the city was captured by Union General Benjamin Butler, called "the Beast" by the citizens after his takeover of the city on May 1, 1862. In spite of several acts of insubordination on the part of the medical officers and board of the hospital after Butler ordered them to take in wounded Federal soldiers, Butler did not seize the hospital or punish the doctor in charge. This had been the expected response considering Butler's other drastic actions in taking the city. Butler, in his memoirs, justified his martial-law actions in New Orleans by saying "the poor had to be fed, the streets had to be cleaned, the protection from yellow fever had to be made sure."[76] However, this same man gave $500 a month to the hospital for the seven months he remained in New Orleans.[77] The hospital historians believe that Butler's compassionate attitude probably came from the great respect he felt for the Daughters of Charity running the hospital, who would have shared the sufferings caused by any stringent means he might have evoked.[78]

Butler's attitude toward the sisters can also be seen in a letter to Sister Maria Clara, Superior of the Daughters of Charity in Donaldson, Louisiana, in September of 1862. In it, he apologized for the damage done by Rear-Admiral Farragut to their buildings in the general bombardment of the city, saying:

No one can appreciate more fully than myself the holy, self-sacrificing labors of the Sisters of Charity. To them our soldiers are daily indebted for the kindest offices. Sisters of all mankind, they know no nation, no kindred, neither war nor peace. Their all-pervading charity is like the boundless love of "Him who died for all," whose servants they are, and whose pure teachings their love illustrates.... Your Sisters in the city will also farther [sic] testify to you, that my officers and soldiers have never failed to do them all in their power to aid them in their usefulness, and to lighten the burden of their labors.[79]

He also promised to repair the damage as far as he could by doing as they asked—filling the order sent for provisions and medicine.[80] That his sentiments were probably more than mere appeasement may have derived from his early experience of seeing the burning of the Ursuline Convent in Massachusetts in 1834. This disaster later motivated him to introduce a bill into the state legislature, which ultimately failed, to make restitution for that act.[81]

In addition to Butler and other famous officers, such as General William Sherman,[82] recording their own views of the sisters, the sisters themselves also noted the reactions, both positive and negative, of some of the officers. For example, some Daughters of Charity, including a number who had been in the South for some time, were on a Union boat on its way to Richmond, where a flag of truce would take them to Maryland. When an officer visited the sisters, he exclaimed, "I need not question you, Sisters; all is right with you. You mind your own business and don't meddle with government affairs. Your society had done great service to the Country and the authorities in Washington hold your community in high esteem."[83] He further stamped the sisters' passes "Examined" without ever reviewing them and arranged for them to stay free on his boat, since he said he did not often have the honor of having Sisters of Charity as his guests.[84] The same officer also chartered a train for them from Annapolis to Baltimore, and the sisters said they "felt his kindness the more as he knew that we have been nursing the Southern soldiers. . . . To be sure," they added, "he may have seen us also at Portsmouth, serving the North; at least he knew that 'part' did not influence us in our labors for the men."[85]

This officers' attitude was echoed by government officials, who publicly expressed their gratitude for the sisters' services, and praise and admiration for their work. Among the most famous are those of Lucius E. Chittenden, an officer of the Treasury during Lincoln's administration.[86] This statement, incorrectly attributed to the President himself, included the following tribute: "Of all the forms of Charity and benevolence seen in the crowded wards of the hospitals, those of some Catholic sisters were among the most efficient. I never knew whence they came or what was the name of their order. [Because of the sisters] these scenes which were altogether the most painful I have ever witnessed, have . . . a beautiful side."[87]

The efficiency and devotion noticed by Chittenden were also observed by other officials. The governor of Pennsylvania, Andrew G. Curtin, praised the efforts of the Sisters of St. Joseph at Camp Curtin. There, he said, "During a period of several weeks amidst the confusion of a constantly changing camp, and amidst an epidemic of measles with typhoid fever, the . . . neatness, order, and sufficient ministrations immediately followed the sisters' arrival in camp."[88]

In spite of the general attitude of gratitude, praise, or at least respect afforded the sisters by the doctors, female nurses, soldiers, military personnel, and governmental officials, the sisters' work among prisoners or in the prisons sometimes drew suspicion and censure. The situation of the Daughters of Charity at the St. Louis prison in Alton, Illinois, is an interesting case in point. The sisters recalled that their first visit to the prison was by no means welcome. "Prejudice greeted us everywhere," they explained. "The patients would not even speak to us, though bereft of every consolation of soul and body." The sisters, however, were not discouraged, and they persevered. At their hospital they prepared broth and other delicacies that the sick were in need of and carried the food every day at noon to the prisons. Eventually, the sisters recorded, the "porrige pot" was hailed by the poor prisoners and caused many of them to bless God.[89]

Finally, arrangements with Colonel Ware were made by the sisters to visit daily in an ambulance provided for them.[90] Because of earlier experience, the sisters worked "with great prudence in the beginning in order to avoid misunderstanding." Eventually, the officers and the Sanitary Commissioners began to approve of their work, setting up a one-hundred-bed ward for the sick prisoners. In addition, the authorities proposed to give the sisters a place to stay where they could "remain day and night to attend more leisurely the wants of the sick."[91]

Unfortunately, though, according to the sisters' accounts, Colonel Ware was eventually removed and replaced with a prejudiced officer who did all he could to displace the sisters. Thus, they could no longer get what was necessary from the prison resources. The new guards at the gates sometimes even prevented them from going to the hospital. When some of the old guards noticed the difficulty, they became indignant and stepped forward, saying, "They are not ladies or women, but Sisters of Charity." Thus, the sisters were permitted to go on without further trouble.[92]

Official records provide a different perspective on this incident. In June 1864, about the time of the sisters' accounts of their dismissal, a Colonel W. Hoffman, Commissary General of Prisoners, wrote to Brigadier General Joseph T. Copeland, Commander of the Military Prison at Alton. Hoffman said, "As you will perceive by my letters to Colonel Sweet the employment of these sisters has not been authorized by me and as their services can be obtained only on unusual conditions viz, the renting and furnishing a house for them and the hire of a servant, their continued employment at the hospitals is not approved."[93] He then suggested that the general find men among the prisoners to serve as nurses, unless female nurses were absolutely necessary. If so, that fact would need to be reported back. In conclusion, he said, "I am under the impression that the Sisters [Daughters] of Charity take advantage of their position to carry information from and to prisoners which is contraband, and if this is so they cannot under any circumstances be employed at the hospital. Please furnish me a list of the articles purchased to furnish their house, with remarks to show where they now are."[94]

A week later, Copeland replied that he had notified the sisters that their continued employment was not approved, and their services would be dispensed with at the end of the present month. Copeland, however, concluded, "I feel that I ought in justice to these persons to express my conviction that the impression, under which you write, that they carry information to and from prisoners which is contraband, is not well founded."[95]

From the sisters' perspective, this event was not without its rewards. "Notified that our services were no longer required at prison," the sisters recorded that "the citizens were anxious for us to remain in Alton, and to convert our house into a hospital." Thus, they received full permission to open a civilian hospital for the citizens of Alton. The hospital, St. Joseph, continues today, though no longer under the direction of the Daughters of Charity.[96]

Another accusation that the Daughters of Charity were spies had been made earlier in December of 1861. Archbishop Francis Kenrick was apprised by Major General John A. Dix that "ladies in the costume of Sisters of Charity furnished by the Convent of Emmitsburg have passed the lines into Virginia, for the purpose of keeping up communication with the Confederate States." Concerned, Kenrick wrote to Father Francis Burlando, superior of the sisters. Kenrick acknowledged to Burlando that Dix "professes himself unwilling to believe that they [the sisters] have been guilty of so gross an act of infidelity to the Government which protects them in their persons and property."[97] Kenrick also indicated that he had explained to Dix that the sisters' "journeys were open and with formal passports from the Government at Washington and wholly unconnected with politics and not intended in any way to aid the rebellion."[98] However, Burlando requested the superior of the sisters, Mother Ann Simeon Norris, to draw up a short statement to be signed by himself and three of the administrative council to send to Dix.

The sisters' reply not only explained what might have caused the misunderstanding, but also reiterated the work that they had done for the Federal soldiers at the request of the Government. The letter stated that "at no time, under no circumstances directly or indirectly, have any of the sisters gone to Virginia or any other State for political purposes, or carried documents or messages, having political tendencies." Further, the letter clearly explained that the only object for which the sisters were sent to Viriginia was to nurse the sick and wounded soldiers.

After explaining several specific instances in which sisters did cross the lines for health or community reasons, Mother Ann Simeon stated:

The fact that the sisters went to nurse the soldiers in the South, could not be interpreted as a disaffection for the Government since sisters from the same society were at the request of General Rathbone sent to Albany where they took care of sick soldiers and remained at the hospital until their services were no

longer required.... In a word, the sisters have responded to every call without
distinction of creed or politics, and are ready at any moment to give their services
if asked by proper authority, nay they are willing to suspend their schools, and
diminish their number in Hospitals and orphan asylums for the purpose of
nursing the sick and wounded—of about eight hundred Sisters of Charity, there
is not one but would readily obey the first summons for the same work of
Charity.[99]

She concluded that the Superiors of the Daughters of Charity "are quite
at a loss how to account for the odious charge." She suggested, however,
that the accusation might have arisen from some ill-disposed source, or
from some misguided female assuming a costume similar to that of the
sisters, thereby obtaining a pass and abusing the privileges of the government. Mother Ann Simeon acknowledged this could have been possible since, a few months earlier, two individuals alleging to be from the
South, and dressed like sisters, were seen in Baltimore feigning to be
nieces of the Honorable Edward Everett, both of whom were members
of the Community. Nevertheless, she emphatically concluded, "We take
the liberty to remark that the duty of the Sisters of Charity is to strive
to save their souls by the exercise of Charity towards their fellow crea-
tures, the poor and suffering of every nation, independent of creed or
politics."[100]

The belief that sisters might be spies or that others might dress as
sisters in order to pass more easily through the lines plagued other
communities beside the Daughters of Charity. For example, Bishop Augustine Verot, of Florida, whose territory was partially in Federal hands,
had frequent difficulties passing between the lines of the two armies. In
1862, when he wanted to take five Sisters of Mercy from St. Augustine,
Florida, to a school in Columbus, Georgia, he initially had difficulty
obtaining a pass. Finally, receiving one, he was faced with a rumor that
he was transporting slaves disguised as sisters. The fact that two of the
sisters—one from Cuba and one from Virginia—were dark-skinned
added to the rumor. After the sisters' fingernails were examined to see
the natural skin color, however, they and Bishop Verot were allowed
through the lines. In 1863, he and some sisters managed another trip
without incident, but the following year, going to Columbus, he again
had difficulty.[101]

Despite the prejudice, mistrust, and suspicion they met from some
they worked with or served, the sisters, generally, were accepted and
appreciated. While the change from a negative to a positive attitude
toward the sisters and their religion is difficult to document, the sisters'
own perceptions at the end of the war support the view that change did
occur. As one sister working in a Washington, D.C., hospital noted:
"Here we did not have the annoyances we had experienced in the be-

ginning of the war since now our calling and costume were better known and understood."[102]

Regardless of the attitude toward them, the sisters themselves almost universally had a positive attitude toward their work. The Baltimore Mercy Sisters, after their offer to nurse at the Douglas Hospital in Washington, D.C., was gratefully accepted, summed up the attitudes of most people the sisters encountered. They noted the friendships they made with the doctors, the consideration they received from the chief of staff, the services from the orderlies who would do anything for them, and the appreciation of the patients. The soldiers, the sisters noted, seemed to regard them as holding the place of their mothers. When they came to know the sisters, they really loved them and could not understand why such noble services should receive no pay from the government. The sisters, of course, tried unsuccessfully to explain that the day would come when they would be "handsomely remunerated" in heaven. But, as the sisters said, their explanation was "all in mystery."[103]

Ultimately aware of the good they accomplished, the Daughters of Charity, recalling their Washington, D.C., hospital experience, expressed the feelings of most sisters. "Of the thousands who were under the sisters' care, we are able to assure you that nearly all were, not only well pleased, but also most grateful for the attentions given them by the sisters. They who at first spurned our kindest efforts, would tell us afterwards that our religion was so calumniated by those who were ignorant of it, that they had looked on us with horror, until they saw for themselves what Catholics were."[104] Nevertheless, the poignancy of the war experience was summarized well by a Vicksburg Sister of Mercy who wrote: "We had the consolation of the return of some to the faith, who had been negligent, and the baptism of others, sick and dying, but the demoralizing effect of the war was such that it was easier to die well, than to live well."[105]

Most of these reflections of the sisters on their experiences were written shortly after the war rather than during the actual events. As one sister explained, when asked later to write down information from her time of service, the sisters hadn't kept records, but rather did what needed to be done and let God keep the record.[106] Or, as another observed, "Sister was too busy in her young days rolling bandages and dressing wounds to be at all concerned about who came and went from Richmond."[107]

Nevertheless, because the sisters did see their primary role as one of spiritually ministering to the men, they were aware of and grateful for the positive effects their work had on changing attitudes about Catholicism. As one sister astutely observed:

Independent of what was done for individuals, thousands returned to their homes, impressed with kind feelings toward the sisters, consequently, towards our Holy Faith, also, which will benefit not only themselves but render in some degree our travel through the different states easier. The officers, doctors, and public authorities all concurring in their unlimited confidence in the sisters must, and did have, its silent effect on all.[108]

This increased tolerance for the sisters, their religion, and their activities, and the unlimited confidence in the sisters' dedicated work were the two predominant and lasting attitudes of those who became acquainted with the sisters because of the Civil War. The sisters' ability to establish cleanliness, quiet, and good order out of the dirt, noise, and confusion of war conditions, and their personal concern and hard work for the Union and Confederate wounded were all qualities that were noted by those who had contact with the sisters.

Understandably, those who requested the sisters' services expressed the most positive attitudes about the sisters' dedication and quiet, efficient service. Female nurses or other women who desired the prestige or attention the sisters generally received from doctors and soldiers expressed the greatest range of attitudes about the sisters. Soldiers, initially perplexed or confused by the sisters' external dress or what they had heard about Catholics, grew to love and appreciate them and their attentive care. Officers and other governmental officials, except those who suspected them of spying for one side or another, noted positively the sisters' willingness, competence, and commitment.

In spite of accusations about spying, the sisters, conscious of the fact that soldiers of either side were wounded and sick, were notably impartial in their care and treatment of them. The sisters' own attitude was that they were in the war to care for the wounded in body and soul, primarily as an extension of their religious commitment to serve those in need in the name of Christ.

Whether these qualities elicited praise, as was generally the case with the doctors, soldiers, and other military and governmental authorities, or were mistrusted or the source of conflict as was often the case with Dorothea Dix and her nurses, no one doubted that sisters of all communities possessed these qualities. This significant fact demonstrates clearly, then, that the effect of the sisters being called into service by many different people to perform a multitude of duties resulted in a consistent impression on other people and often caused a change in attitude about the sisters.

This change in attitude was noted on various levels. After the war, Catholic bishops, as well as doctors, Protestant soldiers, and noncivilians all attested to the impact of the sisters. In a pastoral letter of the American Catholic bishops, gathered for the Second Baltimore Council on October 21, 1866, the question of the condition and needs of the Catholic church were addressed. While not directly mentioning the Civil War the document's final section on religious communities concluded, "We discharge a grateful duty, in rendering a public testimony to the virtue and heroism of these Christian Virgins [Sisters], whose lives shed the good odor of Christ on every place, and whose devotedness and spirit of self-sacrifice have, more perhaps than any other cause, contributed to effect a favorable change in the minds of thousands estranged from our faith."[109] In addition, Dr. Samuel Gross, president of the American Medical Association, lamented at the 1869 annual meeting that the Catholic orders were still the only ones who seemed to see the importance of training for nurses.[110]

Changed attitudes were also apparent from the innumerable letters of support from Union officers who were prisoners in Charleston during the war and cared for by the Sisters of Charity of Our Lady of Mercy. These letters were included in the petition of the South Carolina legislature to Congress for funds for the sisters' orphanage. A representative response was that of a Michigan lawyer, formerly a Federal officer. In 1865, after acknowledging that his life and that of other Union officers had been saved by the Confederate sisters bringing food, clothing, medicine, and supplies to them, often at a great sacrifice to themselves, he said, "I am not of your Church and have always been taught to believe it to be nothing but evil; however, actions speak louder than words, and I am free to admit that if Christianity does extist on the earth, it has some of its closest followers among the ladies of your Order."[111] Other letters particularly pointed out that though most men were Protestant, the sisters made "no distinction between us on account of religion or nationality."[112] This fact changed the men's attitude toward the sisters. Thus, they were willing to acknowledge this change and publicly support the sisters after the war.

More than anything else, then, the Civil War gave the sisters greater exposure to the lay public. The experience both revealed the religious values and beliefs that motivated their lives and also expanded the boundaries of their service in ways that could only happen in a national emergency. In the chaotic state of the country, the sisters willingly and easily moved from their often restrictive convent lives and Catholic institutions to constantly changing medical facilities caring mainly for Protestant soldiers. Yet, because the sisters saw this work primarily as an extension of their ministry to care for those in need, the adjustments to their lifestyle and work were smoothly made. Thus, the composite of attitudes toward them reveals a recognition that the sisters had both important skills and a pragmatic approach in applying them to immediate social needs. These skills, practically applied, stemmed clearly and directly from religious values and training that was uniquely acquired in a community of Roman Catholic women religious.

NOTES

1. John Brinton, *Personal Memoirs of John H. Brinton* (New York: The Neale Publishing Co., 1914), pp. 294, 199.

2. Brinton, pp. 44–45.

3. Brinton, p. 45.

4. Charleston Diocesan Archives (CDA), 27H6, Letter of Sr. De Sales to Bishop Lynch, July 11, 1862.

5. CDA, 28K4, Letter of Sr. De Sales to Bishop Lynch, Jan. 9, 1862. See also 27T4, Letter of Sr. De Sales to Bishop Lynch, Sept. 30, 1862.

6. CDA, 28S2, Letter of Sr. De Sales to Bishop Lynch, Mar. 12, 1863.

7. Archives of the Daughters of Charity, Emmitsburg, MD (ADC), *Annals of the Civil War*, vol. I, p. 13.

8. ADC, "Annals of the Civil War," Manuscript, p. 583.

9. ADC, *Annals of the Civil War*, vol. I, p. 30.

10. Jane Woolsey, *Hospital Days* (New York: D. Van Nostrand, 1868), p. 44. The nurse in question did not last with Woolsey, either.

11. Mary Livermore, *My Story of the War* (Hartford, CT: A.D. Worthington, 1887), p. 218.

12. CDA, 26W7, Letter of Rev. Lawrence O'Connell to Bishop Lynch, Jan. 11, 1862. He recommended that both parties be removed. See also 27P7, Letter of O'Connell to Sr. De Sales, Aug. 30, 1862.

13. Louisa May Alcott, *Hospital Sketches*. Ed. Bessie S. Jones (Cambridge: Harvard University Press, 1960), p. xxxi.

14. Congregational Archives of the Sisters of the Holy Cross, Saint Mary's, Notre Dame, IN (ACSC), Copy of General Order 351, Oct. 29, 1863.

15. ADC, *Annals of the Civil War*, vol. I, p. 23.

16. ADC, *Annals of the Civil War*, vol. I. p. 23.

17. Archives of the Sisters of Charity of Cincinnati (ASCC), Letter of Sr. Anthony O'Connell to Bishop John Purcell, Oct. 25, 1863.

18. ASCC, Letter of Sr. Anthony O'Connell to Bishop Purcell, Nov. 16, 1863.

19. ASCC, *The Catholic Telegraph*, Nov. 15, 1863, reprint.

20. Anna L. Boyden, *Echoes from Hospital and White House* (Boston: Lathrop, 1884), pp. 140–141.

21. Sophronia Bucklin, *In Hospital and Camp* (Philadelphia: John E. Potter, 1869), pp. 79–80.

22. Livermore, pp. 246–247.

23. Woolsey, pp. 42–43.

24. Lew Wallace Collection, Indiana Historical Society Library, Letter of Mrs. Lew Wallace to her mother, Dec. 18, 1861.

25. Kate Cumming, *Kate: The Journal of a Confederate Nurse* (Baton Rouge: Louisiana State University Press, 1959), p. 262.

26. Cumming, pp. 125–126.

27. William Q. Maxwell, *Lincoln's Fifth Wheel: The Political History of the United States Sanitary Commission* (New York: Longmans, Green, 1956), p. 68.

28. Jane Hoge, *The Boys in Blue* (New York: Treat, 1867), p. 280.

29. Livermore, pp. 224–225.

30. Livermore, pp. 204–205.

31. Livermore, pp. 218–219.

32. Hoge, p. 38.

33. Livermore, pp. 218–219.

34. Livermore, pp. 204–205.

35. ADC, *Annals of the Civil War*, vol. III, p. 125.

36. C. Vann Woodward, ed., *Mary Chestnut's Civil War* (New Haven: Yale University Press, 1981), p. 171.

37. Archives of the Sisters of Mercy, Vicksburg, MS (ARSMV), Sr. M. Ignatius Sumner, "Register of the Events from the Foundation of the Community of the Sisters of Mercy, Vicksburg, Miss.," p. 39.

38. ARSMV, p. 39.

39. ARSMV, p. 39.

40. Sr. Teresa Austin Carroll, ed., *Leaves from the Annals of the Sisters of Mercy* (New York: Catholic Publication Society, 1881–88), vol. III, p. 163.

41. ASCC, "Memoirs of Sr. Bernadine," n.p.

42. Carroll, ed., *Annals*, vol. III, p. 161.

43. ADC, *Annals of the Civil War*, vol. III, p. 111.

44. ASCC, "Memoirs of Sr. Cecilia," n.p.

45. ADC, *Annals of the Civil War*, Vol. I, p. 6.

46. ADC, *Annals of the Civil War*, Vol. I, p. 9.

47. ASCC, "Memoirs of Sr. Gabriella," n.p.

48. Livermore, pp. 218–219.

49. Gannon, p. 176.

50. ADC, *Annals of the Civil War*, vol. III, p. 116.

51. ADC, *Annals of the Civil War*, vol. I, p. 9.

52. ADC, *Annals of the Civil War*, vol. I, p. 16.

53. ADC, *Annals of the Civil War*, vol. I, p. 16.

54. ADC, *Annals of the Civil War*, vol. I, p. 28.

55. ADC, *Annals of the Civil War*, vol. I, p. 31.

56. ADC, *Annals of the Civil War*, vol. III, p. 111.

57. ADC, *Annals of the Civil War*, vol. III, p. 111.

58. ASCC, "Memoirs of Sr. Ambrosia," n.p.

59. ADC, *Annals of the Civil War*, vol. III, p. 125.

60. ADC, *Annals of the Civil War*, vol. III, p. 125.

61. Mother Teresa Barry had sent a letter disapproving the action of quarantining a sister, and Sr. De Sales had written to both Lynch and Mother Teresa. See CDA, 28M2.

62. CDA, 28M2, Letter of Sr. De Sales to Bishop Lynch, Jan. 27, 1863.

63. ADC, *Annals of the Civil War*, vol. I, p. 12.

64. CDA, 28K2, Letter of Sr. De Sales to Bishop Lynch, Jan. 6, 1863.

65. ADC, *Annals of the Civil War*, vol. I, p. 12.

66. ASCC, "Memoirs of Sr. Jane De Chantal," n.p.

67. ASCC, "Memoirs of Sr. Theodosia," n.p.

68. ASCC, "Memoirs of Sr. Agnes," n.p.

69. CDA, 29R2, Letter of Bishop Augustine Verot to Bishop Lynch, Oct. 5, 1863.

70. ADC, "Annals of the Civil War," Manuscript, pp. 478–81.

71. ADC, "Annals of the Civil War," Manuscript, pp. 478–81.

72. ADC, "Annals of the Civil War," Manuscript, pp. 478–81.

73. ADC, "Annals of the Civil War," Manuscript, pp. 478–81.

74. Archives of University of Notre Dame (ANDU), I–4-b, Letter of Mother Angela Gillespie to Orestes Brownson, Mar. 19, 1862.

75. Archives, Sisters of Charity of Our Lady of Mercy (ASCOLM), Annals of Sister Mary Charles Curtin, 1841–1892, n.p.

76. Benjamin F. Butler, *Autobiography and Personal Reminiscences of Major-General Benj. F. Butler: Butler's Book* (Boston: A. M. Mayer, 1892), p. 426.

77. Butler, p. 422.

78. Sheilla O'Connor, "The Charity Hospital of Louisiana," *The Louisiana Historical Quarterly*, 31 (Jan. 1948), p. 62.

79. Butler, p. 422.

80. Butler, p. 422.

81. Butler, p. 113.

82. Sherman's admiration of the Holy Cross Sisters, whom he knew through his wife's cousin, Mother Angela Gillespie, did not seem to extend to sisters in the South. In his famous "March to the Sea," the Ursuline convent in Columbia, South Carolina, was burned in spite of a promise by Sherman to the Superior, Sr. Baptista Lynch, Bishop Lynch's sister. See CDA, 32M4.

83. ADC, *Annals of the Civil War*, vol. I, pp. 17–18.

84. ADC, *Annals of the Civil War*, vol. I, pp. 17–19.

85. ADC, *Annals of the Civil War*, vol. I, pp. 17–19.

86. This quote was first misappropriated in Ellen Jolly, *Nuns of the Battlefield*, pp. 188–189, and subsequently quoted by almost every author writing about the sisters in the Civil War. However, the error was pointed out by Sr. Mary Ewens in her dissertation and Betty Perkins in her master's thesis. See bibliography.

87. Lucius E. Crittenden, *Recollections of President Lincoln and His Administration* (New York: Harper and Brothers, 1891), p. 259.

88. Logue, p. 125.

89. ADC, *Annals of the Civil War*, vol. I, p. 1.

90. ADC, *Annals of the Civil War*, vol. I, pp. 4–5.

91. ADC, *Annals of the Civil War*, vol. I, p. 5.

92. ADC, *Annals of the Civil War*, vol. I, p. 5.

93. US War Dept. *The Wars of the Rebellion: A Compilation of the Official Records of the Union and Confederate Armies* (Washington: US Government Printing Office, 1880–1901), Part II, vol. 7, p. 221 (Hereafter cited as *Official Records*).

94. *Official Records*, Part II, vol. 7, p. 221.

95. *Official Records*, Part II, vol. 7, p. 373.

96. ADC, *Annals of the Civil War*, vol. I, p. 6.

97. ADC, Letter of Bishop Francis Kenrick to Rev. Francis Burlando, Dec. 17, 1861.

98. ADC, Letter of Kenrick to Burlando, Dec. 17, 1861.

99. ADC, Letter of Mother Ann Simeon Norris, et al., to General Dix, Dec. 17, 1861.

100. ADC, Letter of Mother Ann Simeon Norris.

101. Willard E. Wight, "Bishop Verot and the Civil War,"*The Catholic Historical*

Review 47 (July 1961): 159–161. See also CDA, 27R5, Letter of Bishop Verot to Bishop Lynch, Sept. 2, 1862.

102. ADC, *Annals of the Civil War*, vol. I, p. 11.

103. Archives of the Sisters of Mercy of Baltimore (ARSMB), "Memoirs of a Sister," n.p.

104. ADC, *Annals of the Civil War*, vol. I, p. 27.

105. ARSMV, Sr. M. Ignatius Sumner, p. 17.

106. ADC, "Annals of the Civil War," Manuscript, various accounts. See especially p. 297.

107. ADC, "Annals of the Civil War," Manuscript, p. 119.

108. ADC, *Annals of the Civil War*, vol. I, pp. 7–13.

109. Peter Guilday, ed., *The National Pastorals of the American Hierarchy*, 1792–1919 (Westminster, MD: The Newman Press, 1954), p. 223.

110. Dr. Samuel Gross, quoted in Mary Adelaide Nutting and Lavinia Dock, *A History of Nursing*, vol. II (New York: Putnam, 1907–12), pp. 366–368.

111. "The Petition of the Members of the Legislature of South Carolina to the Congress of the United States in Favor of the sisters of Our Lady of Mercy, Charleston, S.C. for the Rebuilding of Their Orphan Asylum" (Charleston, SC: Edward Perry, 1870), pp. 16–17. Hereafter cited as "The Petition."

112. "The Petition," p. 20.

Conclusion

When the Civil War was over, the sisters returned home and took up again the tasks of teaching, care of the orphans, and nursing that they had engaged in before the conflict began. Those communities already in nursing continued to care for returning soldiers in their own hospitals, or sometimes remained for a time in government hospitals or homes for infirm soldiers. In addition, as a direct result of their war experience, the Sisters of the Holy Cross and the Sisters of Providence added nursing to their other educational and charitable works. Special recognition was also given to other sisters. For example, the Sisters of Charity of Cincinnati, who were nurses, were given a building which became Good Samaritan Hospital because of Sr. Anthony O'Connell's fame.[1]

The sisters in the South, however, found some of their convents and institutions damaged or destroyed. For instance, the Sisters of Mercy returned to Shelby Springs, Alabama, in May 1864 under a flag of truce to reclaim their convent in Vicksburg, Mississippi. The convent, though standing, was partially damaged by shells and had been occupied as headquarters by a Union general, whose servants had taken furniture and other articles.[2] In Charleston, South Carolina, a fire during one of the bombardments partially destroyed the orphanage of the Sisters of Charity of Our Lady of Mercy. However, supported by action of the South Carolina legislature and scores of grateful letters from Union prisoners the sisters had cared for, the community eventually received $13,000 from Congress for damages done to the orphanage.[3]

Though the sisters in the North did not have their buildings damaged, they sometimes suffered other hardships. The Sisters of St. Joseph, whose hospital in Wheeling, West Virginia, was turned into a government hospital during the war, recounted that they had to beg supplies from the market to make soup for the unemployed since food and money were so scarce.[4] These hardships, however, were typical of all the citizens of the war-torn states. Still, all communities of sisters, even those who did not directly serve in the war, received esteem and recognition from Protestants and Catholics alike for the quality of the work done.

Thus, Roman Catholic sisters emerged from the Civil War clearly identified in the minds of American Catholics and of the American population at large as women whose dedicated service deserved gratitude and praise and whose nursing skills offered a model for other women. Both the praise for their service and the recognition of their skills came as a result of the obvious contrast between the sisters and other female nurses, and from firsthand knowledge of the sisters gained by the experience of military and medical authorities and the soldiers. Both the striking contrast and the positive experiences resulted in improved attitudes about Roman Catholic sisters immediately after the war and increased recognition for their lives and work.

Three major but interwoven issues emerging from this study are the convergence of the sisters' values and skills with battlefield needs, the contrast between the sisters' abilities and those of other female nurses, and the resulting positive attitudes about the sisters. A careful examination of these themes clearly reveals the unique contribution of the Roman Catholic sister to the history of nineteenth-century women, of US nursing, and of American Catholicism. The sisters' place in these histories would not have been secured had not the sisters been concerned primarily about the religious purposes of their community lives. They were, as Protestant South Carolina Congressman C. C. Bowen said in a speech in the House of Representatives after the war, "faithful to their vows as the needle to the pole."[5]

When the war began, no one, least of all the sisters, realized that the Roman Catholic religious communities in the United States clearly had the values, experience, and skills needed to address the medical needs of the war. Unlike anyone else, however, the sisters had a sharply defined purpose and mission to care for other people, especially the sick and suffering—a mission that was religious in nature. Furthermore, the sisters, as they had demonstrated in other crises, notably the cholera epidemics, were willing to expand that religious mission to respond to new needs. In addition, the sisters had the experience of living and working in groups of women specifically organized to meet social needs. Many sisters also had the necessary nursing skills learned within their religious community through caring for the sick at home or in the hospitals they had established.

In sharp contrast to the antebellum situation of inmates or scrub-women giving minimal care to people in public almshouses or private city hospitals, the sisters regarded nursing as a religious calling, not a menial task. They saw the patient as a person in need of compassionate care, and they devoted their lives to giving that kind of care. The main purpose of the sisters' service, in peacetime as well as in war, was to serve people in need in the name of Jesus Christ and in imitation of His work through a life of dedicated service lived in community and expressed by public vows of poverty, celibacy, and obedience. Significantly for the wartime medical needs, the vows that the sisters took, which supported their religious mission and structured their lives, insured that they would be obedient to orders of legitimate authority, accustomed to living simply, and committed to celibacy. Thus, more than other female nurses, the sisters were used to following rules and regulations, would not demand special accommodations or other scarce resources, and would not be interested in the soldiers except as patients.

In contrast to the sisters, other women, whether motivated by patriotism or religious zeal, did not have the experience of directing their whole lives to the service of others. Neither were they accustomed to living and working in organized groups. Married women might be accustomed to obeying their husbands, making do with limited material resources, and being sexually faithful to their husbands, but they made up a distinct minority of those serving as nurses. Most of the female nurses in the war were single, and many may have been looking for a soldier-husband. More importantly, these lay women rarely had nursing skills, let alone experience, in establishing and staffing hospitals. Thus, though these women were eager to address the medical needs of the war, their presence in what was definitely a male environment was neither desired nor sought after by most medical and military authorities. Not only was nursing not a recognized job outside the home, but the idea of women attending to personal needs of strange men also was not considered acceptable for nineteenth-century women. Further, many doctors, though in need of assistance, found themselves unable or unwilling to cope with most of these women, whose enthusiasm far outweighed their organization, skills, or experience.

Thus, in retrospect, it is not surprising, but almost predictable, that against a background of weaknesses of the medical staff, (especially at the beginning of the war), the confusion of the nursing efforts, and the often negative attitudes of the doctors toward most women as nurses that the sisters would be sought after by military and medical authorities. Despite the Know-Nothing and nativist anti-Catholic sentiments of the decades before the Civil War, and despite popular literature depicting Catholic clergy, and especially sisters, as either engaged in various nefarious sexual activities or ignorant and bound by a corrupt clergy and foreign pope, the nursing experience, hospitals, dedication, and willingness of the sisters to serve was recognized. Certainly, the twenty-one communities of sisters responded differently to a variety of requests for service on battlefield, transport boat, and general hospital. While there are isolated instances of communities not responding to requests, the overwhelming evidence indicates that sisters everywhere in the Union and the Confederacy responded immediately.

In fact, nowhere is there a record of any community previously engaged in health care declining to serve in the war if asked. Rather, communities that had sisters in health care, especially the Daughters of Charity, responded generously. Even more significantly, perhaps, is the response of sisters who did not have a history of hospital work or nursing, notably the Sisters of the Holy Cross and the Sisters of Providence. Both responded to requests, nursed for a considerable part of the war, and then started hospitals and continued nursing after the war. Of even greater importance is the fact that the sisters' religious values and beliefs were generally not a deterrent to their being asked to nurse. Rather, those who asked for the sisters, whether government official, military officer, or doctor, were willing to accept the sisters on their own terms, something the authorities certainly were not willing to do for most other female nurses.

It has been suggested that unlike the sisters, the female nurses of the Civil War clashed with most doctors because the nurses' presence challenged male authority generally and the medical field specifically.[6] This theory perhaps implies that the sisters were preferred beause of their greater conformity to the image and ideals of domesticity. However, the situation may have been more complex. It appears that the sisters did challenge doctors and other authorities when they felt nursing care, nutrition, cleanliness, good order, and their religious practices demanded it. In addition, they were often able to get supplies that doctors or military authorities were not able to procure.

Although a certain tension and challenge did exist between other female nurses and the sisters, much of this was due to the fact that both before and after the war, appeals were made to American Protestant women to emulate Sisters of Charity. For example, Catharine Beecher in *The American Woman's Home* recounted a conversation she had with a woman who had seen much of military hospitals during the Civil War. Beecher asked, "Are the Sisters of Charity really better nurses than most other women?" "Yes, they are," the woman replied. "I think it is because with them it is a work of self-abnegation, and of duty to God, and they are so quiet and self-forgetful in its exercise that they do it better while many other women show such self-consciousness and are so fussy!" While aspects of Roman Catholicism or convent life may not have appealed to the American woman, the dedication, commitment, organization, training, and ability of sisters to meet various social needs did. Beecher challenged American women to emulate the Sisters of Charity: "Is there any reason why every Protestant woman should not be trained for this self-denying office as a duty owed to God?"[7]

There may have been no reason why Protestant women could not be trained, but certainly the four years of the war were too short a time to acknowledge a role of women in health care, let alone to turn nursing into a profession. Nevertheless, the Roman Catholic sisters, in that short period, did become known for the way their religious values, which were developed in community life, could contribute to an American need, and for the way their social-service experience and nursing skills could contribute to the medical field. These two contributions created a more positive view of the sister, her religion, and her Church and clearly demonstrated what a group of dedicated religious women could accomplish. All this might well have come about in time even if there had been no Civil War. However, the Civil War gave the Roman Catholic sister an unexpected opportunity to exercise these skills and values in a context larger than their own Catholic institutions. Because of the wider exposure of many Protestants and Catholics to the sisters' dedication and practical skills, the sisters were better known and more appreciated and respected at war's end than they had been four years before.

The sisters, of course, were not inherently professionals, reformers, or feminists, nor were they seen that way by themselves or others. Basically, the Roman Catholic sisters who nursed in the Civil War, while contributing a high level of care to the soldiers, saw their role (or the religious community saw its role) as continuing the mission of serving where needs and requests were greatest; thus, rather than believing that they were charting new paths and directions for moving nursing toward the status of a profession, they saw themselves as following in the long tradition of nursing care done from religious motivation. This is true partly because many of the sisters with special training themselves just passed this on as a matter of course to other members of their communities who served in the hospitals. This practice obviated the need for special training schools until such time as there were not enough sisters to handle the nursing. Also, in spite of some significant women religious who established health care and other institutions serving social needs of people, nursing for the sisters (as well as education and social service) was considered a "ministry," a service to and for others, rather than a profession.

These largely Irish and German immigrants and native-born women, living in a freely chosen, alternative lifestyle of a single-sex community rather than in marriage, and sometimes circumscribed by rules and regulations of a European, male-dominated hierarchical church, served as an example of what a skilled nurse could accomplish. This example helped pave the way for the beginning of professional training for female nurses within a decade after the Civil War. The familiarity with the sisters that the circumstances of the war provided also served to greatly enhance the positive image of the sisters and consequently of the Roman Catholic church during and after the war. It seemed to make little difference whether the sisters were from Union or Confederate states or nursed Northerners or Southerners. As Confederate nurse Kate Cumming observed, the six hundred Roman Catholic sisters who nursed in the Civil War on battlefields, in hospitals, and on transport ships seemed able to "do with honor"[8] what other women desired to do. This "honorable" work clearly has earned the Civil War nursing sisters a unique place in the history of nineteenth-century American women's history.

NOTES

1. Archives Sisters of Charity of Cincinnati (ASCC), file of Sr. Anthony O'Connell.

2. William H. Elder, *Civil War Diary* (Natchez-Jackson Diocese: Gerow, n. ed.), p. 112; p.57. See also Archives of Sisters of Mercy, Vicksburg (ARSMV), Sr. M. Ignatius Sumner, "Register of the Events from the Foundation of the Convent of the Sisters of Mercy, Vicksburg, Miss.," pp. 26–28.

3. "The Petition of the Members of the Legislature of South Carolina to the Congress of the United States in favor of the Sisters of Our Lady of Mercy, Charleston, SC for the Rebuilding of Their Orphan Asylum" (Charleston, SC: Edward Perry, 1870). Hereafter cited as "The Petition." See also *Congressional Globe*, Second Session of the Forty-first Congress, Mar. 21, 1870, pp. 171–173; Third Session of the Forty-first Congress, Mar. 3, 1871, pp. 2007–2010; First Session of the Forty-second Congress, April 18, 1871, pp. 767–812.

4. Sr. Rose Anita Kelly, *Song of the Hills: The Story of the Sisters of St. Joseph of Wheeling* (Wheeling, WV: Sisters of St. Joseph, 1962), p. 220.

5. Archives Sisters of Charity of Our Lady of Mercy, Charleston, SC (AS-COLM), "Rebuilding Orphan Asylum in Charleston, S.C.: Speech of Hon. C.C. Bowen," delivered in the House of Representatives, Mar. 21, 1870.

6. Ann Douglas Wood, "The War Within a War: Women Nurses in the Union Army," *Civil War History* 18 (Sept. 1972), 197–212.

7. Catharine Beecher, *The American Woman's Home* (New York: J. B. Ford, 1870), p. 346.

8. Kate Cumming, *Kate: The Journal of a Confederate Nurse*, ed. Richard B. Harwell (Baton Rouge: Louisiana State University Press, 1959), p. 178.

Selected Bibliography

ARCHIVAL SOURCES

AAC	Archives, Archdiocese of Cincinnati
ACSC	Archives, Sisters of the Holy Cross, Saint Mary's, Notre Dame, Indiana
ADC	Archives, Daughters of Charity, Emmitsburg, Maryland
ANDU	Archives, Notre Dame University, South Bend, Indiana
AOPK	Archives, Sisters of St. Dominic, St. Catharine, Kentucky
AOPT	Archives, Sisters of St. Dominic, Memphis, Tennessee
ARSMB	Archives, Sisters of Mercy, Province of Baltimore, Maryland
ARSMC	Archives, Sisters of Mercy, Chicago, Illinois
ARSMC	Archives, Sisters of Mercy, Cincinnati, Ohio
ARSMNYC	Archives, Sisters of Mercy, New York City, New York
ARSMP	Archives, Sisters of Mercy, Pittsburgh, Pennsylvania
ARSMV	Archives, Sisters of Mercy, Vicksburg, Mississippi
ASCC	Archives, Sisters of Charity of Cincinnati, Cincinnati, Ohio
ASCN	Archives, Sisters of Charity, Nazareth, Kentucky
ASCNYC	Archives, Sisters of Charity, New York City, New York
ASCOLM	Archives, Sisters of Charity of Our Lady of Mercy, Charleston, South Carolina
ASOLMC	Archives, Sisters of Our Lady of Mt. Carmel, New Orleans, Louisiana
ASP	Archives, Sisters of Providence, St. Mary of the Woods, Indiana

ASPSF   Archives, Sisters of the Poor of St. Francis, Cincinnati, Ohio

ASSJP   Archives, Sisters of St. Joseph, Philadelphia, Pennsylvania

ASSJW   Archives, Sisters of St. Joseph, Wheeling, West Virginia

AUNG   Archives, Ursuline Nuns, Galveston, Texas

CDA   Charleston Diocesan Archives, Diocese of Charleston, S.C.
            Bishop Patrick Lynch papers

NA   National Archives, Washington, D.C. Dr. John Brinton papers

SECONDARY SOURCES

History of Religion in America

Ahlstrom, Sydney E. *A Religious History of the American People*. New Haven: Yale
      University Press, 1972.
Gaustad, Edwin Scott. *Historical Atlas of American Religion*. New York: Harper
      and Row, 1975.
————, ed. *A Documentary History of Religion in America*. 2 vols. Grand Rapids:
      William B. Eerdmans, 1982.
Handy, Robert. *A History of the Churches in the United States- and Canada*. New
      York: Oxford University Press, 1977.
Hudson, Winthrop. *Religion in America: An Historical Account of the Development
      of American Religious Life*. 3rd ed. New York: Charles Scribner's Sons, 1981.
Marty, Martin E. *Pilgrims in Their Own Land: 500 Years of Religion in America*.
      New York: Penguin, 1984.
Noll, Mark, et al. *Eerdman's Handbook to Christianity in America*. Grand Rapids:
      William B. Eerdmans, 1983.

History of Catholicism in America

Dolan, Jay. *The American Catholic Experience: A History from Colonial Times to the
      Present*. Garden City, NY: Doubleday, 1985.
————. *Catholic Revivalism: The American Experience, 1830–1900*. Notre Dame,
      IN: University of Notre Dame Press, 1978.
————. *The Immigrant Church: New York's Irish and German Catholics, 1815–1865*.
      Notre Dame, IN: University of Notre Dame Press, 1975.
Ellis, John Tracy. *American Catholicism*. Chicago: University of Chicago Press,
      1956; rev. ed., 1969.
————. *Catholics in Colonial America*. Baltimore: Helicon Press, 1965.
————. *Documents of American Catholic History*. 2 vols. Milwaukee: Bruce Pub-
      lishing, 1956; rev. ed. Chicago: University of Chicago Press, 1969.
Ellis, John Tracy and Robert Trisco, eds. *A Guide to American Catholic History*.
      2nd ed. Santa Barbara: ABC-Clio, 1982.
Gannon, Michael. *The Cross in the Sand: The Early Church in Florida, 1513–1870*.
      Gainsville: University of Florida Press, 1967.
Guilday, Peter, ed. *The National Pastorals of the American Hierarchy (1792–1919)*.
      Westminster, MD: The Newman Press, 1954.

Hennesey, James J. *American Catholics: A History of the Roman Catholic Community in the United States*. New York: Oxford University Press, 1981.

————, ed. *American Catholic Bibliography, 1970–1982*. Series 12, No. 1. Fall, 1982. Notre Dame: Cushwa Center Working Papers, 1982.

————, ed. *Supplement to American Catholic Bibliography, 1970–1982*. Series 14, No. 1. Fall, 1983. Notre Dame: Cushwa Center Working Papers, 1983.

Hutter, Donald, ed. *Mirror of 150-Year Progress (1810 to 1960) of the Catholic Church in the United States of America*. Cleveland, OH: Mirror Publishing, 1964.

The Metropolitan Catholic Almanac and Laity's Directory for the United States, Canada, and the British Provinces. Baltimore: John Murphy, 1861.

O'Grady, John. *Catholic Charities in the United States*. Washington, D.C.: National Conference of Catholic Bishops, 1930; rpt. New York: Arno Press, 1971.

Pillar, James J. *The Catholic Church in Mississippi, 1837–65*. New Orleans: The Hauser Press, 1964.

Sadlier's Catholic Almanac and Ordo for Year of Our Lord, 1864. New York: D. J. Sadlier Co., 1864.

Sadlier's Catholic Almanac and Ordo for Year of Our Lord, 1865. New York: D. J. Sadlier Co., 1865.

Shaw, Richard. *Dagger John: The Unquiet Life and Times of Archbishop John Hughes of New York*. New York: Paulist Press, 1977.

Shea, John Gilmary. *History of the Catholic Church in the United States*. 4 vols. New York: John G. Shea, 1886–92.

Wakelyn, Jon L. and Randall Miller, eds. *Catholics in the Old South: Essays on Church and Culture*. Macon: Mercer University Press, 1983.

Women and Religion in the United States—Nineteenth-Century America

Beaver, R. Pierce. *All Loves Excelling*. Grand Rapids, Mich: Eerdmans Publishing, 1968. (Revised edition *American Protestant Women in World Mission: History of the First Feminist Movement in North America*. 1980).

Cott, Nancy F. "Young Women in the Second Great Awakening in New England." *Feminist Studies* 3 (1975): 15–29.

Gifford, Carolyn DeSwarte. "Sisterhoods of Service and Reform: Organized Methodist Women in the Late Nineteenth Century. An Essay on the State of the Research." *Methodist History* 24 (Oct. 1985): 15–30.

James, Janet Wilson, ed. *Women in American Religion*. Philadelphia: University of Pennsylvania Press, 1980.

Porterfield, Amanda. *Feminine Spirituality in America*. Philadelphia: Temple University Press, 1980.

Ruether, Rosemary Radford and Keller, Rosemary Skinner, eds. *The Nineteenth Century: A Documentary History*. vol. 1 of *Women and Religion in America*. San Francisco: Harper and Row, 1981.

————. *The Colonial and Revolutionary Periods: A Documentary History*. vol. 2 of *Women and Religion in America*. San Francisco: Harper and Row, 1983.

Roman Catholic Religious Women in Nineteenth-Century America

Brewer, Eileen Mary. *Nuns and the Education of American Catholic Women, 1860–1920.* Chicago: Loyola University Press, 1987.

Byrne, Sr. Patricia. "Sisters of St. Joseph: The Americanization of a French Tradition." *U.S. Catholic Historian* 5 (Summer/Fall 1986): 241–272.

Code, Joseph B. "A Selected Bibliography of the Religious Orders and Congregations of Women Founded Within the Present Boundaries of the United States (1727–1850)." *The Catholic Historical Review* 23 (Oct. 1937): 331–351.

————, "Up-Date of 'A Selected Bibliography'." *The Catholic Historical Review* 26 (July 1940): 222–245.

Dehey, Elinor T. *Religious Orders of Women in the United States: Accounts of their Origin, Works, and Most Important Institutions.* Hammond, IN: W. B. Conkey, 1930.

"Destruction of Charlestown Convent from Contemporary Newspaper Accounts." *United States Catholic Historical Records and Studies* 13 (May 1919): 106–119.

Ewens, Mary, OP. "The Leadership of Nuns in Immigrant Catholicism." In Rosemary Ruether and Rosemary Skinner Keller, eds. *Women and Religion in America: The Nineteenth Century. Vol. 1* San Francisco: Harper and Row, 1981, pp. 101–149.

————. *The Role of the Nun in Ninetheenth Century America: Variations on the International Theme.* New York: Arno, 1978.

Kenneally, James J. "The Burning of the Ursuline Convent: A Different View." *Records of the American Catholic Historical Society* 90 (Mar-Dec. 1979): No. 1–4, 15–22.

————. "Eve, Mary, and the Historians: American Catholicism and Women." In Janet W. Jones, ed. *Women in American Religion.* Philadelphia: University of Pennsylvania Press, 1980, pp. 191–206.

Mannard, Joseph G. "Maternity . . . of the Spirit: Nuns and Domesticity in Antebellum America." *U.S. Catholic Historian* 5 (Summer/Fall 1986): 305–324.

Monk, Maria. *Awful Disclosures of the Hotel Dieu Nunnery in Montreal.* New York: Howe and Bates, 1836.

Reed, Rebecca. *Six Months in a Convent.* Boston: Russell, Odeorne and Metcalf, 1835.

Ryan, Maria Alma, IHM. "Foundations of Catholic Sisterhoods in the U.S. to 1850." *American Catholic Historical Society Records.* Vols. 12–14, (1941–1943); vol. 12, 34–61; 87–109; 174–184; 219–243; vol. 13, 21–32; 96–100; 169–178; 250–257; vol. 14, 66–73; 134–146; 159–175.

Sullivan, Sister Mary Christiana. "Some Non-Permanent Foundations of Religious Orders and Congregations." *United States Catholic Historical Society Records and Studies* 31 (Jan. 1940): 7–118.

Thomas, Evangeline, CSJ. *Women Religious History Sources: A Guide to Repositories in the United States.* New York: R. R. Bowker, 1983.

Thompson, Margaret Susan. "Discovering Foremothers: Sisters, Society, and the American Catholic Experience." *U.S. Catholic Historian* 5 (Summer/Fall 1986): 273–290.

Women in Nineteenth-Century America

Beecher, Catharine. *The American Woman's Home: or The Principles of Domestic Science.* New York: J. B. Ford, 1870.

Clinton, Catherine. *The Other Civil War: American Women in the Nineteenth Century.* New York: Hill and Wang, 1984.

Cott, Nancy. *The Bonds of Womanhood: "Woman's Sphere" in New England, 1780–1835.* New Haven: Yale University Press, 1977.

Douglas, Ann. *The Feminization of American Culture.* New York: Alfred A. Knopf, 1977.

Freedman, Estelle. "Separatism as Strategy: Female Institution Building and American Feminism, 1870–1930." *Feminist Studies* 5 (Fall 1979): 513–529.

Hales, Jean Gould. "Co-Laborers in the Cause: Women in the Antebellum Nativist Movement." *Civil War History* 25 (June 1979): 119–138.

Hogeland, Ronald W. "The Female Appendage: Feminine Life-Styles in America, 1820–1860." *Civil War History* 17 (June 1971): 101–114.

James, Edward T., Janet W. James, and Paul S. Boyer. *Notable American Women 1607–1950: A Bibliographical Dictionary.* 4 vols. Cambridge, Mass.: Harvard University Press, 1971.

Livermore, Mary A. *What Shall We Tell Our Daughters?: Superfluous Women and Other Lectures.* Boston: Lee and Shepard, 1883.

Melder, Keith E. "Ladies Bountiful: Organized Women's Benevolence in Early Nineteenth Century America." *New York History* 48 (July 1967): 231–254.

McDannell, Colleen. *The Christian Home In Victorian America, 1840–1900.* Bloomington: Indiana University Press, 1986.

Riegel, Robert E. *American Feminists.* Lawrence: University of Kansas Press, 1963.

Ryan, Mary. *The Empire of Domesticity: American Writing About Domesticity 1830 to 1860.* New York: Haworth Press and the Institute for Research of History, 1982.

Sklar, Kathryn. *Catharine Beecher: A Study in American Domesticity.* New Haven: Yale University Press, 1973.

Smith-Rosenberg, Carroll. *Disorderly Conduct: Visions of Gender in Victorian America.* New York: Alfred A. Knopf, 1985.

Treudley, Mary B. "The Benevolent Fair: A Study of Charitable Organizations Among Women in the First Third of the Nineteenth Century." *Social Service Review* 14 (Dec. 1940): 509–522.

Vicinus, Martha. *Independent Women: Work and Community for Single Women, 1850–1920.* Chicago: University of Chicago Press, 1985.

Walsh, Mary Roth. *Doctors Wanted: No Women Need Apply.* New Haven: Yale University Press, 1977.

Welter, Barbara. *Dimity Convictions.* Athens: Ohio University Press, 1976.

———. "The Cult of True Womanhood, 1802–1860." *American Quarterly* 18 (Summer 1966): 151–174.

History of Nursing

Austin, Anne L. *History of Nursing Source Book*. New York: G. P. Putnam's Sons, 1957.

Bullough, Vern L. and Bonnie Bullough. *The Care of the Sick: The Emergence of Modern Nursing*. New York: Prodist, 1978.

Dolan, Josephine A. *Nursing in Society: A Historical Perspective*. 14th ed. Philadelphia: W. B. Saunders Co., 1978.

Dowling, Harry. *City Hospitals: The Undercare of the Under-privileged*. Cambridge: Harvard University Press, 1982.

Kalish, Philip and Beatrice J. Kalish. *The Advance of American Nursing*. Boston: Little, Brown, 1978.

Lagemann, Ellen Condliffe, ed. *Nursing History: New Perspectives, New Possibilities*. New York: Teachers College Press, 1983.

Nightingale, Florence. *Notes on Nursing; What It Is and What It Is Not*. 1860: rpt. New York: Churchill Livingston, 1969.

Nutting, Mary Adelaide and Lavinia Dock. *A History of Nursing: The Evolution of Nursing Systems from the Earliest Times to the Foundation of the First England and American Training Schools for Nurses*. 4 vols. New York: G. P. Putnam's Sons, 1907–12.

O'Connor, Robin. "American Hospitals: The First 200 Years." *Hospitals* 50 (Jan. 11, 1976): 62–71.

Reverby, Susan M. *Ordered to Care: The Dilemma of American Nursing, 1850–1945*. Cambridge, England: Cambridge University Press, 1987.

Rosenberg, Charles E. *The Care of Strangers: The Rise of America's Hospital System*. New York: Basic Books, 1987.

————. *The Cholera Years: The United States in 1832, 1849, and 1866*. Chicago: The University of Chicago Press, 1962.

————. "The Origins of the American Hospital System." *Bulletin of the New York Academy of Medicine* 55, No. 1 (Jan. 1979): 10–21.

Shryock, Richard H. *The History of Nursing: An Interpretation of the Social and Medical Factors Involved*. Philadelphia: W.B. Saunders, 1959.

Starr, Paul. *The Social Transformation of American Medicine*. New York: Basic Books, 1982.

Woodham-Smith, Cecil. *Florence Nightingale*. New York: McGraw-Hill, 1951.

Woolsey, Abby H. *A Century of Nursing with Hints Toward the Organization of a Training School*. 1916: rpt. New York: Putnam, 1950.

Roman Catholic Sisters and Nursing

Doyle, Ann. "Nursing by Religious Orders in the United States" *American Journal of Nursing* 29 (July-Sept. 1929): 775–786, 959–969, 1085–1095, 1197–1207, 1331–1343; 1466–1484.

Dwight, Thomas. "The Training Schools for Nurses of the Sisters of Charity." *Catholic World* 61 (May 1895): 187–92.

Jameson, Anna Brownell (Murphy). *"Sisters of Charity"* and *"The Communion of*

Labour": Two Lectures on the Social Employment of Women. London: Longman, Brown, Green, Longmans and Roberts, 1859.

"Sisters in the History of Nursing." *America* 92 (6 Nov. 1954): 144.

Stepsis, Sr. Ursula and Sr. Dolores Liptak, eds. *Pioneer Healers: The History of Women Religious in American Health Care*. New York: Crossroad Continuum, 1989.

"Who Shall Take Care of Our Sick?" *Catholic World* 7 (Oct. 1868): 42–55.

Civil War—General

Beitzell, Edwin W. *Point Lookout Prison Camp for Confederates*. Abell, Maryland: E. W. Beitzel, 1972.

Billings, John D. *Hardtack and Coffee or The Unwritten Story of Army Life*. Boston: G. M. Smith, 1887.

Butler, Benjamin. *Autobiography and Personal Reminiscences of Major General Benj. F. Butler*. Boston: A. M. Mayer, 1892.

Chittenden, Lucius E. *Recollections of President Lincoln and His Administration*. New York: Harper and Brothers, 1891.

Confederate States of America. *Official Reports of Battles*. New York, 1863; rpt. New York: Kraus Reprint Co., 1973.

Davis, William, ed. *The Image of War, 1861–1865*. 3 vols. Garden City, NY: Doubleday, 1981.

Glazier, Capt. Willard. *The Capture, the Prison Pen and the Escape, Giving a Complete History of Prison Life in the South*. New York: R. H. Ferguson, 1870.

Fredrickson, George. *The Inner Civil War: Northern Intellectuals and the Crisis of Union*. New York: Harper and Row, 1965.

Hesseltine, William B. *Civil War Prisons: A Study in War Psychology*. New York: Frederick Ungar, 1930; rpt. 1964.

Johnson, Robert and C. E. Buel, eds. *Battles and Leaders of the Civil War*. 4 vols. New York: Century Co., 1884, 1888.

Livermore, Thomas L., ed. *Numbers and Losses in the Civil War in America*. Boston: Houghton, Mifflin, 1901.

Moore, Frank, ed. *The Rebellion Record*. 7 vols. New York: G. P. Putnam's Sons, 1861–1866.

Thompson, Holland, ed. *Prisons and Hospitals*. Vol. 7 in Miller, Francis Trevelyan, ed. *The Photographic History of the Civil War in Ten Volumes*. New York: The Review of Reviews Co., 1911.

United States War Department. *The War of the Rebellion: A Compilation of the Official Records of the Union and Confederate Armies*. 70 vols. in 128 books. Washington, D.C.: U.S. Government Printing Office, 1880–1901.

Wiley, Bell I. *The Life of Billy Yank: The Common Soldier of the Union*. Garden City, NY: Doubleday, 1971.

―――――. *The Life of Johnny Reb: The Common Soldier of the Confederacy*. Garden City, NY: Doubleday, 1971.

Civil War—Medicine

Adams, George Worthington. *Doctors in Blue: The Medical History of the Union Army in the Civil War*. New York: Henry Schuman, 1952.

Barnes, Joseph K., et al. *The Medical and Surgical History of the War of the Rebellion, 1861–65.* 6 vols. Washington, D.C., Government Printing Office, 2nd issue, 1875–1888.

Blackwell, Elizabeth. *Pioneer Work in Opening the Medical Profession to Women.* London: Longmans, 1895.

Brinton, John Hill. *Personal Memories of John H. Brinton, Major and Surgeon USV, 1861–1865.* New York: The Neale Publishing Co., 1914.

Brooks, Stewart. *Civil War Medicine.* Springfield, Illinois: C.C. Thomas, 1966.

Cunningham, Horace H. *Doctors in Gray: The Confederate Medical Service.* Baton Rouge: Louisiana State University Press, 1958.

Letterman, Jonathan. *Medical Recollections of the Army of the Potomac.* New York: D. Appleton, 1866.

Loomis, E. Kent. "History of the U.S. Navy Hospital Ship *Red Rover.*" Washington, D.C.: Navy Department Division of Naval History, 1961.

Mitchell, S. Weir "The Medical Department in the Civil War." *The Journal of the American Medical Association* 62, No. 19 (May 9, 1914): 1445–1450.

Shryock, Richard Harrison. "A Medical Perspective on the Civil War." In Richard Shryock, ed. *Medicine in America: Historical Essays.* Boston: The John Hopkins Press, 1966, pp. 91–108.

Stevenson, Isobel. "Medical Literature of the Civil War." *CIBA Symposia* 3, No. 2 (July 1941): 908–918.

US Surgeon General's Office. *Reports on the Extent and Nature of the Materials Available for the Preparation of a Medical and Surgical History of the Rebellion.* Circular No. 6, Nov 1, 1865. Philadelphia: J. B. Lippincott, 1865.

Whitman, Walt. *Memoranda During the Civil War [and] Death of Abraham Lincoln.* rpt. Bloomington: Indiana University Press, 1962.

————. *The Wound Dresser: A Series of Letters written from the Hospitals in Washington during the War of the Rebellion,* ed. R. M. Burke. Boston, 1898; rpt. Folcroft, Pa.: Folcroft Library Editions, 1975.

Civil War—US Sanitary Commission

Hoge, Mrs. A. H. *The Boys in Blue.* New York: Treat, 1867.

Maxwell, William Q. *Lincoln's Fifth Wheel: The Political History of the United States Sanitary Commission.* New York: Longmans, Green, 1956.

Olmsted, Frederick Law. *Hospital Transports: A Memoir of the Embarkation of the Sick and Wounded from the Peninsula of Virginia in the Summer of 1862.* Boston: Ticknor and Fields, 1863.

Stille, Charles. *History of the U.S. Sanitary Commission.* Philadelphia: J. B. Lippincott, 1866.

Thompson, William Y. "The U.S. Sanitary Commission." *Civil War History* 2 (June 1956): 41–63.

The United States Sanitary Commission: A Sketch of Its Purpose and Work. Boston: Little Brown, 1863.

Wormely, Katharine Prescott. *The Cruel Side of the War.* Boston: Roberts, 1898.

Civil War—Catholics

Blied, Benjamin. *Catholics and the Civil War*. Milwaukee: Bruce, 1945.

Conyngham, Major D. P. "The Soldiers of the Cross: Heroism of the Cross, or Nuns and Priests on the Battlefield." Typescript. n.d. University of Notre Dame Archives.

Elder, Bishop William Henry. *Civil War Diary, 1862–1865*. Natchez-Jackson, Mississippi: Most Rev. R. O. Geron. n.d.

Gannon, Michael V. *The Cross in the Sand: The Early Catholic Church in Florida, 1513–1870*. Gainsville: University of Florida Press, 1967.

Meehan, T. F. "Army Statistics of the Civil War." *U.S. Catholic Historical Records and Studies* 13 (Oct. 1919): 129–139.

Murphy, Robert J. "The Catholic Church in the U.S. During the Civil War Period 1852–1866." *Records of the American Catholic Historical Society of Philadelphia* 39 (Dec. 1928): 271–346.

Shannon, James P., ed. "Archbishop Ireland's Experiences As a Civil War Chaplain." *Catholic Historical Review*. 39 (Oct. 1953): 298–305.

Spalding, David. "Martin John Spalding's 'Dissertation on the American Civil War'." *Catholic Historical Review* 52 (Jan. 1966): 66–85.

Stock, Leo F. "Catholic Participation in the Diplomacy of the Southern Confederacy." *Catholic Historical Review* 16 (Jan. 1930): 1–18.

Wight, Willard. "Bishop Elder and the Civil War." *Catholic Historical Review* 44 (Oct. 1958): 290–306.

————. "Bishop Verot and the Civil War." *Catholic Historical Review* 47 (July 1961): 153–163.

————, ed. "Some Wartime Letters of Bishop Lynch." *Catholic Historical Review* 43 (April 1957), 20–37.

————, ed. "War Letters of the Bishop of Richmond." *The Virginia Magazine of History and Biography* 67 (July 1959): 259–270.

Civil War—Chaplains

Buckley, Cornelius. *A Frenchman, A Chaplain, A Rebel: The War Letters of Père Louis-Hippolyte Gaché, SJ*. Chicago: Loyola University Press, 1981.

Corby, William. *Memoirs of Chaplain Life*. Chicago: LaMonte, O'Donnell, 1893.

Durkin, Joseph T., SJ, ed. *Confederate Chaplain: A War Journal of Rev. James B. Sheeran*. Milwaukee: Bruce, 1960.

King, T. S. "Letters of Civil War Chaplains." *Woodstock Letters* 43 (1914): 24–34, 168–180.

"Letters of Kenrick to Hughes and to Lincoln." *Catholic Historical Review* 4 (Oct. 1918): 385–388.

Pitts, Charles F. *Chaplains in Gray: The Confederate Chaplains' Story*. Nashville: Broodman Press, 1957.

Quimby, Rollin W. "The Chaplain's Predicament." *Civil War History* 8 (March 1962): 25–37.

Trumbull, H. Clay. *War Memories of a Chaplain*. New York: Charles Scribner's Sons, 1898.

Wight, Willard E. "The Churches and the Confederate Cause." *Civil War History* 6 (Dec. 1960): 361–373.

————. "The Bishop of Natchez and the Confederate Chaplaincy." *Mid-America* 39, No. 2 (April 1957): 67–72.

Civil War—Women

Brockett, L. P. and Mary C. Vaughan. *Women's Work in the Civil War: A Record of Heroism, Patriotism, and Patience*. Philadelphia: Zeigler, McCurdy, 1867.

Collis, Septima. *A Woman's War Record, 1861–1865*. New York: G. P. Putnam's Sons, 1889.

Endres, Kathleen. "The Women's Press in the Civil War: A Portrait of Patriotism, Propaganda, and Prodding." *Civil War History* 30 (March 1984): 31–53.

Hancock, Cornelia. *The South after Gettysburg: Letters of Cornelia Hancock, 1863–1868*. Ed. Henrietta Stratton Jacquette. New York: Thomas Y. Crowell, 1937, reprint 1956.

Marszalek, John F., ed. *The Diary of Miss Emma Holmes, 1861–1866*. Baton Rouge: Louisiana State University Press, 1979.

Massey, Mary Elizabeth. *Bonnet Brigades: American Women and the Civil War*. New York: Alfred Knopf, 1966.

Moore, Frank. *Women of the War: Their Heroism and Self-Sacrifice*. Hartford, CT: S. S. Scranton, 1867.

Putnam, Sallie. *Richmond During the War*. New York: G. W. Carlston, 1867.

Quattlebaum, Isabel. "Twelve Women in the First Days of the Confederacy." *Civil War History* 7 (Dec. 1961): 370–385.

Simkins, Francis Butler and James Welch Patton. *The Women of the Confederacy*. Richmond: Garrett and Massie, 1936.

Swisshelm, Jane Grey. *Crusader and Feminist*. Ed. Arthur Larsen. Westport, CT: Hyperion Press, 1976.

Woodward, Comer Vann, ed. *Mary Chestnut's Civil War*. New Haven: Yale University Press, 1981.

Woodward, Comer Vann and Elizabeth Muhlenfeld, eds. *The Private Mary Chestnut: The Unpublished Civil War Diaries*. New York: Oxford University Press, 1984.

Civil War—Female Nurses

Alcott, Louisa May. *Hospital Sketches*. Ed. Bessie Z. Jones. Cambridge: Harvard University Press, 1960.

Austin, Anne L. "Nurses in American History: Wartime Volunteers, 1861–1865." *American Journal of Nursing* 75 (May 1975): 816–818.

————. *The Woolsey Sisters of New York: A Family's Involvement in the Civil War and a New Profession (1860–1900)*. Philadelphia: American Philosophical Society, 1971.

Blake, John B. "Women and Medicine in Antebellum America." *Bulletin of the History of Medicine* 39 (March-April 1965): 99–123.

Boyden, Anna L. *Echoes from Hospital and White House, a Record of Mrs. Rebecca R. Pomroy's Experience in War Times.* Boston: Lathrop, 1884.

Bucklin, Sophronia. *In Hospital and Camp: A Woman's Record of Thrilling Incidents among the Wounded in the Late War.* Philadelphia: John E. Potter & Co., 1869.

Brumgardt, John R., ed. *Civil War Nurse: The Diary and Letters of Hannah Ropes.* Knoxville: University of Tennessee Press, 1980.

Cumming, Kate. *Kate: The Journal of A Confederate Nurse.* ed. Richard Barksdale Harwell. Baton Rouge: Louisiana State University Press, 1959.

Livermore, Mary Ashton. *My Story of the War: A Woman's Narrative of Four Years Personal Experience as Nurse in the Union Army.* Hartford, CT: A. D. Worthington, 1887.

Marshall, Helen E. *Dorothea Dix, Forgotten Samaritan.* New York: Russell and Russell, 1937.

Robinson, Victor. *White Caps.* Philadelphia: J. B. Lippincott, 1946.

Schwartz, Gerald, ed. *A Woman Doctor's Civil War: Esther Hill Hawks' Diary.* Columbia, SC: University of South Carolina Press, 1984.

Simkins, Francis B. and James W. Patton. "The Work of Southern Women among the Sick and Wounded of the Confederate Armies." *Journal of Southern History* 1 (Nov. 1935): 475–496.

Stimson, Julia C. and Ethel C. Thompson. "Women Nurses With the Union Forces During the Civil War." *Military Surgeon*, 62 (Jan. 1928): 1–17; (Feb. 1928): 208–230.

Wittenmyer, Anne. *Under the Guns: A Woman's Reminiscences of the Civil War.* Boston: E. B. Stillings & Co., 1895.

Wood, Ann Douglas. "The War Within a War: Women Nurses in the Union Army." *Civil War History* 18 (Sept. 1972): 197–212.

Woolsey, Jane Stuart. *Hospital Days.* New York: D. Van Nostrand, 1868.

Civil War—Sisters

Aubuchon, Marie T. "Sister Nurses in the Civil War." *Hospital Progress* 42 (May 1961): 182, 186, 188–89.

Barton, George. *Angels of the Battlefield.* Philadelphia: Catholic Art, 1898.

"A Brief Account of the Services During the Civil War of the Sisters of St. Joseph of Philadelphia." *American Catholic Historical Society Researches* 35 (Dec. 1924): 345–356.

Carroll, Sr. Teresa Austin, ed. *Leaves from the Annals of the Sisters of Mercy.* 4 vols. New York: Catholic Publication Society, 1881–88.

Code, Joseph B. *Bishop John Hughes and the Sisters of Charity.* (n.c.). Miscellaneous Historical reprint, 1949.

Constitutions of the Daughters of Charity of St. Vincent de Paul. Paris: Motherhouse, 1954.

Costello, Sr. Mary Loretto. *The Sisters of Mercy of Maryland, 1855–1930.* St. Louis: B. Herder, 1931.

Curley, Michael J. "The Nuns of the Battlefield." *Catholic Mind* 22 (Oct. 8, 1924): 179–180.

Donnelly, Eleanor C. *Life of Sister Mary Gonzaga Grace of the Daughters of Charity of St. Vincent de Paul 1812–1897*. Philadelphia: n.p., 1900.

Evans, Mary Ellen. *The Spirit Is Mercy: The Sisters of Mercy in the Archdiocese of Cincinnati, 1853–1958*. Westminster, MD: The Newman Press, 1959.

Franklin, Sr. Mary Lawrence. "Mercy from Eire to Erie: The Sisters of Mercy of the Erie Diocese." n.p., n.d.

A Guide for the Religious Called Sisters of Mercy, Part I and II. London: Robson and Son, 1866.

Harron, Sr. Mary Eulalia. "Work of the Sisters of Mercy in the Dioceses of the South." *Records of the American Catholic Historical Society of Philadelphia* 36 (June 1925): 155–161.

Hilleke, Sr. John Francis. "Holy Cross Sisters as U.S. Navy Nurses." typescript. Archives of the Holy Cross Sisters, South Bend, Indiana.

Jolly, Ellen Ryan. *Nuns of the Battlefield*. Providence, Rhode Island: Providence Visitor, 1927.

Johnston, Sr. M. Francis. *Builders By the Sea: History of the Ursuline Community of Galveston, Texas*. New York: Exposition Press, 1971.

Kelly, Sr. Rose Anita. *Song of the Hills: The Story of the Sisters of St. Joseph of Wheeling*. Wheeling, WV: Sisters of St. Joseph, 1962.

Kennedy, Hon. Ambrose. "Speech of Hon. Ambrose Kennedy of Rhode Island in the House of Representatives, Mon., Mar. 18, 1918." *Federal Register*. Mar. 18, 1918, 3–39. Washington, D.C.: U.S. Government Publications, 1918.

Lennen, Sr. Mary Isidore. *Milestones of Mercy: Story of the Sisters of Mercy in St. Louis, 1856–1956*. Milwaukee: Bruce, 1956.

Logan, Sr. Eugenia. *The History of the Sisters of Providence of St. Mary of the Woods, Indiana*. 2 vols. Terre Haute, Indiana: Moore-Langen Printing, 1978.

Logue, Sr. Maria Kostka. *Sisters of St. Joseph of Philadelphia: A Century of Growth and Development*. Westminster, MD: The Newman Press, 1950.

Ludey, J. M. "Arkansas Sisters of Mercy in the War." In *Confederate Women of Arkansas in the Civil War, 1861–65*. Little Rock, AR: J. Kellog, 1907, pp. 134–140.

Mackin, Aloysius, OP, ed. "Wartime Scenes from Convent Windows, St. Cecilia, 1860 through 1865." *Tennessee Historical Quarterly* 39 (Dec. 1980): 410–422.

Mallon, Edward A. "Sisters of Charity, St. Joseph's Hospital, 1859–1947." *American Catholic Historical Society Records* 68 (Sept. 1947): 209–213.

McAllister, Anna Shannon. *In Winter We Flourish: Life and Letters of Sarah Worthington King Peter, 1800–1877*. New York: Longmans, Green, 1939.

———. *Flame in the Wilderness*. Paterson, NJ: St. Anthony Guild Press, 1944.

McCann, Sr. Mary Agnes. *The History of Mother Seton's Daughters: The Sisters of Charity of Cincinnati, Ohio, 1809–1917*. 3 vols. New York: Longmans, Green, 1917.

McGann, Sr. Agnes Geraldine. *Sisters of Charity of Nazareth in the Apostolate, 1812–1976*. St. Meinrad, IN: Abbey Press, 1976.

McGuire, Mother M. Bernard. *The Story of the Sisters of Mercy in Mississippi, 1860–1930*. New York: P. J. Kennedy and Sons, 1931.

McHale, Sr. M. Jerome. *On The Wind: The Story of the Pittsburgh Sisters of Mercy, 1843–1968.* New York: The Seabury Press, 1980.

Melville, Annabelle. *Elizabeth Bayley Seton, 1774–1821.* New York: Scribner's Sons, 1951.

Metz, Sr. Judith. "150 Years of Caring: The Sisters of Charity of Cincinnati." *The Cincinnati Historical Society Bulletin* 37 (Fall 1979): 151–174.

Mug, Sr. Mary Theodosia. *Lest We Forget, The Sisters of Providence* of *St. Mary of the Woods in Civil War Service.* St. Mary of the Woods, IN: Providence Press, 1931.

O'Connor, Stella. "Charity Hospital at New Orleans: An Administrative and Financial History, 1736–1941." *Louisiana Historical Quarterly* 31 (Jan. 1948): 6–109.

The Petition of the Members of the Legislature of South Carolina to the Congress of the United States in favor of the Sisters of Our Lady of Mercy of Charleston, SC. Charleston, SC: Edward Perry, Printer, 1870.

Rafferty, Sr. Jeanette. *Mercy Hospital, 1847–1972: An Historical Review, Vol. I.* Privately printed typescript.

Roddis, Louis H. "The U.S. Hospital Ship *Red Rover*, 1862–65." *Military Surgeon* 77 (Aug. 1935): 91–98.

Semple, Henry C., ed. *The Ursulines in New Orleans, A Record of Two Centuries, 1729–1925.* New York: Kenedy, 1925.

"A Southern Teaching Order. The Sisters of Mercy of Charleston, SC, A.D. 1829–1904." *American Catholic Historical Records of Philadelphia* 15 (Sept. 1904): 249–265.

Spiritual Writings of Saint Louise de Marillac. Trans. Sr. Louis Sullivan. Albany, NY: De Paul Provincial House, 1984.

Walsh, Sr. Marie DeLourdes. *The Sisters of Charity of New York, 1809–1959.* Vol. I of 3 vols. New York: Fordham University Press, 1960.

Miscellaneous

Campbell, Sr. Anne Francis, OLM. Personal Interview. 12 Feb. 1986. *The Congressional Globe: The Debates and Proceedings of the Second Session of the Thirty-Eighth Congress.* City of Washington: Congressional Globe Office, 1865.

The Congressional Globe: The Debates and Proceedings of the Second Session of the Forty-First Congress. City of Washington: Congressional Globe Office, 1870.

The Congressional Globe: The Debates and Proceedings of the Third Session of the Forty-First Congress. City of Washington: Congressional Globe Office, 1871.

The Congressional Globe: The Debates and Proceedings of the First Session of the Forty-Second Congress. City of Washington: Congressional Globe Office, 1871.

Tocqueville, Alexis de. *Democracy in America.* Eds. J. P. Mayer and Max Lerner. New York: Harper and Row, 1966.

US House of Representatives. *The Treatment of Prisoners of War by the Rebel Authorities during the War of the Rebellion,* Report No. 45, Serial No. 1391, Fortieth Congress, Third Session, 1869.

Unpublished Theses and Dissertations

Andrews, Rena M. "Archbishop Hughes and the Civil War." Ph.D. Diss. University of Chicago, 1935.

Campbell, Sr. M. Anne Francis, OLM. "Bishop England's Sisterhood, 1829–1929." Ph.D. Diss. St. Louis University, 1968.

Cavanaugh, William. "The Hospital Activities of the Sisters During the Civil War and Their Influence on the Catholic Hospital System Movement up to 1875." MA thesis. Catholic University of America, 1931.

Gallagher, Sr. Ann Seton. "A Study of the Nursing Activities of Sister Anthony O'Connell." MA thesis. Catholic University of America, 1957.

Gilgannon, Sr. Mary McAuley, RSM. "The Sisters of Mercy as Crimean War Nurses." Ph.D. Diss. University of Notre Dame, 1962.

Hickey, Sr. Zoe. "The Daughters of Charity of St. Vincent de Paul in the Civil War." MA thesis. Catholic University of America, 1943.

Misner, Sr. Barbara, SCSC. "A Comparative Social Study of the Members and Apostolates of the First Eight Permanent Communities of Women Religious within the Boundaries of the United States, 1790–1850." Ph.D. Diss. Catholic University of America, 1981.

Nolan, Charles E. "Carmelite Dreams, Creole Perspectives: The Sisters of Mt. Carmel of Louisiana, 1833–1903." Ph.D. Diss. The Pontifical Gregorian University, Rome, Italy, 1970.

Perkins, Betty. "The Work of the Catholic Sister in the Civil War." MA thesis. University of Dayton, 1969.

Smith, Nina Bennett. "The Women Who Went to War: The Union Army Nurse in the Civil War." Ph.D. diss. Northwestern University, 1981.

Tully, Sr. Angela. "Maryland in the Civil War." MA thesis. Catholic University of America, 1933.

Index

About the Author

SISTER MARY DENIS MAHER is Associate Professor of English at Ursuline College, Pepper Pike, Ohio, and a member of the Sisters of Charity of St. Augustine.